OUTCOMES

ELEMENTARY
STUDENT'S BOOK

HUGH DELLAR
ANDREW WALKLEY

1 PEOPLE AND PLACES

page 6

IN THIS UNIT YOU LEARN HOW TO:

- describe people and places
- introduce yourself
- explain where you are from
- talk about jobs and where you work
- ask and answer common questions
- say more about your town / city

2 FREE TIME

page 14

- talk about free-time activities
- discuss what you like – and don't like
- arrange to meet
- describe your daily life
- talk about how often – and when – you do things
- use more English in class

VIDEO 1: A famous city page 22   REVIEW 1 page 23   WRITING 1: Forms page 150

3 HOME

page 24

- talk about the area you live in
- name things you often buy and do
- explain where things are
- explain what you need to do
- describe your house / flat
- ask people to do things

4 HOLIDAYS

page 32

- talk about what you did in the past
- comment on what people tell you
- talk about dates and months
- ask and answer questions about holidays

VIDEO 2: Alex the parrot page 40   REVIEW 2: page 41   WRITING 2: Pen friends page 152

5 SHOPS

page 42

- describe what you want
- talk to a shop assistant
- understand prices
- talk about department stores
- talk about things happening now
- give excuses
- follow directions in a store

6 EDUCATION

page 50

- describe classmates and teachers
- name school and university subjects
- talk about courses you're doing
- talk about languages and education
- give opinions about what's better

VIDEO 3: Photo camp page 58   REVIEW 3: page 59   WRITING 3: Cards page 154

7 PEOPLE I KNOW

page 60

- talk about your family
- express surprise
- give opinions about family life
- talk about things that are necessary or not necessary
- talk about people you know

8 PLANS

page 68

- talk about people's plans
- make simple suggestions
- talk about things you'd like to do
- discuss government plans
- give basic opinions and reasons

VIDEO 4: Two Kenyan guys in Texas page 76   REVIEW 4: page 77   WRITING 4: Making arrangements page 156

2

Contents   3

Contents **5**

1 PEOPLE AND PLACES

3

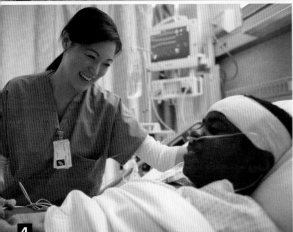

4

9

IN THIS UNIT YOU LEARN HOW TO:

- describe people and places
- introduce yourself
- explain where you are from
- talk about jobs and where you work
- ask and answer common questions
- say more about your town / city

SPEAKING

1   Talk to other students. Tell each other your names.

WORDS FOR UNIT 1

2   Work in pairs. Match the words to the photos.

airport	government	river
beach *1*	mosque	shop assistant
businesswoman	museum	traffic
church	nurse	university
countryside	office	waiter
factory	police officer	

3   ▶ 1 Listen. Check your answers. Listen again. Repeat the words.

4   Work in pairs. Test each other. Cover the words.

Student A: point to a photo.

Student B: say the word.

5   Do you know the English words for anything else in the photos?

10

11

16

17

15

WHERE ARE YOU FROM?

SPEAKING

1   Work in pairs. Try to say the names of everyone in your class.

> That's Yuki.

> That's Carla.

> What's his name?

> Marco.

> What's her name?

> I don't know.

LISTENING

2   ▶ 2 Listen to a teacher and a student at an English-language school. Tick (✓) the sentences that are true.

1   The student's surname is Miguel.

2   He's from Spain.

3   He works in a city called Chihuahua.

4   The city is in the east.

5   It's hot in the city now.

6   He's a businessman.

3   ▶ 2 Listen again. Correct the sentences in Exercise 2 that aren't true.

4   Work in pairs. Look at the audio script on page 197. Practise reading out the conversation.

VOCABULARY Countries

5   Work in pairs. Match the countries in A to the parts of the world in B.

A	B
Costa Rica	Africa
Brazil	North America
Italy	Central America
Canada	South America
China	the Middle East
Saudi Arabia	Europe
Kenya	Asia

6   Write one more country in each part of the world. Use a dictionary if you need to. Then work in pairs.

Student A: say the country.

Student B: say the part of the world.

7   Look at the photos on pages 6 and 7. Say what country or part of the world you think they are in.

For example:

I think the beach in the photo is in Europe.

This photo is in Turkey. It's Istanbul.

DEVELOPING CONVERSATIONS

Which part?

Look at the questions we ask to find out where someone is from.

I: **Where are you from?**

M: *I'm from Mexico.*

I: *Oh, OK. Which part?*

M: *Chihuahua. It's in the north.*

8 Look at the map below. Complete these sentences with places on the map.

1 I'm from _____ – the capital.

2 I'm from _____ – in the north.

3 They're from _____ – in the south.

4 I'm from _____ – in the east.

5 My mum's from _____ – in the west.

6 My dad's from _____ – in the middle.

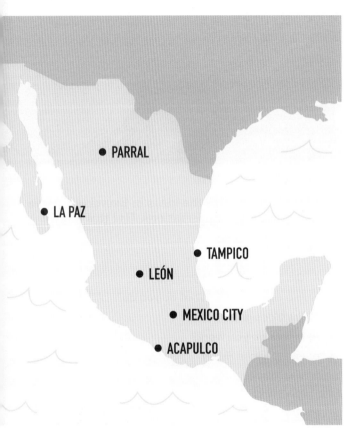

● PARRAL

● LA PAZ

● TAMPICO

● LEÓN

● MEXICO CITY

● ACAPULCO

9 Use countries from Exercises 5 and 6 – or use cities / areas in your country – to have conversations like this:

A: *Where are you from?*

B: *Brazil.*

A: *Which part?*

B: *Recife.*

C: *Where are you from?*

D: *I'm from Rome.*

C: *Which part?*

D: *Morena – in the south.*

GRAMMAR

be

Be has three forms in the present tense: *'m (am)*, *'s (is)*, *'re (are)*.

We add *not* for negatives.

10 Complete the tables with the correct form of *be*.

Statement			
I			30.
He			late.
She			a teacher.
It		(not)	OK.
You			a good student.
We			at the airport.
They			from Moscow.

Question		
	I	
	you	OK?
	they	
	it	

 Check your ideas on page 166 and do Exercise 1.

11 Complete the sentences with the words in brackets and the correct form of *be*.

1 How _____? (you)

2 Where _____ from? (your granddad)

3 _____ from Spain. (my parents)

4 _____ a receptionist in a hotel. (I)

5 It _____ a good job. (not)

6 _____ a very big city. (Tokyo)

7 How old _____? (Miguel)

8 _____ late? (we)

9 _____ cold? (you)

10 _____ a boring place. (it)

12 ▶ 3 Listen and check your answers. Repeat the sentences.

13 Work in groups. Ask students where their parents / grandparents are from.

 For further practice, see Exercise 2 on page 166.

CONVERSATION PRACTICE

14 Look at the questions. Write one more question to ask. Then use all the questions and have conversations with other students.

• Hi. How are you?

• What's your name?

• And where are you from?

• Oh, OK. Which part?

🎥 1 To watch the video and do the activities, see the DVD-ROM.

WHAT DO YOU DO?

VOCABULARY Jobs and workplaces

1   How many jobs can you write in English in one minute?

2   Find out what jobs people in your class do. Ask: *What do you do?*

3   Match the jobs (1–8) to the places people work (a–h).

1 a receptionist	5 a police officer
2 a teacher	6 a waiter
3 a shop assistant	7 a designer
4 a nurse	8 a civil servant

a   in a clothes shop / in Harrods

b   in a clinic / in a hospital

c   in a tax office / in a local government office

d   at home / in a studio

e   in a big hotel / in a small company

f   in a school / in a university

g   at a local police station / in the traffic department

h   in a café / in a restaurant

> We use **a** / **an** with jobs.
>
> *I'm **a** teacher.   My sister's **a** designer.   My dad's **an** artist.*

4   Work in pairs. Use the ideas in Exercise 3. Have three different conversations. Use this model:

A: *What do you do?*

B: *I'm a waiter.*

A: *Oh, yes? Where do you work?*

B: *In a café in town. What do you do?*

A: *I'm a designer.*

B: *Where do you work?*

A: *In a studio in Berlin.*

LISTENING

5   ▶4 Listen to four conversations. Circle the words you hear.

1   Jan is *a doctor* / *a nurse* in *a clinic* / *a hospital* in Warsaw.

2   Lara is *a designer* / *a teacher* in *a school* / *an office* in Bristol. She *enjoys* / *doesn't enjoy* it.

3   Marta is *a civil servant* / *a receptionist*. She works in *an office* / *a company* in the north of Brazil. Her job is *great* / *OK*.

4   Filippo is *a waiter* / *a shop assistant* in *a department store* / *a café* in the centre of town. He doesn't like it. He wants to become *a police officer* / *a nurse*.

6   Work in pairs. Look at the audio script on page 197. Choose one of the conversations and practise reading it out.

7 Read these sentences. Do the people like their job? Write ✓ or ✗.

1 I want a different job.
2 It's great.
3 The people are really nice.
4 The money's bad.
5 It's interesting.
6 I do very long hours.
7 It's boring.
8 I work at night. It's not good.

8 Ask different students these questions.

- What do you do?
- Where do you work?
- Do you enjoy it?

GRAMMAR

Present simple

Look at these examples of the present simple.

*I **live** in Rio Branco.*   *She **works** in an office.*
*I **don't speak** French.*   *He **doesn't like** it.*
*Where **do** you **work**?*
***Do** you **enjoy** it?*

9 Complete the table with *-s, do, does, don't* and *doesn't*.

I / You / We / They **live** there. He / She / It **live** ¹_____ there.
Negatives
I / you / we / they + ²_____ + infinitive he / she / it + ³_____ + infinitive
Questions
⁴_____ + I / you / we / they + infinitive? ⁵_____ + he / she / it + infinitive?

G Check your ideas on page 166 and do Exercise 1.

10 Complete the text with the correct form of the verbs in brackets.

My wife's a journalist. She ¹_____ (work) for a local newspaper. I ²_____ (not see) her a lot because she ³_____ (do) very long hours. She ⁴_____ (get up) early and she sometimes works all night. When she ⁵_____ (have) free time, we ⁶_____ (not go out), because she only wants to sleep! But she ⁷_____ (not want) a different job because her job ⁸_____ (be) very interesting and she ⁹_____ (like) it a lot.

11 Write about three people you know. Then tell a partner.

For example:

*My friend Juan **is a** teacher. He **works in** a school. He **likes** his **job because** the people are nice. / He **doesn't like** his **job because** the pay is bad.*

12 Put the words in the correct order to complete the questions. The first one is done for you.

1 What — do / you / in / free time / do / your / ?
   What do you do in your free time?
2 Where — live / do / you / ?
3 Who — with / you / do / live / ?
4 How — go / do / there / you / ?
5 What time — you / do / get / up / ?
6 When — to bed / you / go / do / ?
7 How many — languages / you / speak / do / ?
8 Do — you / to go / out / want / ?

13 Match the answers (a–h) to questions 1–8 in Exercise 12.

a I live on my own.
b At about twelve o'clock most nights.
c I go swimming, I play football, I read.
d In Belváros, near the river.
e I take the bus.
f Two – French and Spanish.
g Sure. Where do you want to go?
h At half past seven.

PRONUNCIATION

14 ▶ **5** Listen to 'do you' – first fast, then slow. Then listen to five questions from Exercise 12 – first fast and then slow. Repeat them.

15 Work in pairs.

Student A: ask the questions in Exercise 12.

Student B: say the answers in Exercise 13.

G For further practice, see Exercises 2 and 3 on page 167.

SPEAKING

16 Choose five questions from these pages. Write one more question. Then work in pairs. Ask and answer your questions.

A NICE PLACE TO LIVE

VOCABULARY Describing places

1 Work in pairs. The first page of this unit has ten words for places. How many do you remember?

2 Look at page 7 and check. Say the plural of the words. Which word has an irregular plural? Which two words have no plural?

3 Choose the correct words.

  1 It's a *small / big* city. Ten million people live there.

  2 I don't go swimming there because the beaches are very *quiet / dirty*.

  3 It's very *hot / cold* in the summer: 35 or 40.

  4 It's a very *expensive / famous* town. Everyone knows it.

  5 It doesn't have any shops. It's *busy / boring*!

  6 It's very *cheap / safe*. My house is only 400 euros a month.

  7 A lot of people visit in the summer. It's very *busy / quiet*.

  8 I really like it. It's a *great / boring* place to live.

  9 The countryside is very nice. It's a *dirty / beautiful* area.

  10 It's very *famous / safe*. I walk everywhere – day and night.

4 Work in pairs. Say places you know using the ideas below. Do you agree?

  • _____ is a very big city.

  • _____ is very quiet.

  • _____ is very cold in the winter.

  • _____ is very expensive.

  • _____ is a beautiful area.

  • _____ is a very famous town.

READING

5 Work in pairs. Describe the places in the photos. Use words from Exercise 3.

a

b

c

d

6 Read the four texts. Match the texts to the photos on page 12. Then decide which person is:

1 a designer.   3 a businessman.
2 a nurse.   4 a teacher.

7 Work in pairs. Answer these questions.

1 Is each place nice? Why? / Why not?
2 Which place is best / worst for you? Why?
3 Which job is best / worst for you? Why?

MY HOME TOWN

JEFF 🇬🇧 I'm from New Romney, in the south of England. It's near the sea, so there's a nice beach, and the countryside near here is lovely, but there isn't a lot to do. There aren't any cinemas or art galleries or museums. It's a small town. One good thing is it's cheap! I work at home and I do jobs for different companies and magazines. I don't get a lot of money because I don't have a lot of work, but I enjoy it. It's interesting.

NANCY 🇺🇸 I'm from Pinedale, in the middle of California. I work in a school and I walk to work every day. That's nice. I love my job and I love my students, but I don't like the area. It's not very nice. Crime is a problem here. It's not very safe – and there aren't a lot of jobs now, but houses are cheap.

ROLANDO 🇪🇸 I'm from Seville, in the south-west of Spain. It's a great place to live. There are a lot of nice cafés and restaurants and there's a great cathedral as well. I work in a hospital near there. My job isn't easy, but I enjoy it. There are some beautiful parks in the city and there's a river as well. I sometimes walk there after work to relax.

YU TSAN 🇨🇳 I'm from Shenyang. It's in the north-east of China. It's not a bad place to live. There are a lot of places to go shopping, so that's nice – and there are some great old buildings as well. There's a palace called Mukden Palace. It's very famous. One bad thing is the traffic. There are a lot of factories too. I have three – and one hundred and fifty people work for me.

GRAMMAR

there is / there are

Look at these examples from the texts.

There's a nice beach.
There aren't a lot of jobs now.

8 Complete the table with the missing words.

With singular nouns			
1 _____	's	a / an	cinema.
			great museum.
			old church near here.
	isn't		park near here.
2 _____	there	a / an	café near here?
			airport?

With plural nouns			
There	are	two	cinemas.
		some	parks near here.
		a lot of	shops in town.
	3 _____	any	places for kids.
		a lot of	shops.
Are	4 _____	any	shops near here?
			people there?

Ⓖ Check your ideas on page 167 and do Exercise 1.

9 Complete the sentences with words from the table in Exercise 8.

1 *There are* a lot of nice shops near my house.
2 _____ a university in your town?
3 _____ a beautiful old mosque in the town centre.
4 _____ any hospitals in the area.
5 _____ an expensive restaurant near here. It's famous!
6 _____ some beautiful houses in the old part of the city.
7 _____ some nice little places to eat on the beach.
8 _____ an airport outside town.
9 _____ any cinemas in your town?
10 _____ any schools in the village. We go to the next town.

PRONUNCIATION

10 ▶️ 6 Listen to the sentences from Exercise 9 said slowly and then faster. Listen again. Practise saying them.

11 Work in groups. Discuss these questions. Try to use *there's / there are.*

- Which sentences in Exercise 9 describe the place you are from?
- What's the best thing about the place you are from?
- Which places in your country are very good / bad to live in? Why?

Ⓖ For further practice, see Exercise 2 on page 167.

SOUNDS AND VOCABULARY REVIEW

12 ▶️ 7 Listen and repeat the sounds with /l/, /r/, /w/ and /j/. Are any of them difficult for you to hear or say?

13 ▶️ 8 Work in groups. Listen to eight sentences using these words. Together, try to write them down. Then listen again and finish writing them.

languages	receptionist	river	wants
like	restaurant	university	work

Ⓖ For further revision, see Exercises 1–3 on page 167.

2 FREE TIME

1

2

5

6

7

8

12

13

14

14

3

4

IN THIS UNIT YOU LEARN HOW TO:

- talk about free-time activities
- discuss what you like – and don't like
- arrange to meet
- describe your daily life
- talk about how often – and when – you do things
- use more English in class

WORDS FOR UNIT 2

1   Work in pairs. Match the activities to the photos.

cooking	meeting new people
dancing	playing computer games
doing sport	playing the guitar
drawing	reading
going out for dinner	singing
going to a concert	swimming
going to the cinema	walking
listening to music	watching TV

2   ▶ 9 Listen. Check your answers. Listen again. Repeat the words.

3   Work in pairs. Test each other. Cover the words.

Student A: point to a photo.

Student B: say the activity.

4   Do you know the English words for anything else in the photos?

9

15

10

11

16

DO YOU WANT TO COME?

SPEAKING

1 Complete the sentences with activities from page 15.

   1 _____ is boring.   4 _____ is great.

   2 _____ is interesting.   5 I'm bad at _____.

   3 _____ is expensive.   6 I'm good at _____.

2 Work in pairs. Tell your partner your ideas. Does your partner agree?

LISTENING

3 Look at the people in the pictures. What activities do you think they like / don't like?

4 ▶ 10 Listen to the two people talking. Complete the table with *doesn't like*, *thinks it's OK* and *loves*.

	Woman	Man
doing sport		
walking		doesn't like
playing computer games		
going to the cinema	loves	

5 Work in pairs. Look at the audio script on page 198. Practise reading out the conversation.

SPEAKING

6 Work in groups. Ask *Do you like …?* questions. Reply with *I love it, It's OK* or *No, not really*.

   A: *Do you like cooking?*

   B: *Yes, I do. I love it. What about you?*

   A: *It's OK, but I'm not very good at it.*

GRAMMAR

Verb patterns

a After some verbs, we often use *-ing*.

I love **playing** tennis.

b After some verbs, we often use *to* + infinitive.

Do you want **to see** Love Train?

7 Which sentences are the same as pattern a above, and which are the same as pattern b?

   1 He really likes swimming.

   2 I need to go now.

   3 I enjoy working on my own.

   4 I want to learn to drive.

   5 Try to use the words you learn.

   6 I hate living in the city.

Ⓖ Check your ideas on page 168 and do Exercise 1.

8 Write full sentences from the notes.

   1 My daughter / want / get / a new phone.

   2 My sister / love / play / tennis.

   3 you / like / dance?

   4 I / try / study English / every day.

   5 I / not / enjoy / shop.

   6 We / need / buy / some things later.

   7 I / really hate / cook.

   8 I / really want / learn / draw.

PRONUNCIATION

9 ▶ 11 Listen and repeat six sentences with *to* + infinitive. Notice how we often say *to* as /tə/.

10 Complete the sentences so they are true for you.

   1 I love _____.

   2 I don't really like _____.

   3 This week I need _____.

   4 I want to learn _____.

   5 I don't really enjoy _____.

11 Work in pairs. Tell your partner your ideas.

Ⓖ For further practice, see Exercise 2 on page 168.

DEVELOPING CONVERSATIONS

Arrangements

We can make future arrangements using the present simple.

A: *Do you want to go shopping on Saturday?*

B: *OK. Where do you want to meet?*

A: *Outside Harrods – the big department store.*

B: *OK. What time?*

A: *Is ten OK?*

B: *Yeah. Fine.*

12 Match the questions in the box to the pairs of possible answers in 1–5.

Do you like going to the cinema?
Do you want to see *Monsters 6* on Sunday?
What time do you want to meet?
Where?
What time does the film end?

1 A: _____

    B: Is four good? / Is seven OK? The film starts at eight.

2 A: _____

    B: I'm not sure. About seven, I think. / About 11.30.
    It's a long film.

3 A: _____

    B: OK. That sounds nice. / Sorry. I'm busy then.

4 A: _____

    B: Yes, it's OK. / No, not really.

5 A: _____

    B: Outside the train station. / Outside the cinema.

13 ▶ **12** Listen to two conversations where people make arrangements. Choose the correct words in the notes.

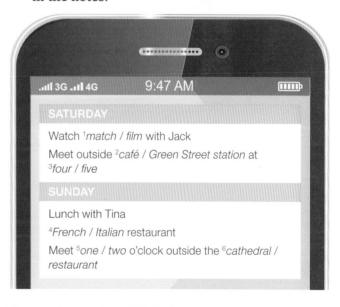

.ıll 3G .ıll 4G   9:47 AM

SATURDAY

Watch [1]*match / film* with Jack

Meet outside [2]*café / Green Street station* at [3]*four / five*

SUNDAY

Lunch with Tina

[4]*French / Italian* restaurant

Meet [5]*one / two* o'clock outside the [6]*cathedral / restaurant*

14 Work in pairs. Which day in the conversations do you think sounds best – Saturday or Sunday? Why?

CONVERSATION PRACTICE

15 Decide two things you want to do at the weekend (on Friday night, Saturday or Sunday). Decide where you want to meet and what time.

16 Work in pairs. Have conversations like the ones in the box in Developing Conversations.

▶ 2 To watch the video and do the activities, see the DVD-ROM.

I USUALLY FINISH AT FIVE

VOCABULARY Daily life

1   When do people usually do the activities below?
    Put them in the three groups in the table.

do homework	have a coffee
finish school	have a shower
get home from work	have lunch
get up	leave work
go to bed	watch the news
go to the theatre	write emails

in the morning	in the afternoon	in the evening

2   Work in pairs and compare your answers. Do
    you always agree? If not, why not?

3   Look at the words in Exercise 1 for two minutes.
    Close your books. Work in pairs. See how many
    words you remember.

GRAMMAR

Adverbs of frequency
We use some adverbs to show how often we do
something. Notice their position in the sentence.

I **always** have a shower in the morning.

I **usually** go to bed at midnight.

4   Complete the table below with the adverbs in
    the box. Then translate all the adverbs into your
    language.

| always | never | often | sometimes |

100%	1 _____
	usually
	2 _____
	3 _____
	occasionally
	hardly ever
0%	4 _____

G Check your ideas on page 168 and do Exercise 1.

5   Tick (✓) the sentences that are true for you.
    Change the adverbs in the other sentences to
    make them true for you.

    1 I always watch the news in the evening.

    2 I usually have a coffee after my lunch.

    3 I never drink beer or wine.

    4 I hardly ever read novels.

    5 I often listen to music when I go to sleep.

    6 I occasionally go to rock concerts.

    7 I always do my homework for my English class.

    8 I sometimes go swimming at the weekend.

6   Work in groups. Take turns saying your
    sentences. Who is most similar to you?

7 Write four true sentences using the phrases in the box and an adverb. Then say them to a partner.

cook dinner for friends	use English outside class
sleep in the afternoon	work at the weekend

G For further practice, see Exercise 2 on page 168.

READING

8 Read an article about how three people spend their free time. Answer these questions.

1 Who is most similar to you? Why?

2 Who do you think is the happiest person? Why?

9 Read the article again. Decide which person:

1 does sport or exercise.

2 spends a lot of money.

3 is tired at the weekend.

4 likes TV.

5 seems quiet.

6 has a busy social life.

7 goes to bed quite early.

8 works long hours.

10 Complete the sentences with the prepositions in bold in the article.

1 I'm always very busy _____ Mondays.

2 I always go running _____ Sunday mornings.

3 I don't usually work _____ Fridays. It's great. I get up _____ nine or ten.

4 Our school day finishes _____ four.

5 The film starts _____ eight and ends _____ 10.30.

6 We don't usually do very much _____ the weekend – just relax.

7 I sometimes have a short sleep _____ the afternoon.

8 I'm usually very tired _____ the morning. I need to have a coffee!

SPEAKING

11 Work in groups. Ask each other these questions.

• What do you normally do on Friday nights?

• What do you normally do on Saturdays?

• What do you normally do on Sundays?

• Do you go out in the evening during the week? When? What do you do?

Which person in the group has the best social life?

DO YOU HAVE ANY FREE TIME?

BIRGIT FROM GERMANY

I do something most nights. On Mondays and Wednesdays, I go to my English class, and on Tuesdays, I usually go to the cinema with friends, because the tickets are cheap then. **On** Thursdays, I always go to the gym. I usually go out dancing **on** Saturday nights. I often get home at four or five in the morning, so on Sundays, I sleep! I sometimes get up at three **in** the afternoon.

FRANKIE FROM THE UK

Free time? I don't have any free time because I have my own business. I occasionally go to a rock concert – about once or twice a year – and I sometimes go shopping **at** the weekend. I like buying expensive things with the money I earn. I have a very nice car and a very big TV. I like watching sport.

SVETLANA FROM RUSSIA

I don't go out much during the week. I usually study for two hours **in** the evening. I never watch TV, really. I usually play the piano every day. It helps me to relax. Then I go to bed **at** nine or ten and read. At the weekend, I go out with my family to a park or the countryside, and we go for a walk. I sometimes go to a shopping centre with friends, but I hardly ever buy anything!

A LOT OF HOMEWORK!

SPEAKING

1 **Work in pairs. Discuss these questions.**

- Do you like doing courses in your free time?
- Is this your first English course?
- Do you like learning English?
- Do you like …
  - … doing homework?
  - … watching films or TV shows in English?
  - … listening to songs in English?
  - … reading in English?
  - … finding new words in a dictionary?
  - … practising your pronunciation?

VOCABULARY In an English class

2 **Match 1–5 with a–e and 6–10 with f–j.**

1	listen	a	a break / notes
2	take	b	the text / the questions
3	turn off	c	in pencil / the words in your notebook
4	write	d	to the conversation / and write what you hear
5	read	e	your mobile phones / the light
6	do	f	the words / what you think
7	check	g	a film / the video and take notes on what you see
8	close	h	Exercise 1 / a lot of homework
9	say	i	your book / the window
10	watch	j	the answers / the meaning in your dictionary

3 **Work in pairs.**

Student A: close your book.

Student B: say a verb.   *write*

Student A: say a phrase.   *write the answers*

4 **Do you need these things for your English class? Explain why / why not.**

a dictionary	paper	scissors
a mobile phone	a pen	tissues
money	a rubber	water

For example:

I always need a pen because I need to take notes.

I don't need scissors because I don't cut things in class.

LISTENING

5 ▶ **13** **Listen to three conversations in an English class. Decide which conversation (1–3) happens:**

a at the beginning of the class. _____

b in the middle of the class. _____

c at the end of the class. _____

6 ▶ **13** **Listen again. Decide if the sentences are true (T) or false (F).**

1 Camilla has money for two coffees.

2 The break is 25 minutes long.

3 They need to do two exercises for homework and learn some words.

4 Simon wants a lot of homework.

5 Simon sits next to Camilla.

6 Camilla gives him her dictionary.

7 ▶ **13** Listen again. Complete the sentences with one word. Contractions (*it's, isn't,* etc.) are one word.

1 It's a break. He says _____ a café next door.

2 OK, thanks. How _____ is the break?

3 B: This is a lot of homework.

   A: Do you _____ so?

4 Simon – _____ to do it. Do some every day. Five or ten minutes.

5 Hi. _____ I'm late.

6 Teacher! What does 'turn off' _____?

8 Work in pairs. Discuss the questions.

- Are Camilla and Simon good or bad students?
- Do you like the way Matty teaches? Why? / Why not?
- How often are you late / do you forget things / do you do homework?

GRAMMAR

Countable and uncountable nouns

We usually use *a / an* with singular nouns and *some / a lot of* with plural nouns.

Nouns with both singular and plural forms like this are called countable nouns.

some pencils

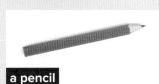
a lot of pencils | a pencil

Some nouns have no plural form.

These nouns are called uncountable nouns.

We use *some* or *a lot of* with them.

some money

a lot of homework

Here are some nouns that are often uncountable:

countryside   food   help   paper   time   traffic   water

9 Complete the sentences with *a / an, some* or *a lot of.*

1 I want to be _____ English teacher.

2 Do you have _____ rubber?

3 Do you want _____ water?

4 I need _____ paper to take _____ notes.

5 Sorry I'm late. There's _____ traffic today.

6 There's _____ nice countryside near here.

10 Look at each pair of sentences in the box and circle the differences. In pairs, discuss what things are different when you use an uncountable noun instead of a countable noun.

	Countable	Uncountable
1	*I don't need a dictionary.*	*I don't need any help.*
2	*There aren't any cars.*	*There isn't any traffic.*
3	*There aren't many cars.*	*There isn't much traffic.*
4	*Do you have a rubber?*	*Do you have any paper?*
5	*Do you have any tissues?*	*Do we have any homework?*
6	*Do you want some chips?*	*Do you want some water?*

G Check your ideas on page 169 and do Exercise 1.

11 Work in groups. Look at the words in Exercise 4. Find out:

- who has the most things.
- how many of the things you have between you.

For example:

A: *Do you have a pen?*

B: *Yes, here. Do you have any paper?*

A: *No. I don't.*

12 Use these ideas to write sentences that are true for you.

1 I / have / free time

2 There / be / thing(s) to do here

3 I / do / homework

4 I / want to have / kid(s)

5 I / drink / coffee

6 I / like / rock music

13 Work in pairs. Say your sentences to each other. How similar are you?

G For further practice, see Exercise 2 on page 169.

SOUNDS AND VOCABULARY REVIEW

14 ▶ **14** Listen and repeat the sounds with /k/, /g/, /s/ and /z/. Are any of them difficult for you to hear or say?

15 ▶ **15** Work in groups. Listen to eight sentences using the words in the box. Together, try to write them down. Then listen again and finish writing them.

break	countryside	get	relax
closes	games	homework	seems

G For further revision, see Exercises 1–3 on page 169.

VIDEO 1

A FAMOUS CITY

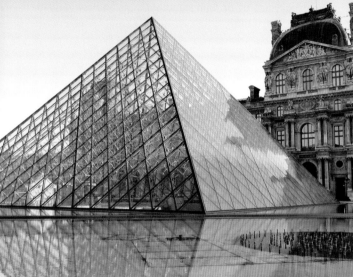

1 **Work in pairs. Look at the photos. Discuss these questions.**

   1 Which city do you think this is?

   2 Do you know the places in the photos?

   3 Do you think this is a good city to live? Why? / Why not?

2 📹 3 **Watch the first part of the video (0.00–0.58). Answer these questions.**

   1 What city is in the video?

   2 What does the speaker like about the city?

   3 In the video, the woman talks about the open spaces – parks, gardens and squares. As a class, say ten things people do in parks.

3 📹 3 **Watch the rest of the video (0.58–2.18). Does the speaker say the same ten things as you?**

4 **In pairs, say:**

   • the six different parks the woman talks about.

   • ten things the woman says people do in parks.

5 **Work in groups. Do you have any photos of your town / city? Show the other students in your group. Say something about each photo.**

UNDERSTANDING FAST SPEECH

6 📹 4 **Read and listen to this extract from the video said fast, then slow. Stressed sounds are in CAPITALS.**

   For TOUrists, PAris is the EIffel TOwer, the musEums, the CHURches. But for ME, PAris is the Open SPAces – the PARKS, GARdens and SQUARES.

7 **You try! Practise saying the extract with the same stressed sounds.**

REVIEW 1

GRAMMAR

1 Choose the correct option.

1 A: Where *are / is* he from?

   B: France.

2 A: Do you want *to go / going* to the cinema later?

   B: OK. What time?

3 A: Do you have *a / any* tissues?

   B: Yes. There are *one / some* in my bag.

4 A: *Are / Is* you OK?

   B: Yes, *I'm / am* OK, thanks.

5 A: Do you like *play / playing* tennis?

   B: Yes, *it's / he's* great.

6 A: *Does / Is* your town big?

   B: Not really. There *is / are* only about 10,000 people.

7 A: What *you do / do you do* at the weekend?

   B: I usually stay at home. *I don't / I'm not* earn much money.

8 A: *Do / Does* your son like football?

   B: He *love / loves* watching, but he doesn't play very *often / sometimes*.

2 Write full questions to complete the dialogue. Use the words in brackets.

A: ¹_____? (do)

B: I'm a doctor.

A: ²_____? (work)

B: At a hospital in the north of Rome.

A: ³_____? (enjoy)

B: Yes. It's a great job.

3 Put the word(s) in bold in the correct place in the sentence.

1 I need do some shopping. **to**

2 I play computer games. **hardly ever**

3 Sorry, I understand. What does 'journalist' mean? **don't**

4 Do you have pencil and paper? **a**

5 There's a palace near the river. It's great. **beautiful**

6 She speaks English very well, but she's from the UK. **not**

4 ▶ **16** **Listen and complete the sentences with one word in each space. Contractions (*I'm, don't,* etc.) are one word.**

1 _____ you _____ _____ money?

2 _____ _____ need _____ help, _____.

3 _____ time _____ _____ want _____ _____?

4 There _____ _____ _____ _____ places to visit _____.

5 I _____ need _____ _____ _____ homework _____.

6 _____ _____ gets up _____ six and _____ work _____ seven.

5 ▶ **16** **Work in pairs. Compare your ideas. Listen again and check.**

VOCABULARY

6 Match the verbs in the box to the groups of words they go with in 1–8.

check	help	play	turn off
close	live	say	watch

1 ~ the news / ~ a football game / ~ a film

2 ~ in the countryside / ~ in the capital / ~ on my own

3 ~ in the park / ~ the piano / ~ a game

4 ~ what you think / ~ no / ~ a lot

5 ~ the TV / ~ your phone / ~ the light

6 ~ my grandparents / ~ me / ~ to do my homework

7 ~ the answers / ~ the word in a dictionary / ~ it's OK

8 ~ your book / the shop ~s at nine / ~ the window

7 Put the words into three groups – places, jobs or free time.

assistant	countryside	factory	officer
church	dancing	guitar	receptionist
clinic	department	the Middle East	swimming
concert	draw	nurse	waiter

8 Match each adjective in italics in 1–8 with its opposite in a–h.

1 It's a *boring* job.   a cheap

2 I have a *busy* social life.   b best

3 He has a *big* car.   c quiet

4 It's an *expensive* restaurant.   d interesting

5 It's the *worst* place to live in the UK.   e west

6 It's in *east* Paris   f old

7 It's a *long* film.   g small

8 I have a *new* mobile phone.   h short

9 Complete the text with the verbs in the box.

finish	go	like	spend
get	have	listen	work

I ¹_____ in a department store in town. I usually start at eight o'clock and ²_____ at four. I leave the house at seven and ³_____ home at five or six. I ⁴_____ doing sport. I often ⁵_____ to the gym after work. I usually ⁶_____ about an hour there. Then, in the evening I just ⁷_____ dinner with my wife and watch TV. We sometimes sit and ⁸_____ to music.

3 HOME

3

IN THIS UNIT YOU LEARN HOW TO:

* talk about the area you live in
* name things you often buy and do
* explain where things are
* explain what you need to do
* describe your house / flat
* ask people to do things

WORDS FOR UNIT 3

1 Work in pairs. Match the words and phrases to the photos.

the bathroom	a post office
clean the house	put on make-up
a department store	set the table
dry my hair	share food
get dressed	sit in the kitchen
go to a chemist	a sports centre
hang up the washing	a supermarket
the living room	wash some clothes

2 ▶ 17 Listen. Check your answers. Listen again. Repeat the words.

3 Work in pairs. Test each other. Cover the words.

Student A: point to a photo.

Student B: say the words.

4 Which photos do you like / not like?

4

9

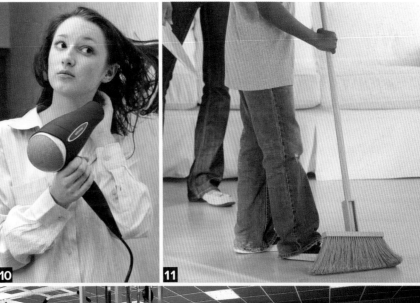

10

11

15

16

IS THERE ONE NEAR HERE?

SPEAKING

1 Work in pairs. Say the shops, restaurants and other facilities that are near your home – and the place you work or study. Decide which area is best.

For example:

A: *There's a really good supermarket near my home, and there are lots of different restaurants and there's a sports centre.*

B: *Near my house there's a small café, a bank and two shops. There's a small park.*

A: *I think my area is best, then.*

B: *Maybe.*

VOCABULARY Local facilities

2 Match the things people do (1–8) to the places in the box.

a bank	a chemist's	a shoe shop
a bookshop	a clothes shop	a sports centre
a café	a post office	

1 buy some toothpaste / buy some aspirins

2 buy a novel / buy a phrasebook

3 have something to eat / have something to drink

4 buy a shirt / buy a jacket

5 buy some boots / buy some shoes

6 play tennis / go swimming

7 buy some stamps / send a package

8 change some money / get some money

3 Work in groups. Discuss these questions.

• Which of the places in Exercise 2 do you go to most?

• What do you usually buy – or do – in each one?

GRAMMAR

Prepositions of place

We use these prepositions, and phrases with prepositions, to describe where things are:

in   on   between   behind   opposite   next to   in front of

4 Work in pairs. Label the balls in the picture with the prepositions in the box above.

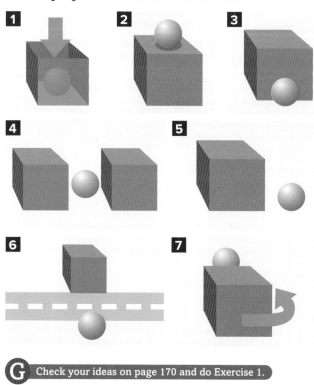

G Check your ideas on page 170 and do Exercise 1.

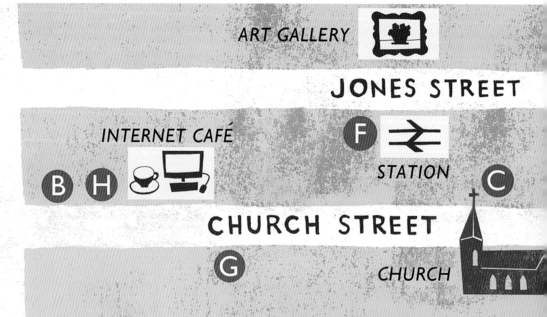

5 Read the sentences and label A–H on the map.

1 There's a bank on this road – next to the supermarket.

2 There's a hotel on the next street – on the left.

3 There's a great museum on this road – on the right.

4 There's a post office on the next road opposite the church.

5 There's a café on Jones Street – next to the station.

6 There's a cinema at the end of this road.

7 There's a big department store on the corner of Church Street and Jackson Lane.

8 There's a clothes shop between the internet café and the department store.

6 Work in pairs. Cover Exercise 5. Look at the map. Ask and answer questions like this:

A: **Is there a** post office **near here?**

B: **Yes, there's one** opposite the church.

For further practice, see Exercise 2 on page 170.

LISTENING

7 ▶ **18** Listen to three conversations where people ask about local places. Answer the questions for each conversation.

a What places do they want to find?

b What do they want to buy / do?

8 ▶ **18** Listen again. Tick (✓) the sentences that are true.

Conversation 1

1 The clothes shop is on New Street.

2 It's on the left.

3 It's next to a bookshop.

Conversation 2

4 There are lots of good places to eat in the area.

5 The supermarket is on Dixon Road.

6 It's next to a small park.

Conversation 3

7 The department store is on the corner of Chester Street and Hale Road

8 It's on the right.

9 It's opposite a clothes shop.

DEVELOPING CONVERSATIONS

Asking for information

When we ask friends for information about places, we often explain why we want to go there. Our friends can then give suggestions. For example:

A: *I need to buy some shoes for my son. Are there any shoe shops near here?*

B: *Try Kids Stuff – it's a clothes shop for kids. They sell nice shoes.*

C: *Are there any restaurants near here? We want to get something to eat.*

D: *There aren't really any places in this area. Try the supermarket on Dixon Road. They have sandwiches and salads.*

9 Look at the questions below. Think of two reasons to go to each place.

I need to ... I want to ...	Is there	a clothes shop a sports centre an internet café a chemist's a post office a bank	near here?

10 Work in pairs. Ask each other questions and give your reasons from Exercise 9. Answer with suggestions of places you know.

For example:

A: *I want to buy a jacket. Is there a clothes shop near here?*

B: *Yeah, try Topshop on Oxford Street.*

or

No, but try the big supermarket – they sell some clothes.

CONVERSATION PRACTICE

11 Choose one of these tasks.

a Work in pairs. Student A: look at File 1 on page 192. Student B: look at File 3 on page 193. Take turns to ask **Is there a ... near here?** to find the places you want. Explain why you need to go to each place. Your partner should answer with information from their map.

b Work in groups. Think of five things you want to buy or do. Then ask other students **Is there a ... near here?** The other students give true answers about the place you are now.

🎥 5 To watch the video and do the activities, see the DVD-ROM.

BOOKSHOP D

PARK ROAD

A

SUPERMARKET E

YOU ARE HERE

FAMILY HOME

VOCABULARY In the house

1 Complete the descriptions of two places with the words in the box.

apartment	bed	kitchen	sofa
balcony	bedrooms	sink	table
bathrooms	cupboards		

Description 1

We have a house. It's really nice. We have four
¹_____ and two ²_____. We have a lovely
living room and a big ³_____. We also have a small
garden, and I have a study because I work from home.

Description 2

I live in an ⁴_____. It has one bedroom, and a very
small bathroom with only a shower, ⁵_____ and
toilet. I have a small kitchen with a ⁶_____ where
I eat. I also have a ⁷_____ where I hang my
washing. The place is OK for me, but I don't have any
space for friends to stay. I only have two chairs and I
don't have many ⁸_____ to keep things in. I usually
watch TV lying in ⁹_____, because I don't have a
living room or a ¹⁰_____ to sit on!

2 Work in pairs. Describe where you live. Use some of the language in Exercise 1.

You need to spend time learning words. Here are three
ways to help you remember them:

– learn short phrases or pairs of words

– connect words to rooms in your house

– connect words to people

3 On a big piece of paper, draw a plan of your house. Write these phrases in different rooms. Then work in pairs and compare your ideas.

brush his teeth	put things in the fridge
cut vegetables	send an email
get dressed	set the alarm clock
get a towel	take an aspirin
lie down	talk on the phone
look in the mirror	wash the dishes
make dinner	watch a film
put on make-up	work on the computer

4 Work in pairs. Make a list of the people in your class. Write sentences like the examples below. Use an *-ing* form for the activity.

Kenji's in the kitchen making dinner.

Sara's on the balcony talking on the phone.

5 Now close your books. How many words and phrases can you remember?

READING

6 Quickly read the blog on page 29, by a young Greek woman, Maria. What places do the photos show?

7 Read again. Answer these questions.

1 What is good / bad about each place?

2 Who does she live with?

3 What problems does she have with each person?

8 Match the verbs with the words they go with in the blog. Then look at the blog and check your answers.

1 live   a an hour to drive there

2 study   b a room with my sister

3 take   c hours putting on her make-up

4 share   d with my sister and brother

5 annoy   e me

6 spend   f Business Management

9 Work in pairs. Say what you remember about Maria and her family, using the language in Exercise 8.

For example:

Maria lives with her sister, Dimitra, and her brother, Costa.

GRAMMAR

Pronouns, possessive adjectives and *'s*

Look at these sentences from the blog.

She spends hours putting on **her** make-up.

Sometimes **my** sister and brother annoy **me**.

My sister's bedroom has **its** own bathroom.

We use pronouns like *she* and *me* to replace nouns and names.

We use person + *'s* or possessive adjectives like *her*, *my* and *its* before a noun.

10 Complete the table.

Subject	Object	Adjective
I	¹_____	my
you	you	²_____
he	him	³_____
she	⁴_____	her
it	it	its
we	us	⁵_____
they	⁶_____	their

G Check your ideas on page 170 and do Exercise 1.

ME AND MY FAMILY

My name's Maria and I live in Thessaloniki. It's a great city. There are lots of things to do. I live with my sister, Dimitra, and my brother, Costa. They both work here, and I study – English and Business Management. We usually stay in the city during the week and then sometimes at the weekend we go back to our family house in the mountains near Askós. My parents live there. They're retired. It takes about an hour to drive there. It's a beautiful place, but the village is very quiet and small and there's not much to do.

In our family home, I think I have the best room because I have a balcony. Sometimes I sit there and listen to music or read or just relax and look at the lovely view. My sister's bedroom is big and has its own bathroom, which is why she thinks her room is the best. But I don't need my own bathroom.

Our flat in Thessaloniki is very small. I share a room with Dimitra, but Costa has his own room. Dimitra and I keep our room nice and tidy, but Costa's is a mess! There are clothes, books and paper on the floor and table. Men!

We take turns to cook, wash the dishes and clean the kitchen. I love living with my family, but sometimes my sister and brother annoy me. My brother sometimes 'forgets' to do his jobs in the house and my sister sometimes spends hours putting on her make-up and washing her hair – and we only have one bathroom there!

11 Complete the sentences. Use the correct object pronoun or possessive based on the words in brackets. The first one is done for you.

1 _____ room is very untidy. (I / sister)
My sister's room is very untidy.

2 I live on _____ own. (I)

3 My room has _____ own bathroom. (it)

4 My mum sometimes annoys _____. (I).

5 My friends keep a cat in _____ apartment. (they)

6 My dad usually makes dinner for _____. (we)

7 We pay someone to clean _____ home. (we)

8 I have a friend who works for _____ company. (he / father)

9 I go to _____ house most weeks. (I / grandparents).

12 Work in pairs. Discuss if the sentences in Exercise 11 are true for you or not.

 For further practice, see Exercise 2 on page 171.

SPEAKING

13 Think about your answers to these questions. Use a dictionary if you need help.

- What's good / bad about living with your parents when you're an adult?
- What's good / bad about sharing a room?
- What's good / bad about living on your own?
- Do you ever have any problems with the person / people you live with? What?

14 Work in groups. Discuss your answers.

CAN YOU HELP ME?

LISTENING

1 Match the sentences (a–h) with the pictures (1–8).

a I can't concentrate.
b I can't get it.
c I can't hear it.
d I can't find my keys.
e I'm cold.
f I'm hot.
g It's a mess.
h It's very dirty.

2 Work in groups. Discuss these questions.
- Which of the problems in Exercise 1 do you sometimes have in your home?
- Imagine you are the people with problems in Exercise 1. What's a good thing to say or ask in each situation?

3 ▶ **19** Listen to three conversations (1–3). Match each one to a situation in Exercise 1.

4 ▶ **19** Listen again. Complete the sentences with one word in each space.

Conversation 1

1 I _____ walk across it without breaking something!

2 Can you _____ it, please?

Conversation 2

3 What temperature is the air-conditioning _____?

4 Can you _____ it up? I'm cold.

5 It's _____ cold.

Conversation 3

6 What did he _____?

7 Can you turn it _____?

8 Is that _____ for you?

UNDERSTANDING VOCABULARY

Collocations

We call words that often go together *collocations*.

The most important kinds of collocations are:
verb + noun: *watch TV, dry my hair, clean the house*
adjective + noun: *a busy week, a famous town, an expensive area*
preposition + noun: *on the corner, at the weekend, in the morning*

When you learn a noun, try to learn verbs and adjectives that go with it.

For new verbs, learn some nouns that go with them.

Learn new preposition + noun collocations when you meet them.

5 Match the verbs in the box to the groups of nouns (1–6) that they go with.

brush	put on	turn up
cut	share	wash

1 ~ my jacket / ~ your shoes / ~ some make-up
2 ~ myself / ~ some vegetables / ~ my hair
3 ~ the TV / ~ the air-conditioning / ~ the music
4 ~ my hair / ~ my teeth / ~ the dog
5 ~ your hands / ~ some dirty clothes / ~ the plates
6 ~ a flat / ~ a room with my sister / ~ a pizza

6 Match the nouns in the box to the groups of verbs and adjectives (1–6) that they go with.

air-conditioning	cupboard	table
alarm clock	sink	towel

1 I need a ~ to dry myself / have a clean ~ / the ~'s wet
2 turn the ~ on / turn up the ~ / turn down the ~ / turn off the ~
3 set the ~ for dinner / clear the ~ / it's on the ~
4 wash your hands in the ~ / leave the dirty plates in the ~ / fill the kitchen ~
5 set the ~ for seven / hear the ~ / the ~ goes off
6 hang it up in the ~ / put it back in the ~ / the ~ under the sink

7 Say things about you and people you live with using the collocations below and *always, usually, hardly ever* or *never*.

For example:
My mum always washes my clothes.
My brother hardly ever washes his hands before dinner.

- wash my clothes
- wash … hands before dinner
- put milk back in the fridge
- leave dirty plates in the sink
- set the table for dinner
- hang up towels after using them
- set the alarm clock
- turn on the air-conditioning

GRAMMAR

can / can't

To say something is impossible, use *can't* + infinitive.

*I **can't get** it.*

*He **can't hear** it.*

To ask (someone) to do something, use *Can I / you*, etc. + infinitive.

***Can** you **turn** the TV down, please? I **can't concentrate**.*

***Can** I **use** this towel? I want to have a shower.*

8 What different ways can you answer the questions in the box above?

 Check your ideas on page 171 and do Exercise 1

9 Put the words in the correct order.

1 sleep / I / can't / .
2 you / can / me / help / ?
3 use / I / can / bathroom / your / ?
4 up / you / turn / can / music / the / ?
5 book / find / I / can't / my / .
6 can / clothes / wash / some / I / ?
7 week / can't / we / next / come / .
8 moment / can't / he / drive / at / the / .

10 ▶ 20 Listen to the sentences in Exercise 9. Notice how we usually say *can* as /kən/ and *can't* as /kɑːnt/. Practise saying the sentences.

11 Use the words in 1–7 to write a question with *can* and an explanation with *can't*. The question sometimes comes before and sometimes after the explanation. The first one is done for you.

1 I / hear you   you / speak louder
   I can't hear you. Can you speak louder?
2 you / move   I / see the board
3 I / do this exercise   you / help me
4 you / turn it up   I / hear the CD
5 I / come to the class   you / tell me the homework
6 I / read the board   I / sit nearer
7 I / go to the toilet   I / wait

12 Work in pairs. Have short conversations using your sentences from Exercise 11.

For example:
A: *I can't hear you. Can you speak louder?*
B: *Yes, of course. Sorry.*

 For further practice, see Exercise 2 on page 171.

SPEAKING

13 Work in pairs. Write four short conversations based on the pictures in Exercise 1.

14 Remember your conversations. Act the conversations for another pair.

SOUNDS AND VOCABULARY REVIEW

15 ▶ 21 Listen and repeat the sounds with /f/, /v/, /p/ and /b/. Are any of them difficult for you to hear or say?

16 ▶ 22 Work in groups. Listen to eight sentences using these words. Together, try to write them down. Then listen again and finish writing them.

bank	living room	plates	sofas
bathroom	package	post office	vegetables

G For further revision, see Exercises 1–3 on page 171.

4 HOLIDAYS

3

4

8

15

IN THIS UNIT YOU LEARN HOW TO:

- talk about what you did in the past
- comment on what people tell you
- talk about dates and months
- ask and answer questions about holidays

WORDS FOR UNIT 4

1 Work in pairs. Match the words and phrases to the photos.

be annoyed	have a picnic
celebrate your birthday	laugh
do some shopping	rent a boat
enjoy the nightlife	see a film
get back home	snow
get some flowers	stay in a hotel
go sightseeing	walk in the mountains
have a cold	watch a football match

2 ▶ 23 Listen. Check your answers. Listen again. Repeat the words.

3 Work in pairs. Test each other. Cover the words.

Student A: point to a photo.

Student B: say the words.

4 Which photos do you like / not like?

9

16

Unit 4 Holidays **33**

I HAD A GREAT WEEKEND

LISTENING

1   Read what four people say about last weekend.
    Do you think each person had a very good time,
    an OK time or a bad time?

    a I was ill. I had a bad cold.

    b We went to a rock festival.

    c Some friends came to visit, so I showed them round
       the city.

    d Nothing much, really. I did some shopping on
       Saturday.

2   ▶ 24 Listen to four conversations. Match
    the conversations (1–4) to sentences a–d in
    Exercise 1. Does each person say the weekend
    was good, OK or bad?'

3   ▶ 24 Listen again. Match a–f below to
    conversations 1–4.

    Conversation 1   _____, _____

    Conversation 2   _____

    Conversation 3   _____, _____

    Conversation 4   _____, _____

    a We had a picnic in the park.

    b I saw The Loons on Saturday night. They were good.

    c I stayed in bed all weekend.

    d I cooked lunch for everyone.

    e I played tennis, watched TV – the usual things.

    f It was fantastic.

4   Work in pairs. Discuss whether you like:

    • busy weekends or quiet weekends.

    • going to music festivals.

    • going to markets.

    • cooking for lots of people.

    • showing people round your town / area.

GRAMMAR

Past simple

The past simple form is usually infinitive + -ed.

If the infinitive form of the verb ends in -e, just add -d.

I **played** tennis and **watched** TV.

I **wanted** to go out yesterday.

She **smiled** to herself.

A lot of common verbs are irregular.

You just need to learn the past simple forms of irregular
verbs when you meet them.

see – saw	take – took	spend – spent
get – got	read – read	buy – bought

5 Look at the past simple forms of some verbs from the listening. Write the infinitive form.

1 showed – *show*
2 cooked – _____
3 stayed – _____
4 played – _____
5 watched – _____
6 went – _____
7 did – _____
8 had – _____
9 was / were – _____
10 came – _____

 Check your ideas on page 172 and do Exercise 1.

6 Work in pairs. Test each other.

Student A: say the infinitive forms in Exercise 5.

Student B: cover the exercise. Say the past simple forms.

Then change roles and repeat.

7 Complete the sentences about things people did last weekend with the past simple forms of the verbs in the box.

be	get	have	stay
come	go	spend	watch

1 I _____ lunch with my grandparents.
2 I _____ to the beach with some friends.
3 We _____ at home and relaxed.
4 I _____ a football match on Saturday.
5 There _____ a free concert in town.
6 Some friends _____ to our house for dinner.
7 I went shopping and I _____ some new shoes.
8 I _____ all weekend studying for an exam.

8 Write three things you did in the past that were great, and three things you did that were bad or boring. Work in groups. Share your ideas.

 For further practice, see Exercise 2 on page 172.

DEVELOPING CONVERSATIONS

That sounds ...
We use *that sounds* + adjective to comment on what people say.

A: *Some friends came to visit, so I showed them round the city.*

B: *That sounds nice.*

9 Write a comment about each sentence using *that sounds* + an adjective in the box.

bad	interesting	great	nice

1 We rented a boat and went on the lake.
2 I went for a walk in the countryside.
3 I had a headache, so I stayed at home.
4 I went shopping with my mum.
5 I saw a documentary about crime.
6 We had a party at home.

10 Practise the conversations.

For example:

A: *What did you do?*

B: *We rented a boat and went on the lake.*

A: *That sounds great.*

PRONUNCIATION

11 ▶ 25 Listen. Circle the form of the verbs you hear in the sentences.

1 visit / visited
2 visit / visited
3 play / played
4 try / tried; play / played
5 want / wanted; rain / rained
6 chat / chatted
7 walk / walked; chat / chatted
8 walk / walked

We usually say past *-ed* endings as /d/ or /t/.

rained	played	walked
/reɪnd/	/pleɪd/	/wɔːkt/

When the infinitive ends in /t/ or /d/, the pronunciation of past *-ed* endings is /ɪd/.

wanted	chatted	visited	decided
/ˈwɒntɪd/	/ˈtʃætɪd/	/ˈvɪzɪtɪd/	/dɪˈsaɪdɪd/

12 Work in pairs. Look at the audio script for Track 24 on page 200 and practise reading out the conversations.

CONVERSATION PRACTICE

13 Think about last weekend. Did you have a nice weekend? Choose an answer from the list below. Write down two or three things you did.

a Yeah, it was great.
b It was OK.
c Not really.

14 Have conversations with different people in your class. Use these two questions.

• Did you have a nice weekend?
• What did you do?

Comment on people's answers about their activities with *that sounds* ...

15 Work in pairs. Decide which person in the class had the best weekend – and why.

 6 To watch the video and do the activities, see the DVD-ROM.

spring

summer

autumn

winter

A PUBLIC HOLIDAY

VOCABULARY
Months, seasons and dates

1 Put the months in the correct order.

August	June	January	December
February	May	October	September
April	July	March	November

2 Work in groups. Discuss these questions.

- Look at the four photos above. Do you have the four seasons in your country?
- What months are they?
- Did you go on holiday this / last year?
- What season was it? What month?

We use ordinal numbers for dates.

March the fourth, May the sixth

To make most ordinal numbers, add *-th* to the number. Some are irregular.

1st – first	*2nd – second*
3rd – third	*5th – fifth*
9th – ninth	*12th – twelfth*
20th – twentieth	*21st – twenty-first*
30th – thirtieth	*31st – thirty-first*

We use *on* with dates: *on October the twelfth.*

3 ▶ 26 Listen and write the dates you hear in 1–6 to complete the information about public holidays.

1	New Year's Day, UK	*Jan 1st*
2	Mother Teresa Day, Albania	_____
3	Women's Day, Russia	_____
4	Day of the Dead, Mexico	_____
5	Sant Joan's Day, Catalonia	_____
6	Martin Luther King Day, USA	_____

4 Work in pairs. Follow the instructions in your file.

Student A: use File 2 on page 192.

Student B: use File 4 on page 193.

5 Work in groups. Discuss these questions.

- Which of the public holidays in Exercises 3 and 4 do you celebrate in your country? How?
- Do you know anything about the other public holidays?
- Do you have any public holidays to celebrate famous people? When? Who is the person?
- Who has a birthday next in your class?

LISTENING

6 ▶ 27 Listen to three stories about what people did on public holidays. Which public holiday from Exercise 3 does each speaker talk about?

7 ▶ 27 Work in pairs. Check you understand the words below from the three stories. Then decide which speaker used each group of words. Listen again to check your ideas.

    a missed – work – nice – presents – flowers – say – room

    b three – drove – clear – cloud – views – traffic – two

    c fire – beach – night – songs – swam – warm – slept

8 ▶ 27 Listen again. Complete the sentences with one word in each space.

Speaker 1

1 We _____ a fire on the beach.

2 We _____ songs and laughed.

3 Some of my friends swam in the _____.

Speaker 2

4 I was in London for work, so I missed the _____.

5 On Women's Day, men usually _____ us very well.

6 I didn't go out for dinner. I didn't get _____ flowers.

Speaker 3

7 We _____ on Saturday the 16th at three in the morning.

8 We drove to the _____.

9 It was very clear and sunny. There wasn't a cloud in the _____.

9 Work in pairs. Say as much as you can about what each speaker did, using the words in Exercise 7.

For example:

*They made a **fire** on the **beach** with some friends.*

GRAMMAR

Past simple negatives

To make past simple negatives, we use *wasn't* / *weren't* for the verb *be*.

For all other verbs, we use *didn't* + infinitive.

10 Complete the sentences from the listening using *wasn't, weren't* or *didn't*.

1 It was good, because there _____ many cars on the road.

2 I _____ go out for dinner.

3 The sea _____ very warm.

Ⓖ Check your ideas on page 172 and do Exercise 1.

11 Write the negative form of the past simple verbs in brackets.

1 I _____ much on Sunday. (did)

2 I _____ until eleven. (got up)

3 I wanted to have breakfast, but there _____ any coffee or bread in the house. (was)

4 I went to the shop, but I _____ my keys. (took)

5 The shops _____ open. It was a holiday! (were)

6 I tried to call my neighbour, but he _____. (answered)

7 I went to a café and I had a coffee, but then I saw that I _____ any money! (had)

8 I went back to my flat. I broke a window to get in. I _____ again after that. (went out)

In negative sentences, we often use *any* + noun after the verb. We can also use *anyone, anything, anywhere*.

I **didn't** get **any** flowers.

I **didn't** have **anyone** to say nice things to me.

12 Complete the sentences by adding *any, anyone, anything* and *anywhere*.

1 I wanted to buy it, but I didn't have _____ money.

2 The film was in English. I didn't understand _____!

3 The beach was very quiet. We didn't see _____ there for maybe three days.

4 We went shopping in the morning, but I didn't buy _____.

5 I had a very quiet weekend. I didn't go _____.

6 We stayed in a very small town. There weren't _____ shops or banks!

7 I didn't enjoy the party. There wasn't _____ I knew there.

8 There wasn't _____ to park the car, so I drove home.

Ⓖ For further practice, see Exercises 2 and 3 on page 173.

SPEAKING

13 Write answers to these questions. Then work in groups and say what you've written.

    • What's your favourite public holiday? What do you normally do?

    • When was the last public holiday? What did you do?

DID YOU GO ANYWHERE NICE?

VOCABULARY Going on holiday

go on holiday

If you go on holiday, you stop working and go away to a different place to relax, usually for a few days or more.

1 Match the verbs (1–6) to the groups of words they go with (a–f).

1 fly	a	a day in Rome / the week relaxing / lots of money
2 stay	b	to Helsinki / with British Airways / first-class
3 take	c	the train / the bus / a taxi
4 spend	d	with friends / in a hotel / in a bed and breakfast
5 rent	e	sightseeing / out for dinner / swimming
6 go	f	a car / a boat / a flat

2 Work in groups. Discuss these questions.

- How often do you / does your family go on holiday?
- Do you usually go to the same place or do you go to different places?
- What do you usually do when you are on holiday?

READING

3 Read an email from a Danish man to his Italian friend. Put the photos in the order they are talked about in the text.

To	mauro1990@shotmail.it
Subject	Re: Ireland

Hi Mauro,

How are you? I hope you and your family are well. How was your trip to Korea? I'm sure it was great.

Helena and I spent three fantastic weeks in Ireland and had a really great time. We flew to Dublin, the capital, and spent a week there. It's a beautiful city. We went sightseeing every day and saw all the old buildings. Then in the evenings, we went out and enjoyed the nightlife. It's a fun city! You'd love it.

After that, we rented a car and spent two weeks driving round the country. It's really beautiful! I was worried about the weather, but it didn't rain once. We stayed in little bed and breakfasts and met some really lovely people.

My favourite place was the west of the country. We went walking in the mountains in County Mayo for a few days. It was lovely and quiet. On the first day we didn't see anyone else – we only saw sheep!

Anyway, now we're back in Copenhagen and back at work! How was your summer? Did you go on holiday anywhere? Did you have a good time?

Please write and tell me everything! Or why not come and visit us? There are some cheap flights in September and the weather is still OK.

Your friend,

Nicklas

4 **Read the email again and answer these questions.**

1 Where did Nicklas go?

2 Did he go on his own?

3 How long was he there for?

4 Was the weather good?

5 What did he do there?

6 Do you think it was a good holiday? Why? / Why not?

5 **Complete the sentences with one word in each space. Look at the email if you need help.**

1 We _____ to Dublin.

2 We _____ a week there.

3 It's a _____ city.

4 I was _____ about the weather, but it didn't rain once!

5 My _____ place was the west of the country.

6 We went _____ in the mountains.

7 On the first day we didn't see _____ else!

8 How _____ your summer?

9 Did you go on holiday _____?

10 There are some cheap _____ in September.

SPEAKING

6 **Work in pairs. Tell each other the best place in your area / country:**

- to go sightseeing.
- to go walking.
- to go swimming.
- to spend a week relaxing.
- for nightlife.
- for driving around.

GRAMMAR

Past simple questions

For the verb *be*, make questions with *was / were*.

How **was** your summer?

How long **were** you there for?

For other verbs, use *did*.

Where **did you go**?

Did you have a good time?

7 **Use the notes below. Write past simple questions you could use to ask a friend about their holiday.**

1 you / go on holiday anywhere?

2 where / go?

3 who / go with?

4 have a good time?

5 how long / there for?

6 where / stay?

7 it very expensive?

8 the weather good?

9 the food good?

PRONUNCIATION

8 ▶ **28** **Listen to** *did you* **– first fast, then slow. Then listen to the** *did you* **questions from Exercise 7 – first fast and then slow. Repeat them.**

1 Did you go on holiday anywhere?

2 Where did you go?

3 Who did you go with?

4 Did you have a good time?

5 Where did you stay?

9 **Match the answers a–i to the questions (1–9) in Exercise 7.**

a Yes, I did. It's a great country.

b Yes, great. They eat lots of fruit, lots of rice. It's lovely.

c I stayed with friends in Rio and then in a hotel.

d Yes, I did. I went to Brazil.

e Two weeks.

f I went on my own.

g No, not really. Most things are quite cheap there.

h Rio de Janeiro and Salvador in the east.

i It was great, yes. Really hot and sunny.

G For further practice, see Exercises 1 and 2 on page 173.

SPEAKING

10 **Choose one of these things to talk about.**

- last weekend
- the last public holiday
- the last time you went on holiday
- your last birthday
- a special day in your life

11 **Write five past simple questions for your partner to ask you about your day / weekend / holiday.**

12 **Work in pairs. Swap questions and interview each other.**

SOUNDS AND VOCABULARY REVIEW

13 ▶ **29** **Listen and repeat the sounds with /d/, /t/, /m/ and /n/. Are any of them difficult for you to hear or say?**

14 ▶ **30** **Work in groups. Listen to eight sentences using the words below. Together, try to write them down. Then listen again and finish writing them.**

drove	missed	rented	time
June	mountains	spent	warm

G For further revision, see Exercises 1–3 on page 173.

VIDEO 2

ALEX THE PARROT

1 Look at the photo. Work in pairs. Discuss these questions.

- Which is the dog, the cat and the parrot?
- For each animal, give a mark 0–5 in each row of the table below.
- Which do you think is the best pet / animal?

	Dog	Cat	Parrot
intelligent			
clean			
friendly			
boring			
beautiful			
easy to keep			

2 ▶ 7 Watch the video about cognitive biologist Irene Pepperberg and the project and tests she does with a parrot called Alex. Which one of the sentences below best explains what the project shows?

1 Parrots are the best pets for children.
2 Parrots are more intelligent than cats.
3 Parrots can repeat sounds but they don't understand the meaning of words.
4 Parrots can show they understand size and colour.
5 Parrots can do the same maths as a five-year-old human.

3 ▶ 7 Complete the summary of the video with these words. Then watch the video and check.

abilities	died	love	smaller
African	different	many	words

Irene Pepperberg worked with an [1]_____ grey parrot called Alex. Alex amazed scientists because he understood words. He could answer questions like *How [2]_____? What colour? What's the same? What's [3]_____? What colour's bigger? What colour's [4]_____?* This showed cognitive [5]_____ similar to four- or five-year-old humans and so the scientists believed adult parrots can think and communicate. Alex [6]_____ in 2007. He learned around 150 [7]_____ in his life and his last ones to Irene were 'I [8]_____ you'.

4 Work in groups. Tell the people in your group about someone you know who has / had a pet. The others ask these questions to find out more.

Do you like it?	Did you like it?
What's its name?	What was its name?
How big is it?	How big was it?
Where does (s)he keep it?	Where did they keep it?
How old is it?	How old was it when it died?

UNDERSTANDING FAST SPEECH

5 ▶ 8 Read and listen to this extract from the video said fast, then slow. Stressed sounds are in CAPITALS.

ALex was ABle to idENtify an OBject MANy WAYS – by COlour, SIZE, and SO on.

6 You try! Practise saying the extract with the same stressed sounds.

REVIEW 2

GRAMMAR

1 Choose the correct option.

1 There's a café *on* / *in* the corner of this road.

2 Our house is *in front* / *next* to a school.

3 *Simon's* / *Simon* parents live on this road.

4 Can you give *he* / *him* the keys?

5 I'm sorry, I *can't* / *can* see the board.

6 Did you *went* / *go* out last night?

7 They *were* / *was* both ill at the weekend.

8 My house is *at* / *in* the end of this road, *opposite* / *between* the church.

2 Complete the text with the past simple form of the verbs in brackets.

We ¹_____ (have) a great holiday in Greece. We ²_____ (fly) to Athens and ³_____ (spend) three days there and ⁴_____ (see) all the famous sights. After that, we ⁵_____ (take) a boat to Mykonos and we ⁶_____ (stay) in a small hotel near the beach.

3 Rewrite the sentences as negatives (-) or questions (?).

1 I can come to the next class. (-)

2 There's a supermarket near here. (?)

3 The hotel was very good. (-)

4 He had a nice time. (?)

5 I understood everything. (-)

6 I can help you later. (?)

4 Write full questions to complete the dialogue. Use the words in brackets.

A: ¹_____? (nice weekend)

B: Yes, it was great.

A: ²_____? (do)

B: I went to stay with my brother.

A: That's nice. ³_____? (live)

B: Leeds. We went to the theatre on Saturday night.

A: ⁴_____? (see)

B: *Othello*.

A: ⁵_____? (good)

B: I liked it, but my brother didn't.

5 ▶ 31 Listen and complete the sentences with one word in each space. Contractions (*I'm, don't,* etc.) are one word.

1 _____ bank's _____ _____ road _____ right.

2 _____ think _____ lives _____ _____ own.

3 _____ _____ turn _____ up? _____ _____ hear it.

4 _____ long _____ you _____ _____?

5 There _____ _____ _____ knew _____.

6 I'm sorry. _____ _____ hear _____ _____ _____.

6 ▶ 31 Work in pairs. Compare your ideas. Listen again to check.

VOCABULARY

7 Replace the adjectives in italics in 1–6 with their opposites in a–f.

1 Do you have any *dirty* clothes?	a bad
2 It's very *hot* in here.	b cold
3 That sounds *great*.	c nice
4 It was *clear and sunny*.	d wet
5 Is that towel *dry*?	e clean
6 People were very *unfriendly*.	f cloudy

8 Put the words into three groups – local facilities, home or time of year.

apartment	chemist's	March	sofa
autumn	cupboard	October	spring
balcony	fridge	post office	sports centre
bookshop	kitchen	sink	winter

9 Match the verbs in the box to the groups of words they go with in 1–8.

cut	send	share	turn down
get	set	show	wash

1 ~ a flat with a friend / ~ a pizza / ~ your ideas

2 ~ an email / ~ a package / ~ a message

3 ~ some money / ~ dressed / ~ back home

4 ~ the table / ~ your alarm clock / ~ a rule

5 ~ the vegetables / ~ yourself / ~ it with scissors

6 ~ your hair / ~ your hands / ~ the plates

7 ~ the air-conditioning / ~ the TV / ~ the temperature

8 ~ me on the map / ~ us round town / ~ him what to do

10 Complete the text with the words in the box.

annoys	mess	rents	songs	visited
lay	nightlife	sightseeing	view	watched

My brother now lives in Rome and I ¹_____ him in the summer. He ²_____ a small flat in the centre of town, so it was great to go ³_____ and enjoy the great ⁴_____. And his flat is on the top floor of the building, so there was a nice ⁵_____ from his balcony. That was all good, but sometimes my brother really ⁶_____ me. The flat was a ⁷_____ when I arrived. I tidied it, but he didn't say thanks. I made dinner and he just ⁸_____ on the sofa and ⁹_____ a film. He also sings ¹⁰_____ in the shower in the morning – very badly! So at the end of the holiday I was happy to leave!

5 SHOPS

1

2

5

6

7

8

12

13

42

14

3

IN THIS UNIT YOU LEARN HOW TO:

- describe what you want
- talk to a shop assistant
- understand prices
- talk about department stores
- talk about things happening now
- give excuses
- follow directions in a store

4

WORDS FOR UNIT 5

1   Work in pairs. Match the words and phrases to the photos.

a bar on the top floor	the menswear department
business is growing	queue to pay
the cheese section	steal some jeans
choose a cake	take the lift
fruit and vegetables	a young woman with a blue top
go up the escalator	a woman with a green dress
have a sale	a woman with a leather jacket
look round the market	work in a bakery
a man with a brown jumper	

2   ▶ 32 Listen. Check your answers. Listen again. Repeat the words.

3   Work in pairs. Test each other. Cover the words.

Student A: point to a photo.

Student B: say the words.

4   What other colours can you see in the photos? What other clothes can you see?

9

15

10

11

16

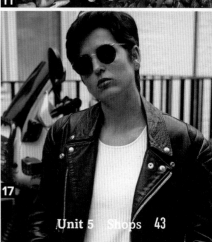

17

HOW MUCH IS THAT RED ONE?

DEVELOPING CONVERSATIONS

Questions in shops
Learning common questions for particular situations will help you understand and have conversations.

1 **Who usually asks each question 1–8: shop assistants (A) or customers (C)?**

1 Who's next?

2 What are those made of?

3 How much are the apples?

4 Can I have some ...?

5 Which one(s)?

6 How much would you like?

7 How many would you like?

8 Anything else?

2 **Match the questions (1–8) in Exercise 1 to the pairs of possible answers (a–h).**

a A: _____
B: Sure. How much?
Of course. How many do you want?

b A: _____
B: 50p each.
One forty-nine a kilo.

c A: _____
B: Me.
This lady, I think.

d A: _____
B: That much.
Half a kilo.

e A: _____
B: Those ones have fish in them and the others have meat.
Leather.

f A: _____
B: No, thanks, that's all.
Yeah, can I have some of that, please?

g A: _____
B: Five or six.
Just one.

h A: _____
B: The blue one.
The ones next to the apples.

3 **Spend two minutes remembering one answer for each question in Exercise 1. Then work in pairs.**

Student A: ask questions.

Student B: close your book and give answers.

LISTENING

4 ▶ **33** Listen to three conversations in markets. Complete the table about what the people buy, including number, size, colour, etc.

	Buys	Total cost
1	¹_____ red _____ ²_____ _____ peaches	³_____
2	⁴_____ cake Coffee cake with ⁵_____	⁶_____
3	⁷_____ _____	⁸_____

5 ▶ **33** Work in pairs and compare your answers. Then listen again and check.

PRONUNCIATION

6 ▶ **34** Listen to these numbers and mark the main stress.

thirteen	fourteen	sixteen
thirty	forty	sixty

7 ▶ **35** Listen to the sentences and write the numbers you hear.

1 That's €_____ exactly.

2 That's $_____ altogether.

3 Everything is reduced by _____%.

4 Those are _____ at the moment, reduced from _____.

5 It costs £_____ new.

6 Our apartment cost _____ when we bought it.

SPEAKING

8 Work in groups. Discuss these questions.

- How important is the price of things? Do you know how much things cost?
- What do you think is the average price of the things below where you live? What's the maximum you think it's OK to pay for them?

a cup of coffee	a new car
a flat with two bedrooms	a nice pair of shoes
a kilo of bananas	a pair of jeans
a litre of petrol	a piece of cake in a café
a meal for two in a restaurant	

- How much would you pay for the things in the photos on page 44?
- Do you ever negotiate the price for things? What things? Are you good at it?

GRAMMAR *this / these / that / those*

9 Match the sentences (1–4) to the pictures (a–d).

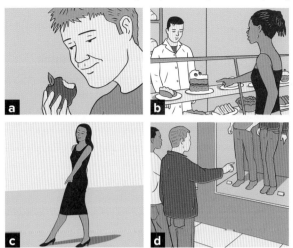

1 I like these ones.

2 This apple is nice.

3 Those jeans are expensive.

4 That cake looks good.

G Check your ideas on page 174 and do Exercise 1.

10 Complete the sentences with one word in each space.

1 A: What _____ this called in English?

B: A shirt.

2 A: What do you call _____ things on your table?

B: They're coins.

3 A: How much _____ those jackets?

B: What? These leather _____?

A: Yes.

B: Well, it depends. _____ brown one's £100.

11 Work in groups. Ask each other the name in English for different things in the classroom. Use these questions.

- What's this called?
- What's that thing there called?
- What are these / those things called?

G For further practice, see Exercise 2 on page 174.

CONVERSATION PRACTICE

12 Work in pairs. Have similar conversations to the ones in the listening. Choose a shop from the photos on page 44.

Student A: you are the shop assistant. Hold your book open for Student B to see.

Student B: you are the customer. Buy two different things in the photo. Try to negotiate the price! Use as much of the language from this page as you can.

Choose a different picture. Change roles and have another conversation.

9 To watch the video and do the activities, see the DVD-ROM.

THEY'RE HAVING A SALE

READING

1 **Work in groups. Discuss these questions.**

- How often do you go shopping? How often do you buy things online? Which do you prefer?
- Do you usually wait for shops to have a sale before you buy things? Why? / Why not?
- Where was the last sale you went to? Did you buy anything?
- Tell a partner about a time you got a bargain. Use sentences like these.

  I bought a coat for the winter. It was €60, reduced from 100.

  I bought a mountain bike. It was reduced by 50%.

  I bought my car for €2,000! I bought it from a friend.

- Who in your group got the best bargain?

2 **Work in groups of four: two As and two Bs. Read about two shops that are having sales.**

Student As: read about Emily.

Student Bs: read about Dalena.

Answer these questions for your text.

1 Where is she from?
2 What does she do?
3 Where does she work?
4 Why is the shop having a sale?
5 How's she feeling? Why?
6 What does she want to do in the future?

3 **Compare answers with the person in your group who read the same text.**

4 **Now work in pairs: one Student A and one Student B. Ask and answer the questions in Exercise 2 to find out about your partner's text.**

5 **Work with the same partner. Complete the sentences with the words in bold from the texts. Put one word in each space.**

1 My granddad had his own business, but he sold it when he _____.
2 My dad works very _____. He has three jobs!
3 It's _____ that small shops are closing in our town.
4 We want to find a new office because the business is _____ fast and we need more space.
5 In the future, I want to start my own business and _____ lots of money!
6 There are lots of _____ to find a good job here.
7 How can I _____ my German?
8 I _____ the toy section in a department store in town. It's a good job.

SPEAKING

6 **Work in pairs. Discuss these questions.**

- Do you know any shops that are closing? Do you know why?
- Are any shops opening where you live? What kind of shops? Are you happy about it?
- Do you know anyone who works very hard? What do they do?
- Do you want to be a manager in a company or shop in the future? Why? / Why not?
- Do you want to make lots of money? If yes, how? If no, why not?
- Are there a lot of opportunities for young people in your country? Why? / Why not?

GRAMMAR

Present continuous

Look at these sentences from the texts.

*I'm **looking** for a job at the moment.*

*We're **having** a sale because we're **closing** the shop.*

*The store opened last year and it's **doing** very well.*

The present continuous uses a form of *be + -ing*. We use the present continuous to talk about present actions or situations that are temporary and not finished.

7 **Complete the sentences with *am / are / is*.**

1 The shops in town _____ having sales at the moment.
2 I _____ working very hard at the moment.
3 My mother's not here. She _____ doing the shopping.
4 The economy _____ growing fast at the moment.
5 My football team _____ doing really well now.
6 You _____ really improving. You didn't know much English when we first met.
7 Some friends _____ staying with me at the moment.
8 My brother _____ studying at university.

PRONUNCIATION

8 ▶ **36** **Listen to the present continuous sentences from Exercise 7. Notice how they use the short forms of *am / are / is*. Listen again and repeat the sentences.**

9 **Look again at sentences 1 and 2 in Exercise 7.**

1 What phrase shows the present actions or situations are temporary and not finished?
2 Make a question and a negative from each sentence.

 Check your ideas on page 174 and do Exercise 1.

A BIG SALE

EMILY, GERMANY

We're having a sale because we're closing the shop. It's **sad**, because my grandfather opened it 60 years ago. When I was small, I came here on Saturday mornings and sat and read the children's books.

When my granddad **retired**, I started to **manage** the shop. Now there's a sale, so there are lots of people and they're buying lots of books, but we don't normally have so many customers. There are lots of very big bookshops now, which sell every book their customers want. They often have cafés and famous writers come and give talks for them, but we can't do that. And then other people look online to get books cheaper, so we don't really **make** much money.

I'm looking for a job at the moment, but I don't really know what I want to do in the future. I don't really want to work in another bookshop after I leave here.

DALENA, SLOVAKIA

I'm a sales assistant in a big clothes store. The store opened last year and it's doing very well. We're having our summer sale at the moment, so I'm working really **hard**. The shop is staying open later than normal. We usually close at seven, but during the sale we're open until nine. I'm tired, but I like my job. I like helping people to find nice clothes and, of course, everyone is happy when they find a bargain.

I want to continue working with the company and maybe become a floor manager and then a store manager. I think it's a good place to work, and the business is **growing** at the moment and opening new stores, so I think there are lots of **opportunities**. Maybe I can get a job in one of their shops in the UK and **improve** my English!

---

10 Work in pairs. Which sentences in Exercise 7 are true for you? Change the other sentences so they are true.

11 You are at a party or meeting. Write an excuse using the present continuous to explain why each of the people in the box can't come.

your mum and dad	Susie (your sister)
your wife or husband	David (a friend / flatmate)
Mr Smith (your boss)	the President!

Now have conversations using your sentences.

For example:

A: *Hi. How are you?*

B: *Fine.*

A: *Are your mum and dad coming?*

B: *No. Some friends of theirs are visiting.*

G For further practice, see Exercise 2 on page 175.

DO YOU SELL ...?

SPEAKING

1   Read the text about the store in the photo. Find out what is unusual about John Lewis.

2   Work in groups. Discuss these questions.
- Do you think it's a good idea to share a company's profits between the workers? Why? / Why not? Do you know any other company that does it?
- What's the biggest department store where you live? Do you ever go there? Why? / Why not? What do you know about the company?
- What's your favourite shop? Why?

VOCABULARY Department stores

3   Label the plan with the words in the box.

an assistant	the main entrance
the basement	the menswear department
the beauty department	the second floor
the changing rooms	the security guard
the escalator	the till
the first floor	the top shelf
the ground floor	the womenswear department
the lifts	

John Lewis is the company with the most department stores in the UK. The company started with one shop in Oxford Street, London, in 1864. The store is still there today. It has around 80 sections and sells everything from cheese to baths, and perfume to foreign holidays. After the war, the business grew a lot and it now has 32 department stores, eleven furniture shops, a small factory and a farm. It also owns a supermarket with over 300 shops. John Lewis is an unusual company because all the workers are partners in the business – when the company makes money, the workers share some of the profits. John Lewis made around £320 million last year and the 93,000 partners shared half of that money between them.

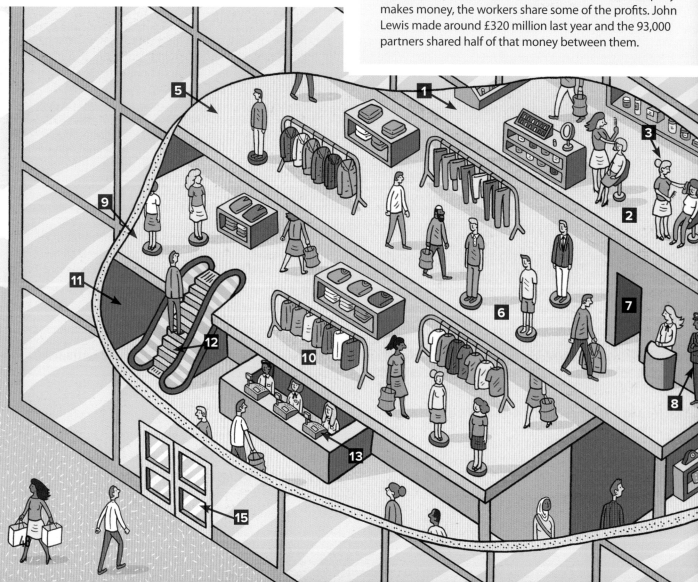

4 Work in pairs. Answer these questions using words from Exercise 3.

1 Where do you try clothes on?

2 Where do you ask 'Are you going up?' or say 'Fourth floor, please'?

3 Where do you go in and go out of the store?

4 Which floor do you always go down to?

5 What floor is the main entrance usually on?

6 Where do you queue to pay?

7 Where do you buy trousers and a shirt?

8 Where do you buy a skirt and top?

9 Where do you buy perfume?

10 Who do you ask for information or help?

11 Who stops people stealing things?

12 What do you get off at the top or at the bottom?

LISTENING

5 ▶ 37 Listen to four short conversations in a department store. Match each conversation (1–4) to one of these situations.

a Someone is stealing something.

b Someone wants to try some clothes on.

c Someone is explaining where to meet.

d Someone is looking for an item in the wrong place.

6 ▶ 37 For each conversation, decide if the sentence is true (T) or false (F). Listen again and check.

1 The man wants some batteries for a toy.

2 The speakers tell a security guard about what they saw.

3 The woman bought some jeans, a skirt and two tops in a sale.

4 You can take six items of clothing to the changing room.

7 Choose the correct option in the sentences. Then look at the audio script for Track 37 on page 202 and check your answers.

Conversation 1

1 *Do you sell* / *Are you selling* batteries?

2 They're there. *On* / *In* the bottom shelf.

Conversation 2

3 She put that perfume *on* / *in* her bag!

4 Someone *talks* / *'s talking* to her.

Conversation 3

5 I'm still *at* / *on* the bus, but *we come down* / *we're coming down* Oxford Street now.

6 When you get *out* / *off* on the fourth floor, it's behind you. It's *at* / *to* the back of the store.

Conversation 4

7 The changing rooms are over there *in* / *on* the corner. Next *to* / *of* the jeans.

8 How *much* / *many* items can I take to try on?

SPEAKING

8 Imagine you're in a department store. Think of some things you want to buy and complete each sentence in two different ways.

Excuse me. Do you sell ...?

Excuse me. I'm looking for ... .

9 Now work in pairs. Roleplay conversations between a customer and a shop assistant in a department store. Change roles for each conversation.

Student A: you are the customer. Ask your questions from Exercise 8.

Student B: you are the shop assistant. Look at the plan and the phrases in the box in File 11 on page 196. Give directions to Student A.

SOUNDS AND VOCABULARY REVIEW

10 ▶ 38 Listen and repeat the sounds with /ŋ/, /ʃ/, /tʃ/ and /dʒ/. Are any of them difficult for you to hear or say?

11 ▶ 39 Work in groups. Listen to eight sentences using the words in the box. Together, try to write them down. Then listen again and finish writing them.

cheaper	everything	jeans	section
choose	improving	manage	shirt

G For further revision, see Exercises 1–3 on page 175.

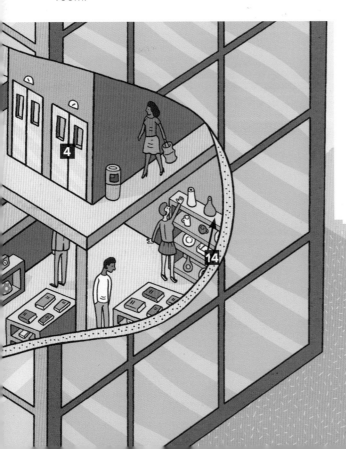

6 EDUCATION

3

4

9

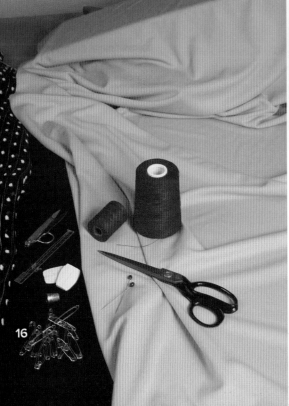

16

IN THIS UNIT YOU LEARN HOW TO:

- describe classmates and teachers
- name school and university subjects
- talk about courses you're doing
- talk about languages and education
- give opinions about what's better

WORDS FOR UNIT 6

1   Work in pairs. Match the phrases to the photos.

an angry boss	learn to ride a bike
a boring class	make clothes
borrow some money	a modern university
cause a problem	pass the exam
a creative person	police training
help each other	solve the problem
a Law student	a strange teacher
a lazy student	study Engineering
learn Arabic	teach PE

2   ▶ 40 Listen. Check your answers. Listen again. Repeat the words.

3   Work in pairs. Test each other. Cover the words.

Student A: point to a photo.

Student B: say the words.

10

11

17

18

Unit 6   Education   51

WHAT ARE YOU STUDYING?

VOCABULARY School and university

1   Match each group of adjectives (1–4) to one of the nouns (a–d).

1	2	3	4
friendly	popular	interesting	helpful
nice	expensive	boring	patient
lazy	modern	difficult	strange
_____	_____	_____	_____

   a   a course

   b   a classmate

   c   a teacher

   d   a university

2   Work in pairs. Compare your ideas. Then add one more adjective to each group above.

3   Choose three adjectives to describe your school / university / college life. Tell a partner.

For example:

Our English teacher is very patient.

My university was very popular – and very expensive!

I was sometimes lazy when I was at school!

4   Work in pairs. Look at the subjects below. Answer the questions.

   1   Which subjects are arts subjects?

   2   Which subjects are science subjects?

   3   Which subject(s) do you usually start studying at school and which do you usually start at university?

Biology	Geography	Marketing
Chemistry	History	Maths
Computing	Law	Medicine
Engineering	Literature	PE

5 Work in groups. Discuss which subjects:

- you think are most / least important.
- you think are easy / difficult.
- you know a lot about.
- you liked / didn't like at school.

LISTENING

6 ▶ 41 Listen to three conversations about studying. Complete the table.

	Subject	Year	How's it going?
1			Really well.
2		2nd	
3			

7 ▶ 41 Listen again. Choose the correct option.

Conversation 1

1 I'm *doing* / *making* a degree in Marketing.

2 I'm really *enjoying* / *liking* it.

Conversation 2

3 I'm a student *at* / *of* university.

4 Not very well, actually. I just find it *boring* / *bored*.

Conversation 3

5 It's a lot of *work* / *works*!

6 Good luck *with* / *for* it.

8 Work in pairs. Discuss these questions.

- Do you know anyone at university / college at the moment?
- What are they studying?
- What year are they in?
- Are they enjoying it?

PRONUNCIATION

9 ▶ 42 Listen to eight questions said fast and then slower. Note how we often pronounce *are* as /ə/. Repeat what you hear.

10 ▶ 42 Listen again and write what you hear.

11 Work in pairs. Take turns to ask and answer the questions.

DEVELOPING CONVERSATIONS

How's the course going?

We can ask *How's the course going?* to find out if someone is enjoying their course or not.

A: *How's the course going?*

B: *Really well. It's great. I'm really enjoying it.*

12 Look at these answers to the question *How's the course going?* Complete each answer with *Really well, OK* or *Not very well.*

1 _____, but it's not very easy.

2 _____. I find it boring.

3 _____. It's very interesting.

4 _____, but it's a lot of work.

5 _____. I don't really like my teacher. He's strange!

6 _____. The other students are very nice and friendly.

7 _____. I did very well in my exams. I found them easy.

8 _____. I think I chose the wrong subject!

9 _____, I suppose, but I'm not sure it's what I really want to do.

13 Work in groups. Discuss these questions.

- How's your English course going?
- What's good about it?
- Is there anything you don't like?

CONVERSATION PRACTICE

14 Work in pairs. Use the guide below to have four conversations like the ones you heard in Exercise 6. Use different ideas from the table below if you need to, and add a reason for how the course is going. Take turns to start. Try to give different answers each time.

Student A	Student B
So what do you do?	*I'm a student at …*
So what're you studying?	Answer the question.
What year are you in?	Answer the question.
How's the course going?	Answer the question and explain why.

Place	Course	Year	How's it going?
University of Rome	Biology	1	Good
Middlesex University	Computing	2	Bad
Le Cordon Bleu, Australia	Hotel Management	3	OK
Harvard	Medicine	4	
Cambridge	Chinese	Final	

🎥 10 To watch the video and do the activities, see the DVD-ROM.

LEARNING AND TRAINING

VOCABULARY Courses

1 Complete the texts (1–5) by putting the words in brackets in the correct space.

1 I do an art class every Tuesday. The class _____ at eight in the evening and _____ at ten. We paint anything we want and the teacher _____ us help and advice. (finishes, gives, starts)

2 I'm _____ a course at the moment. It's for my work, so the company is _____ for it. It's about ways to improve sales. It's very useful and I'm _____ a lot. (learning, paying, doing)

3 My brother's _____ to become a pilot. The course _____ three years and it's very difficult. It _____ about £100,000 altogether. My family's _____ the money from the bank to pay for it. I hope he _____ all his exams! (borrowing, training, passes, lasts, costs)

4 I started learning Russian last year. I _____ to a class on Wednesday evenings. The teacher was very good and patient and I _____ the class, but I was quite lazy and I didn't _____ very much. We _____ an exam at the end of the course and I _____, so I can't do the next level. (study, had, went, failed, enjoyed)

5 We _____ a training session at work every month. The sessions usually _____ for about three hours. We do different things. Sometimes a trainer _____ from outside the company, sometimes our manager _____ us information about changes in the company, sometimes we all _____ our ideas about how to improve things. They're often very useful, but occasionally they're very boring. (comes, gives, have, share, last)

2 Work in pairs. Use verbs from Exercise 1 to say things about your English class. How many of the verbs can you use?

3 Complete the conversation with the questions in the box.

How long does the course last?	Is it good?
What time does the class start?	What's it about?
Do you have any homework?	When are the classes?
Why are you doing it?	How much did it cost?

A: I'm doing an evening course at the moment.

B: 1 _____

A: Speaking in public.

B: 2 _____

A: I want to improve my opportunities at work.

B: 3 _____

A: Every Monday.

B: 4 _____

A: Yeah. I usually watch some videos online and prepare a talk.

B: 5 _____

A: Six, and it ends at eight.

B: 6 _____

A: Ten weeks.

B: 7 _____

A: Two hundred pounds.

B: 8 _____

A: Yeah. It's very useful. I'm enjoying it.

4 Work in pairs. Practise reading the conversation.

LISTENING

5 Match these words and phrases to the photos. Think of one more word for each photo.

an online course	a horse	a training session	fashion

6 ▶ 43 Listen to four people talking about the courses in the photos. Match the speakers to the photos a–d and decide if all the learning experiences you heard about were good. Then compare your ideas with a partner.

7 ▶ 43 Listen again. Decide if the sentences are true (T) or false (F).

Conversation 1

1 The course is 6.30 to ten, twice a week.

2 She works in fashion now.

Conversation 2

3 His manager told him to go to the training session.

4 He learned how to make good decisions.

Conversation 3

5 She always rides twice a week.

6 She rode horses when she was younger, but then stopped.

Conversation 4

7 His wife didn't like the course because there were too many people.

8 He wants to become a journalist.

8 Complete the sentences from the listening with the correct form of the verbs in brackets.

1 I _____ to make clothes. (learn)

2 It _____ for ten weeks. (last)

3 It only _____ about an hour. (last)

4 We _____ any choice. (not / have)

5 I _____ in the countryside and I always wanted _____. (grow up / ride)

6 My teacher _____ very patient and I _____ quite good now. (be / get)

7 My wife _____ it with me, but she _____. (start / stop)

8 I _____ taking exams. I always _____. (hate / fail)

d

9 Work in groups. Discuss these questions.

- Which of the four courses sounds best to you? Why?
- Do you know anyone who changed jobs? If yes, why did they change?
- Did you have any classes after school when you were a child? If yes, what?
- What's good / bad about doing open online courses?

10 Work in pairs. Have conversations like the ones in Exercise 3.

Student A: choose one of the courses from this lesson or think about a course you are doing. Tell your partner.

Student B: choose questions from Exercise 3 to ask.

For example:

A: *I'm doing a training course at the moment.*

B: *What's it about?*

A: *Making decisions.*

GRAMMAR

Modifiers

Very, *really* and *quite* are modifiers. They go before adjectives.

Very and *really* mean 'a lot'.

*It's **really good.***

*The teachers are **very helpful.***

We often make adjectives negative by adding *not very*.

*It **wasn't very long** – only about an hour.*

Quite means 'a little'.

*I was **quite angry** by the end.*

*It's **quite expensive**.*

11 Choose the correct option.

1 Some of my classmates aren't *very / quite* friendly.

2 The course is *quite / really* difficult! I don't understand anything!

3 It's a great university. It's *very / not very* popular.

4 She's nice, but she's *quite / not very* lazy.

5 Most of the students are really friendly, but one or two aren't *really / very* nice.

6 It's a good course. It's *quite / not very* interesting.

7 He's a good teacher, but he's *not very / quite* patient.

8 It's a great university, but it's *quite / really* expensive! I can't study there.

12 Work in groups. Tell each other about things – or people – that you think are:

a really expensive.

b very popular at the moment.

c quite strange.

d not very modern.

e quite boring.

G For further practice, see Exercises 1 and 2 on page 175.

GROWING UP BILINGUAL

VOCABULARY Languages

1 Work in pairs. Say a country or area in the world where each of these are official languages.

Arabic	French	Romanian	Turkish
Chinese	German	Russian	
English	Japanese	Spanish	

2 Work in pairs. Discuss these questions.

- How important is each of these languages in the world:

  - very important?

  - quite important?

  - not very important?

- Which of the languages sound nice to you?

- Do you know any bilingual people? What languages do they speak?

READING

3 Before you read, complete the sentences with the words in the box.

caused	explaining	solving
creative	positive	

1 I'm quite a _____ person. I'm good at arts subjects.

2 I'm good at _____ problems. People often ask me for help.

3 I'm a very _____ person. I always try and think about good things.

4 I'm good at _____ ideas. I'd be a good teacher.

5 I sometimes _____ problems at school and my teacher got angry with me.

4 Work in pairs. Discuss which sentences in Exercise 3 are true for you.

5 Read the first two paragraphs of the article on page 57. Answer these questions.

1 How many languages do the students at Newbury Park speak altogether?

2 What are some of the languages children learn about?

3 Who teaches the words in these different languages?

4 How many students in England are bilingual?

5 Why do some teachers think it's a problem?

6 What do you think of Newbury Park School and the way they teach language? Do you agree with the views in the second paragraph?

7 Read the rest of the article. What's the writer's opinion about the questions in Exercise 6? Work in pairs and compare your ideas. Say the reasons the writer gives for their opinion.

8 Work in pairs. Discuss these questions.

- Did you find any of the ideas surprising? Which ideas?

- Do you agree with *everything* the writer says? If not, why not?

- Do / Did you have people from different countries at your school? Where are / were they from?

- Are there any bilingual schools in your city / region? Do you think they are good? Why? / Why not?

GRAMMAR

Comparatives

You can compare how good two things are using *better than*.

*Growing up bilingual is **better than** only knowing one language.*

We often then use other comparatives to explain why.

*Bilingual children get **higher** grades at school.*

*They are **more creative**.*

9 Choose the best comparative to complete the explanations.

1 Her English is better than mine. She gets *higher / lower* grades.

2 This computer is better than mine. My one's *slower / faster*.

3 Mr Platt is a better teacher than Mrs Jones. He's *funnier / more boring*.

4 I think Biology is better than English. It's *more interesting / more difficult*.

5 They're better students than me. I'm *more helpful / lazier*.

10 Work in pairs. Discuss what the basic adjective is for each option in Exercise 9. When do we add *-er, -ier* and *more* to make comparatives?

G Check your ideas on page 176 and do Exercise 1.

11 Write sentences using comparatives and the ideas below.

1 I'm / good at / swimming / you.

2 My house is / near to / the school / your place.

3 I'm / tall / you.

4 You're / interested / in history / me.

5 My school was / small / your school.

6 It was / warm / last week / this week.

12 Work in pairs. Ask each other questions about the sentences in Exercise 11. Find out who is better at swimming, etc.

For example:

Are you good at swimming?

How far can you swim?

G For further practice, see Exercise 2 on page 176.

EDUCATION

THE WORLD IN A SCHOOL

Janet Scott finds the benefits of knowing two languages

The students at Newbury Park Primary School in London speak over 40 languages! Each month, a teacher films a student and asks the child to say simple things like *hello* and *thank you* in their language. They show the film to the other children in the school to teach them the foreign words. In January and February, the students learned some Turkish and Japanese. This month, they're learning Romanian.

In England, one in seven children now speaks a foreign language at home, and some teachers think it's causing problems. They think teaching is more difficult with bilingual children in the class and that bilinguals can't do well in *any* subject if they don't speak English at home.

It is true that starting school is difficult for some bilingual children. Sometimes, the children had bad experiences before they moved to the UK. Maybe they experienced a war, or a parent died, or they lost their home. Schools can help these children. For example, the students feel more positive about school and their new life if they occasionally do something at school in their first language – like they do at Newbury Park.

But most bilingual children don't have any problems at school. In fact, growing up bilingual is usually *better* than only knowing one language. Research shows that bilingual children are better at solving problems and they usually finish school with higher grades. That's because they are more creative and they're often better at explaining ideas. That's good news, because 70% of the world's population speak two or more languages!

SPEAKING

13 Choose five things from the box. Decide if they are better or worse now than before. Spend two minutes thinking of one or two reasons why. Use a dictionary if you need to.

the economy	parents	transport
exams	schools	universities
hospitals	sport	the weather
old people	teachers	young people

14 Work in groups. Say your ideas. What do the other people in your group think?

SOUNDS AND VOCABULARY REVIEW

15 ▶ 44 Listen and repeat the sounds with /e/, /ə/, /ɔː/ and /ɜː/. Are any of them difficult for you to hear or say?

16 ▶ 45 Work in groups. Listen to eight sentences using these words. Together, try to write them down. Then listen again and finish writing them.

causes	education	learned	spent
course	friendly	popular	work

G For further revision, see Exercises 1–3 on page 176.

VIDEO 3

PHOTO CAMP

1 **Look at the photo of a refugee camp. Discuss these questions.**

  • Why do you think the different people in the photo are there?

  • What things can help refugees in this situation?

  • Are there any refugees in your country? Where are they from?

2 ▣ 11 **Watch the first part of the video (0.00–2.15) about a special course. Answer these questions.**

  1 Who are the teachers? Who do they work for?

  2 Who are the students? Where are they from? Where do they live now?

  3 What is the course for?

3 **Read the sentences (1–4) from the second part of the video. Match them to the follow-up sentences (a–d).**

  1 Life is difficult in the refugee camp.

  2 Photo camp is an inspiration for many of the camp's residents.

  3 Near the end of the programme, the students have an exhibition.

  4 These students received more than a certificate and a new skill at photo camp.

  a They are excited to show their work.

  b Agonzi Grace, for example, wants to become a professional photographer.

  c They also learnt how to document their world.

  d But Reza and the other photographers are showing these young adults how to see their temporary home in a new way.

4 ▣ 11 **Watch the second part of the video (2.16–3.50). Put the pairs of sentences in Exercise 3 in the order you hear them.**

5 **Work in pairs. Discuss these questions.**

  • Do you think the course is a good idea? Why? / Why not?

  • Do you like taking photos? Are you good at it?

  • Do you have any photos on your phone that you like?

6 **Work in groups. Show some photos you like to each other. Ask each other questions like these.**

  • Where was that?

  • When did you take it?

  • What are they doing?

  • Who's that?

UNDERSTANDING FAST SPEECH

7 ▣ 12 **Read and listen to this extract from the video said fast, then slow. Stressed sounds are in CAPITALS.**

THEY are TEACHing SIXty YOUNG REfuGEES HOW to tell the STOries of their LIVES in PHOtographs.

8 **You try! Practise saying the extract with the same stressed sounds.**

REVIEW 3

GRAMMAR

1 Choose the correct option.

1 A: Can you pass me *that / those* cups over there?

   B: Sure. Here.

2 A: *You are / Are you* waiting to pay?

   B: No. Go ahead.

3 A: How was the exam?

   B: Bad! It was *more difficult / difficulter* than last year.

4 A: Hello. Can I speak to Greg, please?

   B: Sorry, *he does / he's doing* his homework.

5 A: Did you enjoy the film?

   B: It was *quite / very* good, but not great.

6 A: Do you like this dress?

   B: I prefer the blue *one / ones* that you tried on before. And it was *more cheap / cheaper*!

7 A: Do you want to try some of *this / that* soup?

   B: Oh, it's nice. It's *more good / better* than my one.

2 Write full questions to complete the dialogue. Use the words in brackets.

A: [1]_____? (do)

B: I'm at university.

A: Oh, right. [2]_____? (studying)

B: Business Management.

A: [3]_____? (going)

B: Great. I'm really enjoying it. I really like Marketing.

A: [4]_____? (What year)

B: My second year. I have two more years after this.

A: So [5]_____ Business Management? (doing)

B: My parents want me to manage their factory.

3 Complete the sentences with one word in each space. Contractions (*he's, don't*, etc.) are one word.

1 I lost my job. I'm _____ working at the moment.

2 I can't help you now. _____ doing my homework.

3 What _____ all those people looking at?

4 Do you have a coat? _____ raining outside.

5 I love _____ shoes. They're _____ nice.

6 A: I can't do _____ exercise. Can you help me?

   B: Sure. It is a _____ difficult.

4 ▶ 46 Listen and complete the sentences with one word in each space. Contractions (*I'm, don't,* etc.) are one word.

1 _____ son's _____ Law _____ university.

2 _____ _____ to _____ a horse _____ _____ moment.

3 Excuse me. _____ _____ _____ _____ changing rooms.

4 _____ _____ my classmates _____ _____ friendly.

5 _____ English _____ _____ _____ mine.

6 _____ _____ _____ warmer last _____.

VOCABULARY

5 Match the verbs in the box to the groups of words they go with in 1–8.

borrow	go up	leave	lasted
give	improve	look for	pay

1 ~ your dictionary / ~ the money / ~ a pen

2 ~ sales / ~ my grades / ~ my English

3 ~ your opinion / ~ us information / ~ me some advice

4 ~ my job / ~ school / ~ home

5 ~ my keys / ~ the toy section / ~ a new flat

6 ~ at the till / ~ for my course / queue to ~

7 ~ a long time / ~ two years / ~ about four hours

8 ~ the escalator / ~ the stairs / ~ the mountain

6 Put the words into three groups – shops, study or clothes.

bakery	fail	leather	shirt
Chinese	History	red top	subject
Engineering	jeans	security guard	training
entrance	jumper	shelf	vegetables

7 Choose the best option.

1 Lots of people do it. It's *very popular / helpful / special*.

2 She's 1.84 m. She's quite *high / slow / tall*.

3 It's an interesting course, but it's quite *friendly / difficult / boring*.

4 Our teacher's nice. He's very *lazy / patient / hard*.

5 I like art. I'm quite *important / average / creative*.

6 His cat died. It was really *sad / warm / modern*.

7 I found a bargain. I was very *strange / happy / young*.

8 I feel a bit *easy / strange / stupid* because I failed the exam.

8 Complete the text with the words in the box.

assistant	ground	section	took
came out	perfume	size	
experience	sale	store	

I went to a big department [1]_____ to buy a dress for my wife. I went to the womenswear [2]_____ and found a really nice dress in the [3]_____. It was reduced by $100, but it was the wrong [4]_____. I asked the [5]_____, but she said it was the only one they had. I decided to buy some [6]_____ instead. I [7]_____ the lift to the [8]_____ floor but it stopped between floors. I waited for 20 minutes! I felt ill and when I [9]_____ I went home. It was a bad [10]_____.

7 PEOPLE I KNOW

60

3

4

9

14

IN THIS UNIT YOU LEARN HOW TO:

- talk about your family
- express surprise
- give opinions about family life
- talk about things that are necessary or not necessary
- talk about people you know

WORDS FOR UNIT 7

1   Work in pairs. Match the words and phrases to the photos.

clever	husband	repair a car
dead	look after children	strict
do some housework	male and female	surprised
do the washing	nursery school	very fit
feed the dog	old friends	a wedding
funny		

2   ▶ 47 Listen. Check your answers. Listen again. Repeat the words.

3   Work in pairs. Test each other. Cover the words.

Student A: point to a photo.

Student B: say the words.

10

11

15

16

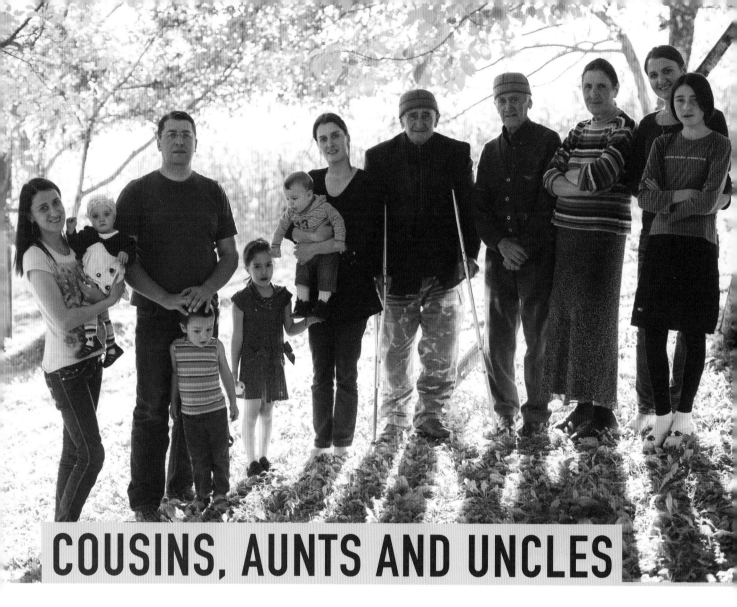

COUSINS, AUNTS AND UNCLES

VOCABULARY Relationships

1   Complete the table with the words in the box.

| daughter | grandmother | mum | uncle |
| girlfriend | husband | sister | |

Male	Female
grandfather	
	wife
dad	
son	
	aunt
boyfriend	
brother	
cousin	

2   Complete the sentences with words from Exercise 1.

1   Pat is my uncle. He's my mum's _____.

2   Clare is my _____. She's my aunt Stella's daughter.

3   Larry is my cousin. He's my uncle Matthew's _____.

4   Tina's my younger _____. I'm two years older than her.

5   Mel is my brother's _____. They met a few months ago.

6   My mum's _____ and _____ are both dead now, and so is my dad's dad, but my _____ is still alive. She's 88!

3 Work in pairs. Look at the photo. Say who you think the people are.

For example:

I think she's the wife of this man here, and probably the mother of these two here.

Maybe these three are sisters – or cousins.

4 Write the names of six people in your family. Then tell your partner who they are.

LISTENING

5 ▶ 48 Listen to three conversations about families. Which relations from Exercise 1 do they mention?

6 ▶ 48 Listen again. What do you learn about the family members?

GRAMMAR

Auxiliary verbs

We often use just auxiliary verbs (e.g. *be, do, can*) to answer questions. We don't need to repeat the main verb and / or words that follow it.

A: *Did you go out yesterday?*

B: *Yeah, I did go out.*

A: *So, are you married, Ted?*

B: *Yes, I am married.*

7 Complete the answers in these short dialogues with the correct auxiliary verbs.

1 A: Do you have any brothers or sisters?

B: Yeah, I _____.

2 A: Is he married?

B: Yes, he _____.

3 A: Does she have a boyfriend?

B: Yes, she _____.

4 A: Do your children still live with you at home?

B: My son does, yes, but my daughter _____.

5 A: Are you very similar?

B: Yes, we _____.

6 A: Are your grandparents still alive?

B: My mum's parents are, yes, but my dad's _____.

7 A: Did you do anything nice at the weekend?

B: Yes, I _____.

8 A: Did it rain?

B: No, it _____.

8 Work in pairs. Take turns reading the questions, but this time give opposite answers.

For example:

A: *Do you have any brothers or sisters?*

B: *No, I don't.*

G For further practice, see Exercises 1 and 2 on page 177.

DEVELOPING CONVERSATIONS

Adding information

In conversations, we don't normally just give short answers to questions. We try to add comments.

9 Match the extra comments to the questions and short answers in Exercise 7.

a Luckily! It was a bit cloudy, but it stayed dry.

b My grandfather had his 80th birthday party.

c A younger brother.

d They died a few years ago.

e She's studying in the United States.

f We're sisters, but we're best friends too.

g The wedding was last month, actually.

h He's a really nice guy. I like him.

10 Work in pairs. Practise the conversations in Exercise 7, adding the comments above.

11 Write short answers to these questions and then add comments. Then ask and answer the questions in pairs.

1 Do you live near here?

2 Do you have any aunts or uncles?

3 Are you married?

4 Did you go anywhere during the holidays?

PRONUNCIATION

We often say *Really?* to show surprise / interest. The intonation goes up high and then down.

Really?

12 ▶ 49 Listen and repeat *Really?* three times.

13 ▶ 50 Work in pairs. Listen to six sentences. After each sentence, say *Really?* if the information is surprising or interesting. If it's not, say *Oh, OK*.

CONVERSATION PRACTICE

14 Write five questions about families to ask other students in your class. Use ideas from these pages.

For example:

Do you have any brothers or sisters?

Are they older or younger than you?

15 Ask your questions to different people in your class. Add comments when you answer their questions. Say *Really?* when you hear interesting or surprising things. Ask extra connected questions if you want to.

🎥 13 To watch the video and do the activities, see the DVD-ROM.

I HAVE TO DO A LOT OF HOUSEWORK

VOCABULARY
Jobs and activities in the home

1   Work in pairs. Which jobs and activities can you see in the photos?

2   Match 1–5 to a–e, and 6–10 to f–j.

1	look after	a	the washing
2	tell	b	songs together
3	sing	c	my baby brother
4	repair	d	jokes to each other
5	do	e	the roof
6	feed	f	my daughter from school
7	pick up	g	a story at bedtime
8	play	h	the dishwasher
9	empty	i	the dog
10	read	j	games together

3   Work in pairs. Discuss these questions.

- Which of the jobs and activities in Exercise 2 do you do? How often?
- Which do you enjoy doing? Which don't you like doing? Why?
- Which do you think are essential?

SPEAKING

4   Work in pairs. Read the introduction to a discussion board on a website. Discuss the three questions at the end.

DEBATE OF THE WEEK: WORKING PARENTS

Family life is changing. In the past, women stayed at home and looked after the children. They did all the housework, and men earned money and maybe repaired a few things in the house. Now, both parents often have full-time jobs. Who does all the housework? How does both parents working affect the kids and family life? Is it a good thing?

READING

5   Read the comments on the message board. Who is writing each comment? Match each name to one of the people below. There is one person you do not need.

a grandmother	_____	a mother	_____
a father	_____	a daughter	_____
a nanny	_____	an uncle	_____
a son	_____		

✉ MESSAGE BOARD

Bertha, Canada My son Travis brings the kids to my house three days a week – when he has to work. They're a bit difficult sometimes, but I love being with them. We sing songs and play games. I also think my son's wife Clara is really great. I'm happy that she has a job and doesn't have to stay at home all the time. She has a very full life.
6 hours ago   Like

José, Chile I'm happy both my parents work because they can buy me nice things.
5 hours ago   Like

Sophie, Germany We have a dishwasher and I have to fill it and empty it. Mum and Dad say they don't have time. It's not fair! My friends don't have to do jobs in the home. Their parents do them or they have a cleaner!
5 hours ago   Like

Hannah, Australia I recently started work again after I had my baby, Lianna. My husband takes her to nursery school at nine and I pick her up at five. I then have to do housework and feed Lianna. I also have to get up at night if she wakes up. It's difficult, but I still want to work. I love my job and I feel like I'm doing something important for society.
3 hours ago   Like

Roberto, Italy I think it's better to have one parent at home, but it doesn't have to be the woman. My wife had a better job than me, so I left my job to stay with our kids.
2 hours ago   Like

David, England Of course both parents want to work. Send your kids to live in a private school. My brother does that and everyone's happy. The kids always have friends and get a good education. The family spends the holidays together.
1 hours ago   Like

6 Read the comments again. Decide if each person thinks both parents working is a good thing, a bad thing, or both good and bad.

7 Work in pairs. Say if you like what each person wrote or not.

GRAMMAR *have to / don't have to*

8 Look at the comments again. Complete the sentences with the missing words.

1 We have a dishwasher and I _____ fill it and empty it.

2 My son Travis brings the kids to my house three days a week – when he _____ work.

3 My friends _____ do jobs in the home.

4 I'm happy that she has a job and _____ stay at home all the time.

9 Complete the explanation in the box by choosing the correct option.

Have to and *has to* + infinitive show it's [1]*necessary / not necessary* to do something.

Don't have to and *doesn't have to* + infinitive show it's [2]*necessary / not necessary* to do something.

 Check your ideas on page 177 and do Exercise 1.

10 Complete the sentences with the correct form of *have to* or *don't have to*.

1 We really _____ do some shopping. We don't have any food.

2 The exam's easy. You _____ study very hard to pass it.

3 I _____ work today, so we can go out somewhere, if you want.

4 She can't play today. She _____ finish her homework.

5 We have lots of time. We _____ leave now.

6 He can't come today. He _____ look after his sister.

7 _____ I _____ go to bed now?

8 What time _____ he _____ be there?

11 Work in groups. Say things you have to do:

• at home.

• at work / school.

• this week.

For further practice, see Exercise 2 on page 177.

SPEAKING

12 On your own, decide if it is good, bad or doesn't matter:

• if both parents have to work.

• if kids have to do lots of homework.

• if kids don't have to do jobs in the home.

• if kids watch TV.

• if families eat together.

• if parents set lots of rules for children.

• if parents send their kids to bed at eight o'clock.

• if parents don't go out on their own.

13 Work in pairs. Take turns saying your ideas. Reply using *I agree, I don't agree* or *it depends*.

For example:

A: *It doesn't matter if both parents have to work.*

B: *It depends. Sometimes it's OK, but sometimes it's a problem.*

14 Write two more opinions you have about family life. Work in groups and tell each other your ideas. Do you all agree?

MY CIRCLE OF FRIENDS

SPEAKING

1 Read the text on page 67. Then discuss these questions in groups.

- Which kind of friend is most / least important? Why?
- What do you talk about with each kind of friend?
- Which kind of friend do you meet / talk to the most?
- What other different kinds of friends can you think of?

LISTENING

2 ▶ 51 Listen to four people talking about friends. Match the descriptions (1–4) to the different kinds of friends in the text.

3 ▶ 51 Listen again. Correct two mistakes in each summary.

1 He met Johan at university. Johan lives in New York now. He's a doctor.

2 Her husband studies with Miguel. She doesn't get on well with Miguel. Miguel is 21.

3 He's a student. He met Claire when he was on holiday. Claire wants to come to England.

4 Liu is her grandmother. Liu is stupid. She lives in Shanghai.

4 Match the verbs (1–6) with the words they went with in the listening (a–f).

1 share		a	stupid things
2 go		b	face-to-face
3 say		c	college
4 meet		d	me feel good
5 leave		e	a house
6 make		f	to parties

5 Work in pairs. Discuss these questions.

- Do you know people who share a house? Do they like it?
- What's a good age to stop going to parties all night?
- Do you know anyone who says stupid things? What kinds of things do they say?
- Who / What usually makes you feel good?

VOCABULARY Describing people

6 Work in pairs. Which of the adjectives in the box do you think are positive? Which do you think are negative? Why?

clever	fit	loud	reliable
confident	funny	quiet	strict

7 Complete the sentences with the adjectives in Exercise 6.

1 She's a very _____ woman. She always makes me laugh.

2 He's really _____. He goes running every day and plays basketball twice a week as well.

3 He's quite _____. He doesn't say very much.

4 She's very _____. She's an engineer, she speaks five languages and she's very good with computers!

5 He's very _____! When he's talking, it's difficult for anyone else to say anything!

6 My dad's quite _____. If I come home late or don't do well at school, he gets angry.

7 She's very _____. She always does what she says. You can trust her.

8 She's very _____. I mean, she's good at what she does – and she knows it.

8 Work in groups. Discuss these questions.

- Which adjectives describe people in your family? Explain why.
- Which adjectives do you think describe you?

SPEAKING

9 Think of four people you know – not family members. Write their names and think about how to answer the questions for each person. There is an example for each question.

1 How did you meet each other?

We were in the same class at secondary school.

2 What kind of person is he / she?

He's great. He's very funny and very clever.

3 How often do you talk?

Two or three times a week. We talk on the phone a lot.

4 How often do you go out together?

Maybe once or twice a month. We go out for dinner or for a drink.

10 Work in groups. Ask and answer questions about the people you know. Start like this:

I have a friend called …

SOUNDS AND VOCABULARY REVIEW

11 ▶ 52 Listen and repeat the sounds with /iː/ and /ɪ/. Are any of them difficult to hear or say?

12 ▶ 53 Work in groups. Listen to eight sentences using these words. Together, try to write them down. Then listen again and finish writing them.

agreed	feed	fit	similar
confident	female	leave	strict

G For further revision, see Exercises 1–3 on page 177.

A LITTLE HELP FROM YOUR FRIENDS

Some friends last a lifetime, but often we make friends for particular reasons at particular times. Here, we look at a few of the different kinds of friends we make during our lives.

THE OLD FRIEND

Old friends are friends you met a long time ago and that you are still close to. You have a shared history. You enjoy talking about the past and always stay in touch.

THE FRIEND OF THE FAMILY

These friends are always happy to help – and they can be very useful. People that our parents or brothers or sisters know can often teach us things or help us to find a job.

THE ONLINE FRIEND

Many people make 'friends' through the internet. Sometimes these friendships move into the real world, but usually they don't.

THE FRIEND OF SOMEONE YOU KNOW

Perhaps this is a friend of a friend or of your husband or girlfriend. The big problem is you don't get on with them. You see them quite a lot and have to be nice to them, but sometimes it's really hard to do.

8 PLANS

1

2

5

6

7

9

10

11

3

4

8

IN THIS UNIT YOU LEARN HOW TO:

* talk about people's plans
* make simple suggestions
* talk about things you'd like to do
* discuss government plans
* give basic opinions and reasons

WORDS FOR UNIT 8

1 Work in pairs. Match the phrases to the photos. Which two phrases do not match a photo?

a big clock	grow fruit
build a house	have a check-up
destroy a building	lose your job
do some exercise	the main square
drive someone round	move house
get married	provide help
get a taxi	a romantic dinner
go fishing	save money
go to the library	win the lottery

2 ▶ 54 Listen. Check your answers. Listen again. Repeat the words.

3 Work in pairs. Match phrases that have a connection. How many different connections can you make? Use your own language to explain if you need to.

For example:

get a taxi / the main square: *You can get a taxi in the main square.*

get a taxi / drive someone round: *Taxi drivers drive people round.*

13

14

12

15

16

WHAT ARE YOUR PLANS?

SPEAKING

1   Work in pairs. Discuss the questions.
    - What entertainment is there where you live?
    - Do you go out much in the evening?
    - When do you go out – and where?
    - What do you do in your free time?

VOCABULARY Common activities

2   Complete each group of collocations with one verb from the box.

do	get	go	go for
go to	have	play	write

1   ~ tennis / ~ baseball
2   ~ a few emails / ~ a letter
3   ~ some shopping / ~ my homework
4   ~ a walk in the park / ~ a run
5   ~ the library / the doctor's for a check-up
6   ~ a meeting with a client / ~ a romantic dinner
7   ~ home / ~ fishing
8   ~ something to eat / ~ a taxi home

3   Work in pairs. Use the language in Exercise 2 to say:
    a   two things people do at work.
    b   two things students do.
    c   two things people do if they feel ill.
    d   two things people do to keep fit.
    e   two things you did yesterday.
    f   two things you are planning to do soon.
    g   two things you really like doing.
    h   two things you never – or hardly ever – do.

LISTENING

4   ▶ 55 Listen to three conversations about plans. Decide which conversation (1–3) happens:
    a   at work.
    b   at university.
    c   on holiday.

5   ▶ 55 Listen again. Find out in which conversation someone:
    a   is going to go to a restaurant.
    b   arranges where to meet.
    c   asks someone out on a date.
    d   is going to tell some colleagues about something.
    e   doesn't want to meet.
    f   is going to fly somewhere soon.

GRAMMAR

6 Look at these sentences from the listening. Then complete the rules in the Grammar box.

A: *What're your plans?*

B: ***I'm going to go*** *running by the river later.*

A: *What about tonight?* ***Are you going to be*** *busy then?*

B: *No. Why?*

going to

We use the present form of the verb [1]_____ + *going to* + [2]_____ to talk about [3]_____ – and especially to talk about plans we have.

G Check your ideas on page 178 and do Exercises 1 and 2.

7 Complete each sentence with the correct form of *be* + *going to* + the verb in brackets.

1 A: My boyfriend _____ me for a romantic dinner tonight. (take)

   B: That's nice. Where _____ you _____? (go)

2 A: I _____ tomorrow. My flight is at six in the morning! (leave)

   B: Really? That's early. What time _____? (get up)

3 A: Some friends _____ next week. (visit)

   B: That's nice. How long _____? (stay)

4 A: I spoke to Sergei. He _____. He's got another bad headache. (not come)

   B: Really? _____ to the doctor's for a check-up? I hope it isn't anything serious. (go)

PRONUNCIATION

8 ▶ **56** Listen to *going to* and six sentences from Exercise 7 — first slow and then fast. Notice how we often say *going to* as /gʌnə/.

9 Work in pairs. Practise reading out the dialogues in Exercise 7. In each dialogue, answer the final question.

10 Tell a partner which things below you are going to do today / tomorrow / this week. Say when. Your partner is going to ask a question to find out more.

meet a friend	cook dinner / lunch
go on holiday	write an email / on my blog
watch TV	do some studying / homework
go shopping	get up early / late

For example:

A: *I'm going to meet some friends tonight.*

B: *Really? Nice. Where are you going to meet?*

A: *In the centre of town. We're going to have dinner somewhere.*

G For further practice, see Exercise 3 on page 178.

DEVELOPING CONVERSATIONS

Making suggestions

We often make suggestions using *How about ...?*

A: *Do you want to meet somewhere?*

B: *Yes, OK. Where?*

A: ***How about*** *in the main square at eight?*

11 Put the sentences in the correct order to make a conversation.

1 ___ 2 ___ 3 ___ 4 ___ 5 ___ 6 ___ 7 ___ 8 ___ 9 ___

a How about in the main square, under the big clock?

b Is six OK?

c Oh, sorry. Well, how about seven thirty?

d What're your plans for later?

e Perfect! See you later. Bye.

f Yes. Great. Where?

g I don't have any. Why? Do you want to meet somewhere?

h It's quite early.

i Yes, fine. What time?

12 ▶ **57** Listen and check your ideas.

13 Write a suggestion with *How about ...?* to respond to each question.

1 What do you want to see at the cinema?

2 What are we going to get her for her birthday?

3 What do you want to eat tonight?

4 Do you know a good place to have a party?

CONVERSATION PRACTICE

14 Work in pairs. Have conversations about your plans. Take turns being Student A and Student B. Use the guide below to help you.

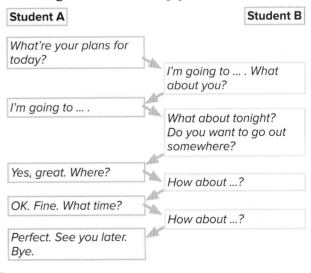

Student A	Student B
What're your plans for today?	
	I'm going to ... . What about you?
I'm going to	
	What about tonight? Do you want to go out somewhere?
Yes, great. Where?	
	How about ...?
OK. Fine. What time?	
	How about ...?
Perfect. See you later. Bye.	

🎥 14 To watch the video and do the activities, see the DVD-ROM.

HOPES AND DREAMS

a

drian

b

c

LISTENING

1 You are going to hear four people talking about things they want to do. The pictures show what each person is thinking. Work in pairs. What do you think they say?

2 ▶ 58 Listen and match each speaker to one of the pictures. Then work in pairs and compare your ideas.

Speaker 1: Picture _____

Speaker 2: Picture _____

Speaker 3: Picture _____

Speaker 4: Picture _____

3 ▶ 58 Listen again. Tick (✓) the sentences that are true.

Conversation 1

1 He's from Manchester.

2 He already does kung fu.

Conversation 2

3 She's planning to leave her job this year.

4 She wants to have children before starting a business.

Conversation 3

5 He thinks that retiring is going to be good.

6 He wants to grow flowers.

Conversation 4

7 She wants to be rich.

8 She wants to learn how to drive.

4 Read the audio script on page 205 to check your answers. Underline the words that helped you decide.

5 Work in groups. Would you like to do any of the things the people talk about? Why? / Why not?

VOCABULARY Life events and plans

6 Complete each pair of sentences with one verb from the box. One sentence is about a past event and one is about a future plan. Use the correct form in each sentence.

become	have	move	stop
get	leave	start	win

1 a My wife's going to _____ a baby in January.

   b My friend _____ a serious accident a few years ago and he can't work now.

2 a We _____ to St Petersburg when I was ten. My dad got a job here.

   b We're going to _____ house next year. We need a bigger place!

3 a My mum _____ working when she had me!

   b My dad says he's going to _____ smoking. I hope so!

4 a My grandparents _____ a restaurant 50 years ago and now I run it.

   b I'd like to _____ my own business when I'm older.

5 a I _____ a writing competition when I was 30, and after that I left my job and became a writer.

   b We're going to _____ the lottery and then we can stop work and travel round the world.

6 a We're going to _____ married next year.

   b My parents _____ divorced when I was younger.

7 a I _____ home when I was 27. I went abroad to work.

   b I want to _____ my job. I'd like to do something different.

8 a I trained to _____ a nurse after I left school.

   b My brother's an actor. He'd like to _____ famous, but he's still waiting for his big opportunity.

7 Work in pairs. Use verbs from Exercise 6 to talk about your life up to now and your plans for the future.

GRAMMAR

would like to + verb

We use *would like to* + infinitive to talk about things we want to do – or hope to do – sometime in the future.

*I'd really **like to learn** Spanish.*

*I'd **like to go** to Iran one day. I'm sure it's interesting.*

Negatives

*I **wouldn't like to do** his job! It's hard!*

*I **wouldn't like to live** there. It's not very nice.*

Questions

***Would you like to go** out with me?*

***Would you like to try** some of this food?*

8 Use the notes to make sentences with the correct form of *would / wouldn't like (to)*.

1 I / really / spend a year in South America.

2 I / really / meet him sometime. I love his music!

3 My brother / learn how to cook.

4 She / change jobs sometime soon.

5 I / not / be famous!

6 It's a nice apartment, but I / not / live in that area.

7 you / get something to eat after class?

8 you / come shopping with me tomorrow?

PRONUNCIATION

9 ▶ 59 Listen and check the answers to Exercise 8. Notice when we use the contraction *'d*.

10 Work in groups. Discuss which of the things below you'd like to do sometime in the future. There is an example for the first sentence.

1 buy my own house

   A: *I'd really like to buy my own house one day.*

   B: *I'm OK just renting. I think it's easier.*

2 get married

3 have kids

4 travel round the world

5 move to a different country

6 speak really good English

7 write a book

8 get fitter

9 learn to play a musical instrument

10 learn another foreign language

11 Now tell other people in your group about:

- a place you'd really like to visit.

- a person you'd really like to meet.

- something you'd really like to do.

- something you'd like to learn.

- something you'd like to stop doing.

G  For further practice, see Exercises 1 and 2 on page 178.

FOR AND AGAINST

SPEAKING

1 **Work in groups. Discuss these questions.**

- How important are the changes below for your town / city?

better water	a new airport
better wi-fi	a new hospital
a bigger library	a new metro line
improved roads	a new museum
more schools	a new shopping mall
more street lights	a new stadium

- Say if they are very important, quite important or not very important. Explain why.

- Look at the photo. Are they building or destroying anything in your city, area or country? What? Where? Is it a good idea?

- Are they planning to build anything? What? Where? Is it a good idea?

VOCABULARY For and against

If you are *for* a plan, you think it's good. If you are *against* a plan, you think it's bad.

When we explain why we think a plan is good or bad, we sometimes use *be going to* to say the results we predict for the future.

*I'm **for** building more schools. There **are going to be** fewer students in each class. That's good for kids.*

2 **Read the comments (1–9) about plans. Are the speakers for or against the plans?**

1 It's going to save time.

2 It's going to provide a useful service.

3 It's going to improve education.

4 It's going to help businesses.

5 It's going to cause a lot of noise and pollution.

6 It's going to be bad for the economy.

7 It's going to create jobs.

8 It's going to cut the number of cars on the road.

9 People are going to lose their jobs.

3 **Work in pairs. Which comments in Exercise 2 could you make about the changes in Exercise 1?**

For example:

A new airport is going to cause a lot of noise and pollution. A new shopping mall is going to provide a useful service.

4 **Spend two minutes trying to remember the verbs in Exercise 2. Then cover Exercise 2 and complete the sentences below with the verbs. The first letter is given.**

1 I don't want the government to cut taxes. It's going to b_____ bad for public services.

2 The government needs to use technology more. It can s_____ a lot of money.

3 I'm for having the Olympic games here. It's going to c_____ lots of opportunities for people here.

4 The government wants to c_____ the number of policemen, but I'm against it. It's going to c_____ problems. There's going to be more crime.

5 It's a good idea to stop cars in the city centre. It's going to i_____ the city and p_____ more space for people. Shopping is nicer when there isn't any traffic.

6 A big car company is going to close down because it's l_____ money. I want the government to h_____ the people who are going to lose their jobs.

READING

5 Look at the extract from a website. Read the comments about three plans the local or national government has. What do you think the plans are? Complete headings 1–3 on the website. Then compare your ideas in pairs.

6 Which person:

1 would like more tourists?

2 would like to improve education?

3 wants to save time?

4 wants to save money?

5 likes sport?

6 is worried about the environment?

7 Work in pairs. Say which people have similar opinions to you and why.

SPEAKING

8 Read the plans below and decide which you are for and which you are against. Write one reason why.

1 The government is going to build new train lines for high-speed trains.

2 The government wants to make a law to stop people building in the countryside or next to the sea.

3 The government is going to increase the age when people retire from 65 to 68.

4 The local government is going to close all the libraries and provide some books online for free.

5 The local government would like to build a shopping mall in your area with 100 shops and a car park.

9 Work in groups. Discuss your opinions about the plans in Exercise 8.

For example:

A: *I'm for the high-speed trains. It's going to create jobs.*

B: *I agree. It's going to save time and provide a useful service for us.*

C: *I'm against it. It's going to be bad for the environment.*

SOUNDS AND VOCABULARY REVIEW

10 ▶ **60** Listen and repeat the sounds with /eɪ/, /aɪ/ and /uː/. Are any of them difficult for you to hear or say?

11 ▶ **61** Work in groups. Listen to eight sentences using these words. Together, try to write them down. Then listen again and finish writing them.

create	exercise	move	saving
drive	library	provides	situation

G For further revision, see Exercises 1–3 on page 179.

YOUR OPINION MATTERS!

 1 The local government wants to _____.

FOR

Jamila

I think it's a good idea. It's going to help business and more people are going to come here. At the moment people have to fly to the capital and then get the train. It takes hours.

AGAINST

Cass

I don't think it's a good idea. It's not going to be near my house, but I still don't want all those planes to come here. There's going to be a lot of noise and pollution. And they want to build it in some nice countryside outside the city.

 2 The government is planning to _____

FOR

Gavin

It's going to improve the situation. The government is spending too much money at the moment. They need to do something about it and I don't want to pay more taxes.

AGAINST

Selina

It's going to cause a lot of problems because there are going to be fewer doctors, fewer policemen, fewer teachers. Maybe some people can pay to see a private doctor, or pay for extra classes for their children, but for a lot of people it's going to be bad for their health and their children's education.

3 Our government wants to _____

FOR

Gloria

It's going to be good for our country and our economy. Lots of people are going to come here and spend money in the hotels and restaurants. And they're going to meet local people and learn about our country too. I think it's a great opportunity. And for me, it's going to be good because I'd really like to go and see the matches – I hope the tickets aren't going to be very expensive.

AGAINST

Elijah

It's going to cost a lot of money and I think we could spend the money on better things. There are more important things than sport. How about providing a computer for every student or providing free English lessons? Those are better ways to spend all that money.

VIDEO 4

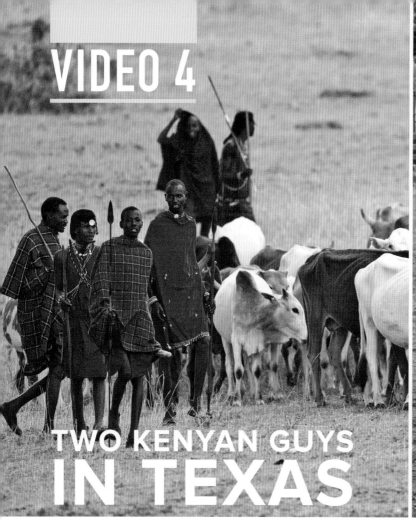

TWO KENYAN GUYS IN TEXAS

1 **Look at the photos. Answer the questions.**
   - Where are the two places?
   - What can you see in each photo?
   - What do you think is similar and what's different about their houses and lifestyles?

2 📹 15 **Read the summary of the first part of the video and check any words you don't know. Then watch the first part of the video (0.00–2.07) and complete the summary with one word in each space.**

Two Maasai men are travelling around ¹_____.
They decide to visit a ranch in ²_____ to see all the cows, because the Maasai believe all the cows in the ³_____ belong to them! They meet a man called ⁴_____. He's famous because he owns a ranch in ⁵_____ as well as his ranch at home. He's going to show the Maasai men around and introduce them to his family. When they are in the car, they try to learn some ways to say 'hello' and 'how are you'. The Maasai men find it ⁶_____ to understand the Texan man's accent.

3 📹 15 **Watch the second part of the video (2.08–4.44). Answer these questions.**
   1 Which members of the family do you see and hear about?
   2 Which rooms do you see?
   3 How different is the Maasai's house? in what ways?

4 📹 15 **Choose the correct option. Watch the second part of the video again to check.**
   1 The ranch was owned by his *grandmother's* / *grandfather's* family.
   2 *A prime minister* / *A famous Hollywood actor* visited them and stayed in the bedroom.
   3 The gun *is not real* / *was used in a war*.
   4 The Maasai move *every year* / *every three years* to look for fresh grass.
   5 *A fire* / *The rain* destroys the Maasai's old house.
   6 The Maasai are going to learn how to *become cowboys* / *cook*.

5 **Work in groups and discuss the questions.**
   - Would you like to visit the two homes? Why? / Why not?
   - Do you ever have visitors to your home?
   - Do you have any paintings or photos of your family on the wall in your home? Who of?
   - Do you have any special objects people can see in your home? What are they? Why are they special?
   - What's your favourite part of your house? Why?

UNDERSTANDING FAST SPEECH

6 📹 16 **Read and listen to this extract from the video said fast, then slow. Stressed sounds are in CAPITALS.**

KINDa like the WOmen in YOUR culture – SHE brought the COWS to the MArriage

7 **You try! Practise saying the extract with the same stressed sounds.**

REVIEW 4

GRAMMAR

1 Complete 1–7 with one word in each space.

1 A: Are you _____ to be here for lunch today?

   B: Yes, I _____. I'm going to leave at about four o'clock.

2 A: Do you have to work at the weekends?

   B: No, I _____.

3 A: Who's going _____ make the dinner?

   B: We _____.

4 A: Your grandmother's 98! Wow! Can she still walk OK?

   B: Yes, she _____, but she's very slow.

5 A: Do you enjoy studying?

   B: No, I _____.

6 I can't talk now. I have _____ speak to my boss.

7 I don't speak much English, but my wife _____.

8 I _____ like to visit Chile next year, but tickets are very expensive.

2 Rewrite the sentences as negatives (-) or questions (?).

1 I'm going to see him today. (-)

2 She has to come to the meeting. (-)

3 You'd like to be famous some day. (?)

4 I'd like to work for that company. (-)

5 He's going to stay here. (?)

6 I have to wait. (?)

7 We have to go to the meeting. (-)

8 She'd like a cup of coffee. (?)

3 Put the word in bold in the correct place in the sentence.

1 She have to drive me to the station. I can take a taxi. **doesn't**

2 My parents speak Chinese and my older brother too. **does**

3 My grandfather's tall and my dad is. **too**

4 It's OK. You don't to do it. You decide. **have**

5 Would you like get something to eat? **to**

6 My husband is going to, but I'm not. **go**

4 ▶ 62 Listen and complete the sentences with one word in each space. Contractions (*I'm, don't*, etc.) are one word.

1 She's _____ _____ _____ _____ the idea.

2 _____ _____ _____ _____ work tomorrow, _____ my wife _____.

3 _____ _____ _____ you _____ _____ _____ tomorrow?

4 _____ really _____ _____ _____ working and travel more.

5 _____ _____ _____ _____ to eat?

6 My daughter still _____ _____ _____, _____ my sons _____.

5 ▶ 62 Work in pairs. Compare your ideas. Listen again to check.

VOCABULARY

6 Complete the texts with the verbs in the boxes.

cut	provide	save	stop

The government wants to [1]_____ the speed limit in cities to 40 km/h. It says the change is going to [2]_____ accidents and [3]_____ money in the health service. The government would also like to [4]_____ more bus services.

build	create	help	improve

The government says it's going to [5]_____ more jobs and opportunities for young people. It wants to [6]_____ education and [7]_____ a lot more schools, roads and houses. It's a big job, but it's going to [8]_____ businesses.

7 Complete the adjectives with the missing letters.

1 My dad's very f_ _. He ran a marathon last year.

2 My sister's very c_ _ver. She always gets A grades.

3 She's doesn't say much. She's very qu_ _ _.

4 You can trust her. She's very re_ _ _ _le.

5 On my birthday, he took me out for a ro_ _ _tic dinner.

6 My granddad is very f_ _ _y. We laugh a lot together.

7 She's very s_ _ _ct with her kids. They can't do anything!

8 It's very l_ _d! Can you turn it down?

9 He's very quiet. He's not very c_ _fi_ _ _t.

10 She's 53? I'm su_ _ _ _ _ed. I thought she was younger.

8 Match the verbs in the box to the groups of words they go with in 1–8.

do	go	lose	pick up	repair
get	have	move	play	start

1 ~ to Germany / ~ house / ~ to a nicer area

2 ~ a meeting with a client / don't ~ time / ~ a check-up

3 ~ my child from school / ~ a friend from the airport /

4 ~ games / ~ an instrument / ~ tennis

5 ~ running / ~ to a party / ~ home

6 ~ my car / ~ a broken chair / ~ the roof

7 ~ something to eat / ~ divorced / ~ a taxi home

8 ~ my homework / ~ the washing / ~ some exercise

9 ~ your job / ~ money / ~ some weight

10 ~ my own business / ~ a family / ~ smoking

9 EXPERIENCES

1

2

5

6

7

10

11

12

78

3

4

8

13

IN THIS UNIT YOU LEARN HOW TO:

- talk about places you've been to
- recommend places
- explain and ask about problems
- talk about experiences

WORDS FOR UNIT 9

1   Work in pairs. Match the phrases to the photos.

break a glass	hurt myself
buy fresh fish	lie on the beach
call an ambulance	lose the game
an exciting ride	make a mess
fall down	start crying
forget to bring	visit a palace
go up a tower	win the match
get a great view	

2   ▶ 63 Listen. Check your answers. Listen again. Repeat the words.

3   Which things do you think are part of a good experience? Which are part of a bad experience?

4   Work in pairs. Test each other. Cover the words.

Student A: point to a photo.

Student B: say the words.

9

14

15

HAVE YOU EVER BEEN THERE?

SPEAKING

1   Work in pairs. Discuss the questions.

- Do you know the building in the photo? If yes, what do you know about it?
- What do you know about the city of Istanbul?

2   Make a list of eight very famous buildings or places around the world – and four very famous ones in your country.

3   Work in groups and compare your lists. Did you think of the same places?

GRAMMAR Present perfect

4   Look at the dialogues below, then complete the rules in the Grammar box.

1   A: **Have you visited** the Hagia Sophia?

B: *No, never.* **Have** *you?*

A: *No, I* **haven't.**

2   A: **Have you tried** Turkish food?

B: *Yes, lots of times. I love it.*

3   A: **Have you been** to Istanbul?

B: *Yes, I* **have. Have** *you?*

We use the present perfect to ask about an action before now when we feel it is connected to the present situation – to ask, for example, if someone has experience of something.

To make the present perfect, we use a form of the verb ¹_____ + a past participle.

Regular past participles end in ²_____.

Some past participles are irregular. For example, *be* – ³_____.

G   Check your ideas on page 179 and do Exercise 1.

5   Work in groups. Ask each other about the famous buildings / places you thought of in Exercise 2, and answer using the phrases in the box.

For example:

A: *Have you (ever) been to ...? / Have you ever visited ...?*

B: *Yes, I have. Have you?*

Yes, I have. Have you?

No, I haven't. Have you?

No, never, but I'd like to.

> To give – or ask about – details of the past action (e.g. exactly when) we use the past simple.
>
> A: **Have you been** to Moscow?
>
> B: *Yes. I* **went** *there* **last year**.
>
> A: **Have you ever tried** English food?
>
> B: *Yes,* **I have**. *I* **had** *it in Manchester* **two years ago**.
>
> A: **Did** *you* **like** *it?*
>
> B: *No, not really.*

6   Choose the correct option.

1   A: Have you ever been to Africa?

   B: Yes. I *went / have been* to Nigeria and Ghana a few years ago.

2   A: Have you tried the restaurant here in the hotel?

   B: No. *Have / Did* you?

   A: Yes. We *went / have been* there last night. It *was / has been* really good.

3   A: Have you ever been to Turkey?

   B: Yes. We *have been / went* there last year on holiday.

   A: Oh, really? *Did you visit / Have you visited* the Hagia Sophia in Istanbul?

   B: No. We *wanted / have wanted* to, but we *were only / have only been* in the city for a day.

4   A: Have you ever tried Thai food?

   B: No, never.

   A: Really? Wow! Well, *have you tried / did you try* any other Asian food?

   B: Yes. Once. *I've been / I went* to an Indonesian restaurant when I was in Holland, but I *haven't really liked / didn't really like* it.

7   Change partners. Have similar conversations to the ones in Exercise 6, but this time, add details when you answer.

 For further practice, see Exercise 2 on page 180.

LISTENING

8   ▶ 64 Listen to a conversation between two tourists in Istanbul and someone who lives there. Put the questions in the order you hear them. The first one is done for you.

1 _e_ 2 ___ 3 ___ 4 ___ 5 ___ 6 ___ 7 ___ 8 ___

a   How long did you spend there?

b   Have you been to Topkapi Palace?

c   What are your plans for this evening?

d   Did you go up the Galata Tower?

e   Have you been to Istanbul before?

f   Have you tried the fish here?

g   Where have you been?

h   When did you arrive?

9   ▶ 64 Work in pairs. Do you remember how the speakers answer the questions in Exercise 8? Listen again and note the answers.

10   Work in groups. Discuss the questions.

- Which countries / cities would you really like to visit? Why?

- Do you know anyone who's been to any of those places already? Did they like them?

- Which tourist places in your country have you never been to? Why not?

DEVELOPING CONVERSATIONS

Recommending

If someone hasn't been to a place that we think is good, we often say *You should!*

If someone hasn't been to a place that we think is bad, we often say *Don't!*

We can then explain why we are recommending (or not recommending) the place.

A: *Have you tried the fish here?*

B: *No, we haven't.*

A: *Oh,* **you should**. *It's very good – very fresh.*

C: *Have you visited the palace?*

D: *No, I haven't.*

C: **Don't! It's really boring.**

11   Think of four places you think are good to visit – and four places that you think are bad. Think about why.

12   Work in pairs. Have conversations about your places. Follow these patterns.

A: *Have you been to the zoo here?*

B: *No, I haven't.*

A: Oh, you should! It's great. They have lions!

C: *Have you been to Harrods?*

D: No, never.

C: *Don't! It's very expensive!*

CONVERSATION PRACTICE

13   You are going to roleplay a conversation like the one you heard in the listening.

Student A: you're a local person. Ask the questions below.

Student B: you're a tourist. Answer Student A's questions. Use language from these pages.

Then change roles and have another conversation.

- Have you been here before?
- When did you arrive?
- Where have you been?
- Did you like it?
- Have you been to …?
- What are your plans for this evening?

 17 To watch the video and do the activities, see the DVD-ROM.

WHAT'S HAPPENED?

VOCABULARY Problems

1 Match the verbs in each group with the correct sentence endings.

1	I forgot	the wrong train.
2	I made	a mess.
3	I took	to turn off the gas.
4	I broke	on the floor.
5	It fell	my glasses.
6	I missed	my flight.
7	I lost	myself.
8	I hurt	a bit ill.
9	I felt	my passport.

2 How serious are the problems in Exercise 1, in your opinion? Work in pairs and write the sentences in the table below.

Very serious	
Quite serious	
Not very serious	

3 Work in pairs. Take turns saying a different sentence ending for each verb in Exercise 1. How long can you continue?

For example:

A: *I forgot to tell you.*

B: *I forgot his name.*

A: *I forgot to turn off the light.*

B: *I forgot the word.*

A: *I don't know another. 1 point to you! OK. You start next.*

B: *I made ...*

LISTENING

4 ▶ **65** Listen to five short conversations where there is a problem. Decide in which conversation (1–5):

a someone has made a mess.

b someone has lost something.

c someone has hurt themselves.

d someone has taken the wrong road.

e someone has forgotten to bring something.

5 ▶ **65** Work in pairs. Look at the sentences from the listening. What are the two missing words in each sentence? Listen again and check.

Conversation 1

1 Have you checked in your _____?

2 I've found them! They were by _____!

Conversation 2

3 _____'s thrown the plate on the floor.

4 Do you have a cloth or some tissues? There's sauce on _____.

Conversation 3

5 _____ a bottle this morning.

6 It's not in _____.

Conversation 4

7 I've cut _____.

8 Do you have _____ or something?

Conversation 5

9 Oh! You've come the _____. Do you have a map?

10 You need to go back and then _____ here.

6 Work in groups. Discuss how often you and people you know:

- lose things.
- forget things.
- break things.
- hurt yourself.
- take the wrong direction.
- make a mess.

For example:

A: *I'm quite good. I hardly ever lose things, but my dad often loses things – especially his keys.*

B: *I think I'm average. I sometimes forget things but I think it's normal. My friend, Kenji – he never forgets things. He hears something once and he remembers it! He's amazing.*

GRAMMAR

Past participles

Regular verbs have the same *-ed* ending for both the past simple tense and the past participle, but many common verbs are irregular.

7 Work in pairs. Decide if the verbs in the box have a regular or irregular past participle. You have seen all the verbs in this unit!

arrive	feel	plan
be	find	see
break	forget	stop
check	happen	study
come	hurt	take
cut	lose	throw
do	make	try
fall	miss	visit

G Check your ideas on page 180 and do Exercise 1.

8 Complete the sentences with the correct present perfect form of the verbs in brackets.

1 _____ my keys? I'm sure I put them down here somewhere. (you / see)

2 I'm really sorry. _____ your name! (I / forget)

3 I don't believe it. _____ my bag! (someone / take)

4 What was that noise? What _____? (you / do)

5 I'm really sorry. _____ a glass. (I / break)

6 Can you help us? _____. (our bags / not arrive)

7 Hi. This is Andrew. I'm really sorry, but _____ our flight. (we / miss)

8 Where _____? Is he going to come back? (Martin / go)

9 _____ the police? (anyone / call)

PRONUNCIATION

9 ▶ **66** Listen to the present perfect forms in Exercise 8 – first fast, then slow. Notice how *have* can sound like /hæv/, /həv/, /əv/ or /v/ and how sometimes you don't hear it at all in fast speech.

10 ▶ **67** Listen to the slower version and repeat the sentences.

11 Work in pairs. Write a response to each sentence in Exercise 8.

For example:

1 Have you seen my keys? I'm sure I put them down here somewhere.

Yes. They're in your hand!

2 I'm really sorry. I've forgotten your name!

That's OK. I've forgotten yours too!

12 Work with another pair. Read out your dialogues.

G For further practice, see Exercises 2 and 3 on page 180.

SPEAKING

13 Work in pairs. Discuss these questions. Give some details.

- Have you lost anything recently?
- Have you broken anything recently?
- Have you taken any exams recently?
- Have you hurt yourself recently?
- Have you missed anything recently?
- Have you seen anything good recently? (TV or films)

MEMORABLE EXPERIENCES

VOCABULARY Describing experiences

1 Match the sentences (1–8) to the pictures (a–h).

1 It was really relaxing.

2 It was really annoying.

3 It was really boring.

4 It was really sad.

5 It was really embarrassing.

6 It was really exciting.

7 It was really scary!

8 It was really stressful.

2 Work in pairs. Discuss which adjectives in Exercise 1 describe good experiences and which describe bad experiences.

3 Work in pairs. Read the sentences about holiday experiences and check you understand the words in bold. Then discuss what adjective from Exercise 1 best describes each experience.

1 We went to a big **theme park** with some amazing rides.

2 The **plane was delayed** and we had to wait for hours.

3 Someone **with a gun** stopped us and **stole our money**.

4 We did nothing for a week. We just **lay on the beach** and swam in the sea.

5 The **airline lost our bags** on the way there.

6 My boyfriend **asked me to marry him**.

7 There was **an accident on the motorway** and several people died.

8 I got up in the night to **get some water from the cooler** and I forgot to take my room key!

9 We **went** over the city **in a helicopter**.

10 My wife's parents stayed with us for **a couple of months** last summer.

READING

4 Work in groups. Discuss the questions.

- Has this been a good year for you or not?

- What are you going to remember from this year?

5 Read about the memorable experiences people had in one year. Which person talks about:

1 a celebration?

2 a theme park?

3 a concert?

4 a football match?

5 a holiday?

6 a baby?

6 Read again. What do you think of the experiences in the text? Rank them from 1 (= the best) to 6 (= the worst).

👍 The best   1 _____

                2 _____

                3 _____

                4 _____

                5 _____

👎 The worst   6 _____

7 Work in pairs. Compare your lists from Exercise 6 and explain your ideas.

UNFORGETTABLE!

 KRISSU, ESTONIA

I went to our national dance and song festival in Tallinn. 18,000 of us sang together and more than 100,000 people watched us. When you sing with so many people, you create an amazing sound. I actually started crying!

 JUANA, MEXICO

This year was very stressful at work, but in November I went to a meditation centre for ten days. In the centre, you don't speak to anyone, you can't use your mobile phone or a computer, or watch TV. You try not to think. You relax completely. It was exactly what I needed.

 LAURA, SCOTLAND

I had a party for my 21st birthday. All my family were there. It was really nice – apart from when my dad gave a speech about me. It was a bit embarrassing.

 MANUELA, ITALY

Having my daughter was obviously unforgettable, but it was extra special because I had her at home. The day it happened, I started feeling her move at six in the evening. We thought we had lots of time, but by seven o'clock I was in a lot of pain! My husband called an ambulance, but my daughter arrived first! It hurt a lot and it was a bit scary without a doctor, but it was very quick, and she's beautiful and healthy!

 **TARIQ,** OMAN

We went to Ferrari World in Abu Dhabi. I love cars – especially Ferraris. It was really good, but there were some long queues. We waited for two hours to go on the fastest roller coaster in the world! Then the ride only lasted a minute, but it was really exciting and I loved it!

 **JACK,** UK

On May the 30th, I went to see my team Hull play in the Cup Final. We lost 3–2. After the game, someone stole my wallet. I went to the police, but they couldn't help. I missed my train, so it took a long time to get home. I would like to forget that day, but I can't!

---

8 **Complete each pair of collocations with a verb from the text.**

1 _____ an amazing sound / more jobs
2 _____ your mobile phone / your computer
3 _____ a speech / him a present
4 _____ an ambulance / the police
5 _____ for two hours / for a bus
6 _____ 3–2 / our last match

9 **Work in pairs. Discuss the questions.**

- Have you ever been to a festival? Where? Was it good?
- Have you ever been to a theme park? Where? Was it good?
- Have you ever given a speech? When? In front of how many people?
- Have you ever queued for a long time? How long for? What for?
- Have you ever called an ambulance or the police? Why? Was everything OK?

SPEAKING

10 **Choose an experience that one of the adjectives from Exercise 1 describes. Plan what you want to say about the experience. Use a dictionary or ask your teacher for help, if you need to. Write:**

- what the experience was.
- when it happened.
- where you were.
- who you were with.
- what happened first, second, etc.

For example:

One time I lost all my bags. Five years ago I went on holiday to America with my family. We went to New York. We arrived late and we missed our next flight. When we got to San Francisco, our bags didn't arrive. It took six days to get them!

11 **Work in groups. Tell the group your story, but don't say the adjective. Can the other students guess which adjective you chose?**

For example:

A: *It sounds very stressful.*   B: *Yes, it was!*

SOUNDS AND VOCABULARY REVIEW

12 ▶ **68** **Listen and repeat the sounds with /æ/, /ɒ/, /aʊ/ and /əʊ/. Are any of them difficult for you to hear or say?**

13 ▶ **69** **Work in groups. Listen to eight sentences using these words. Together, try to write them down. Then listen again and finish writing them.**

broken	found	planned	sad
forgot	lost	round	stole

 For further revision, see Exercises 1–3 on page 180.

1

2

5

6

7

8

12

13

86

14

3

4

9

15

IN THIS UNIT YOU LEARN HOW TO:

- talk about train travel
- buy tickets
- talk about the time
- talk about transport where you live
- recommend places

WORDS FOR UNIT 10

1   Work in pairs. Match the phrases to the photos.

an animal on the line	a lovely pool
change money	park the car
charge for the motorway	pay in cash
cycle in a bike lane	taste delicious
get a haircut	travel first class
get in the car	vote for it
get off the train	wait on the platform
go to the gym	watch a live band
a lot of crime	

2   ▶ 70 Listen. Check your answers. Listen again. Repeat the words.

3   Work in pairs. Test each other. Cover the words.

Student A: point to a photo.

Student B: say the words.

10

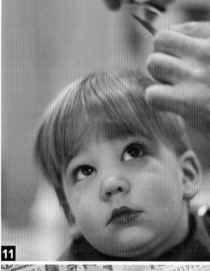

11

16

17

WHEN'S THE NEXT TRAIN?

VOCABULARY Trains and stations

1　Work in pairs. Check you understand the words in bold in the questions below. Then decide who usually asks the question – a passenger (P) or someone who works for the train company (T)?

1　Would you like a **single** or **return?**

2　I'm a student. Do I get a **discount?**

3　Which **platform** is it?

4　Is it a **direct** train?

5　What's causing the **delay?**

6　Which stop do we **get off** at?

7　How would you like to pay?

8　How much is a **first-class** ticket?

2　Match the questions in Exercise 1 to the answers below (a–h).

a　In cash.

b　No, you have to change in Munich.

c　67 pounds – and second class is 39.

d　A return, please, coming back tomorrow.

e　Not the next one, but the one after that.

f　Platform three.

g　There's an animal on the line.

h　Yes, you get 15% off.

3　Work in pairs. Practise saying the questions and answers in Exercises 1 and 2.

LISTENING

4　▶ **71** Listen to a conversation in a train station in Amsterdam, Holland. Answer the questions.

1　What kind of tickets do the passengers buy?

2　How much are the tickets?

3　How do they pay?

4　What time is their train?

5　Which platform do they need?

5　▶ **71** Listen again. Complete the sentences with one word in each space.

1　_____ can I help?

2　The _____ train is at 12.25.

3　It's probably _____ to buy two singles.

4　Please _____ your PIN. Great.

5　You have to _____ at Hilversum.

6　How long does the journey _____?

7　You _____ around three o'clock.

8　Thanks for your _____.

6　Work in groups. Discuss the questions.

• Are trains good or bad in your country? Why?

• Do you have a favourite train journey?

• Are there any train journeys you'd like to make?

DEVELOPING CONVERSATIONS

Telling the time

We can say times in two different ways.

| 12.25: *twenty-five past twelve* | or | *twelve twenty-five* |
| 11.45: *quarter to twelve* | or | *eleven forty-five* |

Both ways are very common.

9 Work in groups. Discuss the questions.
- What time is it now?
- What time did your class start?
- What time does it finish?
- What time do you usually get up?
- What time did you go to bed last night?
- What time do you usually catch the bus / train in the morning?
- What time do you usually get home?
- What time do you usually have dinner?

PRONUNCIATION

10 ▶ 72 Listen to eight phrases and sentences that use *to* between other words. Notice that we often pronounce *to* as /tə/. Listen again and write what you hear.

11 ▶ 72 Listen again. Repeat what you hear.

CONVERSATION PRACTICE

12 Work in pairs. You are going to roleplay a conversation at a station.

Student A: you sell tickets. Look at File 8 on page 195.

Student B: it's nine in the morning. You'd like to buy a ticket to Hull. Ask Student A for information.

13 Now roleplay the conversation. Use the guide below to help you.

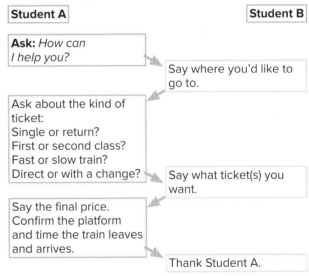

14 Change roles and have another conversation.

Student A: it's four in the afternoon. You'd like to buy a ticket to Hope. Ask Student B for information.

Student B: you sell tickets. Look at File 5 on page 194.

18 To watch the video and do the activities, see the DVD-ROM.

7 Match the times (1–8) to the pictures (a–h).

1 half past three
2 quarter to four
3 four fifteen
4 five to nine
5 five past nine
6 six twenty-five
7 nine o'clock
8 two thirty

8 Work in pairs. Cover the times in Exercise 7. Say the times in the pictures (a–h) in two different ways.

GETTING AROUND

VOCABULARY Transport

1 Complete each group of collocations with one word from the box.

bike	bus	car	flight	taxi	train

1 get the ~ / the 73 ~ / get off the ~ / wait at the ~ stop / the ~es run all night

2 go in the ~ / get in the ~ / park the ~ / my ~ broke down / rent a ~

3 catch a ~ / get the 8.20 ~ / a direct ~ / miss my ~ / pick me up from the ~ station

4 ride a ~ / lock my ~ / fell off my ~ / have a mountain ~ / someone stole my ~

5 get a ~ / stop a ~ / the ~ driver took a long route / the ~ driver charged too much

6 book my ~ / miss my ~ / the ~'s delayed / ~ FR09 to Rome

2 Tick the collocations you knew before and cross the collocations that are new for you. Then work in pairs. Compare what you knew. Check any words you don't know in a dictionary.

3 Work in groups. Discuss these questions.

- What bus routes go near your house? Where do they go? Do you take any of them? If yes, what stops do you usually get off at?

- Do you have a bike? What kind? Is it safe to ride a bike where you live? Do people often steal bikes there? Have you ever fallen off a bike?

- Do you have a car? What kind? Is it easy to park where you live? Has your car ever broken down? Have you ever rented a car?

- How often do you fly? When you book a flight how do you choose the airline? Have you ever missed a flight?

- Do you ever take taxis? Why? / Why not? Is there much competition between taxi companies in your city? Have you ever been charged too much or taken a strange route?

READING

4 Read the article about taxis round the world. Decide which of the ten paragraphs (1–10) is not true.

5 Work in groups. Discuss your ideas about which part of the article is not true. Then check in File 10 on page 195 to see if you were right.

6 Work in pairs. Look at the things, places and numbers below. Can you remember what the article says about these things?

1 320 and 25%

2 the hippocampus

3 Uzbekistan

4 South Africa and 2,000

5 a company in Puebla

6 7,000 and 300

7 Olden and 550

8 Seoul and 17

9 Britain, Europe and 1

7 Read again and check your ideas.

TAXI!

1 **KNOWLEDGE:** London taxi drivers have to take a course to learn 320 routes and all the names of the roads on each route. Only 25% of people finish the course and pass the exam.

2 **BIGGER BRAINS:** On average, taxi drivers have a bigger *hippocampus* than other people. The hippocampus is a part of the brain connected to memory and learning.

3 **EXPENSIVE:** In Muscat, Oman, you can get a one-million-dollar Ferrari Enzo taxi. The driver charges clients $30 per kilometre.

4 **I HAVE A CAR. I AM A TAXI DRIVER:** In Tashkent, Uzbekistan, anyone with a car can be a taxi driver. If they see someone waiting at the side of the road, they can stop and negotiate a price.

5 **DANGEROUS:** In South Africa in the 1990s, competition between different taxi companies caused 'taxi wars' in which more than 2,000 people died.

6 **SAFER:** Many women don't feel safe in taxis if a man is driving. But there aren't enough women taxi drivers because they don't feel safe picking up men! A company in Puebla, Mexico, has found a solution: pink taxis. Women drive them and they only pick up women.

7 **THE LONGEST JOURNEY:** In 1930 two old ladies in Australia took a taxi on a 7,000-mile trip across the desert, with taxi driver Charles Heard. The trip cost around £300.

8 **LOST IN TRANSLATION:** A Spanish couple had to pay $3,000 when they got a taxi in Norway. They wanted to go to Olden but the driver understood Halden – more than 550 kilometres further away!

9 **THAT'S BETTER:** The city of Seoul, South Korea found foreign tourists had difficulty using taxis because they don't know enough Korean. So now it provides a free translating service in seventeen languages. Customers can phone a number and ask a translator to speak to the driver.

10 **THEY'RE THE BEST:** Britain has some of the worst transport problems in Europe. There's too much traffic, there are too many delays on public transport and it costs too much. However, the UK is number one for taxis. International tourists voted on a website. They said Britain's taxi drivers are friendly and reliable: in fact, the best in the world!

GRAMMAR

too much, too many and not enough

Too shows a situation is bad because it's more than we want.

Not enough shows a situation is bad because it's less than we want.

*There's **too much** traffic.*

*There are **too many** delays on public transport.*

*There are**n't** enough women taxi drivers.*

*They do**n't** know **enough** Korean.*

8 Look at the sentences above. Complete these rules with *too much*, *too many* or *not enough*.

1 _____ only goes with uncountable nouns.

2 _____ only goes with plural nouns.

3 _____ can go with uncountable noun or plurals.

 Check your ideas on page 181 and do Exercise 1.

9 Choose the correct option.

1 There *aren't enough / are too many* trains. They need to run more often.

2 The government says there are *too much / too many* accidents here, so it wants to reduce the speed limit.

3 I always travel by car. There *is / are* too much crime on public transport.

4 There *isn't / aren't* enough buses at night. You have to get a taxi after eleven in the evening.

5 Too *much / many* people are flying these days. Flights are too cheap.

6 There are too many cars on the road. Travelling to work takes too much *time / hours*.

10 Work in groups. In three minutes, see how many sentences about the picture you can say using *too / not enough*. Which group can get the most?

 For further practice, see Exercise 2 on page 181.

SPEAKING

11 Work in groups. Talk about where you live using *too much*, *too many* and *not enough*. Think about the things in the box. Say what your town or city needs to make things better.

For example:

*The trains in my city are OK, but **there aren't enough trains** at night. They stop at midnight.*

accidents	cyclists	places to park	taxis
airport	drivers	pollution	traffic
buses	flights	roads and motorways	trains

WHERE'S THE BEST PLACE TO GO?

DEVELOPING CONVERSATIONS

Where's the best place?

When we want to know good places to do things, we often ask *Where's the best place to ...?*

To suggest places, we often say *Try* + the name of a place.

1   **Match the questions (1–8) to the suggestions (a–h).**

   1   Where's the best place to eat?
   2   Where's the best place to stay?
   3   Where's the best place to change money?
   4   Where's the best place to go shopping?
   5   Where's the best place to go dancing?
   6   Where's the best place to go cycling?
   7   Where's the best place to get some exercise?
   8   Where's the best place to get a haircut?

   a   Try the park. There are **bike lanes** there, so it's very safe.
   b   Try Melati's. It's small and friendly, and it has a really nice **atmosphere**. The food is great as well.
   c   Try Embassy. It's always really busy and the music's great. They have **live bands** every Friday as well.
   d   Try the post office. They usually give you a good **rate**, especially for dollars.
   e   Try the Natural Fitness Centre. They have a good gym and a nice **swimming pool**.
   f   Try the big department store in town. They sell a good **selection** of different things.
   g   It depends what **style** you want.
   h   Try the Imperial. The rooms are nice and it's not very expensive. It's **good value for money**.

2   **Work in pairs. Discuss what you think the words in bold in Exercise 1 mean.**

3   **Now practise having conversations.**

   Student A: you are a tourist. Ask questions 1–8 from Exercise 1.

   Student B: suggest good places you know in your town or city.

   Then change roles.

LISTENING

4   **▶ 73 Listen to a conversation in a hotel between two guests and a receptionist. Answer these questions.**

   • Which two questions from Exercise 1 do the guests ask?

   • Which places does the receptionist recommend?

5   **▶ 73 Choose the correct option. Then listen again and check your answers**

   1   How *can I / I can* help you?
   2   *We like / We'd like* to go out for dinner.
   3   It's not *the cheapest / cheaper* place in town.
   4   *Need we / Do we need* to book?
   5   *Which / What time* would you like your table?
   6   What's the *easy / easiest* way to get there?
   7   It *takes / spends* about half an hour to walk there.
   8   *Do / Would* you like me to book one for you?
   9   There's a nice market *in / at* the main square.
   10 No problem. *It's my / It was* pleasure.

6 Work in pairs. Discuss these questions.

- Are you happy to go to a more expensive restaurant if the food there is very good?
- How often do you eat fish and seafood? Do you have a favourite place to eat fish?
- What kind of places do you eat in when you are in a town you don't know?
- Do you prefer walking or taking a taxi? Why?
- Do you like shopping in markets or do you prefer other kinds of places? Why?
- Do you usually buy presents when you go on holiday? If yes, what kind of things do you buy?

GRAMMAR

Superlatives

To compare more than two things, use *the* + a superlative adjective.

To make superlative adjectives:

– add *-est* to short, one-syllable adjectives.

– for short adjectives ending in a consonant, double the consonant.

– for adjectives ending in *-y*, change to *-iest*.

– for longer adjectives (two or more syllables), use *the most* + adjective.

A small number of superlative adjectives are irregular.

7 Read the information in the Grammar box and complete the table with the correct superlative forms.

Adjective	Comparative	Superlative
good	better	
bad	worse	
fast	faster	
small	smaller	
big	bigger	
strange	stranger	
hot	hotter	
early	earlier	
boring	more boring	
interesting	more interesting	

 Check your ideas on page 181 and do Exercise 1.

8 Complete the conversations with the superlative form of the adjectives in brackets.

1 A: What's _____ way to get back to our hotel? (quick)

   B: Take the underground. It's only two stops away.

2 A: How was Vienna?

   B: Amazing. It's one of _____ cities I've ever been to. (beautiful)

3 A: Is it an expensive hotel?

   B: Well, it's not _____ place to stay, but it's not _____ either. (cheap, expensive)

4 A: Is the crime bad there?

   B: Yes. It's one of _____ cities in the world! (dangerous)

5 A: How was your journey?

   D: It was awful   one of _____ flights I've had. (bad)

6 A: How's your course going?

   B: It's impossible! It's _____ thing I've done! (difficult)

 For further practice, see Exercise 2 on page 182.

SPEAKING

9 Work in groups. Make questions by changing the words in italics into superlatives.

1 Where's *good* place to live in your town / city?

2 And where's *bad* place to live?

3 Where's *old* part of your town / city?

4 What's *easy* way to get around your town / city?

5 Where's *cheap* place to eat?

6 What's *big* city in your country?

7 What's *beautiful* part of your country?

8 What are *popular* places for tourists?

9 Who's *famous* person from your country?

10 What's *delicious* food from your country?

10 Now discuss your answers to the questions. Do you agree with the other people in the group?

SOUNDS AND VOCABULARY REVIEW

11 ▶ **74** Listen and repeat the sounds with /ʊ/, /uː/, /ɜː/ and /ɑː/. Are any of them difficult for you to hear or say?

12 ▶ **75** Work in groups. Listen to eight sentences using the words in the box. Together, try to write them down. Then listen again and finish writing them.

booked	half	route	world
car	journey	value	would

For further revision, see Exercises 1–3 on page 182.

VIDEO 5

BARCELONA'S STREET LIFE

1 Look at the photo. Discuss the questions.

- What do you think of this kind of street performer?
- Do you sometimes see similar people where you live?
- What other kinds of street performers have you seen? Where?
- Do you ever give money to people performing on the street?

2 ▶ 19 Watch the video. Decide if these sentences are true (T) or false (F).

1 You see all of the following:
  - a jazz band
  - people dancing
  - a clown
  - a woman performing magic
  - a man selling art
  - a shop selling flowers

2 All the speakers like the Ramblas.

3 All the speakers are from Barcelona.

3 Work in groups. Discuss the questions.

- Have you been to Barcelona? If yes, what did you think of it?
- If no, would you like to go there?
- Did you like any of the performers in the video?

4 ▶ 19 Read the sentences below. Then watch the video again and put the sentences in the order you hear them.

1 ___ 2 ___ 3 ___ 4 ___ 5 ___ 6 ___

a In the Ramblas you can find ... music from Argentina, from Spain, from Africa, from all the world.

b You'll always find a friend on the streets.

c There's never nobody in the Ramblas. Every hour of the day there's life.

d You have traffic, you have people, you have tourists, you have thieves, you have performers.

e It's worth coming to Barcelona.

f If you walk past, by the flower shops, I mean, the way they build it up is beautiful.

5 Work in groups. Make a list of:

- the three best streets where you live.
- the three best places you have ever visited.

Discuss your reasons. Then share your ideas with the class.

UNDERSTANDING FAST SPEECH

6 ▶ 20 Read and listen to this extract from the video said fast, then slow. Stressed sounds are in CAPITALS.

like Any TIME you go OUT of your HOUSE, there's ALways SOMEthing going ON.

7 You try! Practise saying the extract with the same stressed sounds.

REVIEW 5

1 Complete the text with one word in each space.

Have you ¹_____ had Moroccan food? I think it's ²_____ best food in the world! I cooked some a few days ³_____ and it was one of the ⁴_____ delicious things I've ⁵_____ eaten in my life. The only problem was my wife didn't like it. She said it was ⁶_____ hot. She also said I spend too ⁷_____ time cooking – and not ⁸_____ time talking to her.

2 Put the verbs in the questions in the present perfect and the answers in the past simple.

1. A: *you / ever / be* to Brazil?

   B: Yes. *I / go* there last year on holiday.

2. A: *your son / see* the new Disney film?

   B: Yes. *he / see* it at the weekend, actually.

3. A: *they / visit* the USA before?

   B: Yeah, *they / come* to see us here two years ago.

4. A: *she / meet* your parents yet?

   B: Yes. *we / have* lunch with them on Sunday.

5. A: *you / try* Indian food?

   B: Once, in London, but *I / not like* it.

3 Correct the mistake in each sentence.

1. That's her goodest book.
2. He have done this hundreds of times before.
3. The most easy way to get there is by taxi.
4. I've never readed anything by Günter Grass.
5. There not enough time to do it now.
6. There are too much guns in our society.
7. The Alhambra is most beautiful building in Spain.
8. I've played a really good computer game yesterday.
9. There isn't enough places to park in the city centre.
10. His books are too much long.

4 ▶ 76 Listen and complete the sentences with one word in each space. Contractions (*I'm, don't,* etc.) are one word.

1. She's _____ _____ _____ funniest people _____ _____.

2. I've _____ _____ there, but _____ _____ _____ go.

3. _____ _____ _____ pollution and there _____ _____ _____ cars on the road.

4. I _____ _____ in Madrid _____ _____ _____ ago.

5. There _____ _____ chairs here _____ _____.

6. I _____ _____ help. _____ _____ _____ happened.

5 ▶ 76 Work in pairs. Compare your ideas. Listen again to check.

6 Replace each adjective in sentences 1–10 with its opposite from a–j.

1 The mountains are quite *far*.	a stressful
2 We had a very *relaxing* week.	b expensive
3 It's a very *exciting* film.	c right
4 It's very *cheap* there.	d fast
5 We're on the *wrong* platform.	e early
6 I was very *sad* to leave.	f impossible
7 We arrived *late*.	g boring
8 It's *easy* to park the car there.	h dangerous
9 We took the *slow* train.	i happy
10 It's a very *safe* place to live.	j near

7 Put the words into two groups – problems, or trains and stations.

buy a single	get a discount	pay in cash
enter your PIN	hurt myself	steal money
feel ill	lose my bags	
first class	make a mess	

8 Match the verbs in the box to the groups of words they go with in 1–8.

arrive	break	get off	miss
book	charge	lose	take

1. ~ the bus / ~ at the next stop / ~ the train
2. ~ a long route / ~ the wrong train / ~ two and a half hours
3. ~ in London at eight / ~ late / the train ~s at nine
4. ~ a flight / ~ a table / ~ a taxi for you
5. ~ my flight / ~ my train / ~ my bus
6. ~ a glass / ~ a window / ~ my glasses
7. ~ a lot / ~ for the motorway / ~ £60 an hour
8. ~ my keys / ~ the match / ~ money

9 Complete the text with one word in each space. The first letters are given.

My grandfather was born in 1900 and ¹d_____ in 2000, one day after his 100th birthday. He had an ²ac_____ and fell down the stairs. He had several jobs in his life – he was a taxi ³dr_____, a teacher and, for 20 years, he was a politician. He had quite a lot of success. He wanted better ⁴p_____ transport and he wanted more people to ⁵cy_____ when other people just wanted more cars and to build more ⁶mot_____. Because of his work, they created the first bike ⁷la_____ in the country. Lots of people don't like politicians, but my grandfather was very ⁸po_____. I really miss him.

11 FOOD

1

2

5

6

7

11

12

13

3

IN THIS UNIT YOU LEARN HOW TO:

- order and pay in restaurants
- understand menus
- describe different kinds of food
- agree and disagree with statements
- talk about what you eat

4

WORDS FOR UNIT 11

1 **Work in pairs. Match the phrases to the photos.**

ask for the bill	look at the menu	steak and chips
buy some sweets	a lot of garlic	tomato soup
a cookery book	a lot of spices	a vegetable dish
cut some onion	order food online	want to lose weight
fried chicken	a pregnant mum	
a fruit dessert	sell soft drinks	

2 ▶ **77** **Listen. Check your answers. Listen again. Repeat the words.**

3 **Work in pairs. Test each other. Cover the words.**

Student A: point to a photo.

Student B: say the words.

8

9

10

14

15

16

Unit 11   Food   **97**

ARE YOU READY TO ORDER?

SPEAKING

1 Work in groups. Discuss these questions.

- How often do you eat in restaurants?
- Do you have a favourite restaurant?
- What do you usually eat when you go out for a meal?
- Who usually pays?

VOCABULARY Restaurants

2 Complete the dialogues with the pairs of words in the box.

the bill + service	order + the soup
course + like	ready + decide
dessert + the ice cream	a table + booked

1 A: Hello. Do you have _____ for two?

   B: Have you _____?

   A: No, I'm afraid not.

2 A: Are you _____ to order?

   B: Not yet. We're still trying to _____ what we want.

3 A: OK, so can I take your _____ next please, sir?

   B: Yes. Thanks. For starters, I'll have _____, please.

4 A: And for your main _____?

   B: I'd _____ the chicken, please.

5 A: Would you like any _____?

   B: Yes, please. Can I have _____?

6 A: Can we have _____, please?

   B: Yes, of course. Here you are.

   A: Thank you. Oh! It's quite expensive. Does this include _____?

   B: Yes, we add 10%.

3 Work in pairs. For each dialogue (1–6) in Exercise 2, decide whether A is the waiter / waitress or the customer.

LISTENING

4 ▶ 78 Listen to two English people in a restaurant in France. Answer these questions.

a What three problems do they have?

b What do they order?

c Do they enjoy the meal?

d Do you think they are going to leave any extra money for the waiter? Why? / Why not?

5 ▶ 78 Work in pairs. Who / What do these adjectives describe? Discuss your ideas. Then listen again to check.

busy	delicious	finished	full	well-cooked

7 ► **79** Listen to the sentences in the box – first slow, then fast. Repeat what you hear.

8 Put a–f in the correct order in the two conversations.

Conversation 1   1 ___ 2 ___ 3 ___ 4 ___ 5 ___ 6 ___

a   Yes. Thanks. I'll have the salad for starters, please.

b   Can I get the chicken, please?

c   Are you ready to order?

d   Really? Oh. OK. Well, can I have the fish then, please?

e   Certainly. And for your main course?

f   I'm afraid the chicken's finished.

Conversation 2   1 ___ 2 ___ 3 ___ 4 ___ 5 ___ 6 ___

a   Yes, please. Can I get the ice cream?

b   Without, please, so just black.

c   Would you like any dessert?

d   I'm really full. I'll just have a coffee, please.

e   Of course. And for you, madam?

f   With milk – or without?

9 ► **80** Listen and check your answers. Then work in pairs. Practise reading out the conversations.

CONVERSATION PRACTICE

10 Work in pairs. You are going to roleplay a conversation like the one you heard in the listening.

Student A: you are a customer. Look at File 9 on page 195. Decide what you'd like to have.

Student B: you are a waiter / waitress. Choose questions from these pages to ask. Remember them.

11 Now roleplay the conversation. Use the guide below to help you. Then change roles and have another conversation.

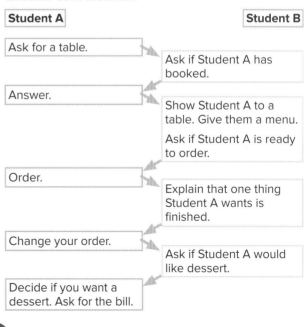

6 Work in groups. Which of these sentences do you agree with? Why? There is an example for the first sentence.

- French food is the best in the world.

  A: *I haven't tried French food, so I don't know. Maybe it's true.*

  B: *I've tried it, but I prefer Japanese food.*

- It's always better to book a table before you go out for dinner.

- Waiters and waitresses usually just recommend expensive things.

- If you have a starter and a main course, it's better not to have a dessert.

- It's better if restaurants include service in the bill.

DEVELOPING CONVERSATIONS

Ordering food and drink

We can use different phrases to order food and drink. They all mean the same thing.

*For starters, **I'll hav**e the soup, **please**.*

***I'd like** the chicken, **please**.*

***Can I get** a steak, **please**?*

***Can I have** the ice cream?*

🔊 **21 To watch the video and do the activities, see the DVD-ROM.**

WHAT'S THIS ON THE MENU?

VOCABULARY Food

1 Match the kinds of food in the box to the photos.

beans	fish	nuts
dairy products	fruit	seafood
drinks	meat	vegetables

2 Work in pairs. Decide which word does not go in each group (1–7). Use the correct sentence from a–g to explain why. The first one is done for you.

1 salt / sugar / pepper / spices / water

They're all things that we add for flavour except water.

2 potatoes / pasta / cream / rice / bread

3 wine / milk / cheese / butter / cream

4 apples / oranges / eggs / kiwis / bananas

5 juice / coffee / carrots / tea / beer

6 lemons / onions / garlic / potatoes / spinach

7 tomatoes / beef / lamb / pork / steak

a They're all basic foods except …

b They're all vegetables except …

c They're all things that we add for flavour except …

d They're all drinks except …

e They're all kinds of meat except …

f They're all dairy products except …

g They're all kinds of fruit except …

3 Which of the foods from Exercise 2 can you see in the photos?

4 Work in pairs. Practise asking about and explaining the names of different foods.

Student A: look at File 7 on page 194.

Student B: look at File 12 on page 196.

LISTENING

5 ▶ 81 Listen to three conversations connected to food. What is happening in each conversation?

a They're discussing a place to go and eat.

b They're discussing a place to go on holiday.

c They're discussing a food programme on TV.

d They're discussing things on a menu.

e They're discussing what they are going to cook.

Conversation 1: _____

Conversation 2: _____

Conversation 3: _____

6 ▶ **81** Listen again and complete the sentences with two words in each space. Contractions (*that's*, *I've*, etc.) are one word.

Conversation 1

1 A: Oh really?

   C: Yeah, but if the restaurant has some fish or _____, that's OK.

2 B: Me neither. What's _____?

   A: It's nice. It's Italian – more or less.

3 B: OK. That's fine _____.

   C: Me too.

Conversation 2

4 A: No? Why not?

   B: It's _____ and I don't like planes.

5 C: Hmm. I'm not sure. What's _____ like? Is it all meat and barbecues?

   B: No, not at all! There's lots of great Asian food and all kinds of different things.

6 B: Yeah. In fact, I had some of the best food I've _____ there.

   A: It sounds great.

Conversation 3

7 B: Me too. Don't you like any seafood?

   A: Not really. _____ prawns before, but I prefer meat.

8 B: Hmm. Good choice. I saw Jamie Oliver on TV last night and he made a prawn curry.

   C: Oh yeah. I saw that too. Maybe _____ I thought of it!

9 A: OK, I think I'll have the steak.

   B: Oh right – _____. OK. I'm going to have the lamb.

7 Work in groups. Discuss these questions.

- What different restaurants are there near your home? What are they like?
- What countries have you been to? What was the food like?
- What cookery programmes do you know? Do you watch them? How often?

GRAMMAR

---

me too, me neither and auxiliaries

Look at two ways speakers in the listening agreed and disagreed with each other.

Agree

A: *I can't decide.*   B: ***Me neither***.

A: *OK. That's fine with me.*   B: ***Me too.***

Disagree

A: *Oh, I **don't like** seafood.*   B: *Really? **I do!***

A: *Really? **I'd** really **like** to go there.*   B: *Oh, **I wouldn't**.*

---

8 Complete the rules with words and phrases in bold from the Grammar box.

1 We use _____ to agree with a statement with *not* or *never*.

2 We use _____ to agree with a positive statement.

3 To disagree with a statement in the present simple we sometimes use *I* _____ or *I don't*.

4 We sometimes use other auxiliary verbs like *have, can* or _____ to disagree.

Ⓖ Check your ideas on page 182 and do Exercise 1.

9 Work in groups of three. Discuss the foods in Exercises 1 and 2. Find things that you *all*:

1 love.

2 don't really like.

3 eat or drink too much.

4 don't eat or drink enough.

Take turns to start. Your partners should agree or disagree.

For example:

A: *I love cheese, I eat it every day.*

B: *Me too.*

C: *Oh, I don't. I don't really like cheese.*

10 Complete these sentences so that they are true for you.

1 I love _____.

2 I've never had _____ food.

3 I can't _____ very well.

4 I've seen _____ several times.

5 I'd really like to _____.

6 I _____ last weekend.

11 Work in pairs. Read out your sentences to each other. Your partner should agree or disagree. Try and find out more by asking a question.

For example:

A: *I've never had Russian food.*

B: *Me neither. Are there any Russian restaurants near here?*

or

A: *I've never had Russian food.*

B: *Oh, I have.*

A: *Really? Was it nice?*

B: *Yes. Delicious.*

Ⓖ For further practice, see Exercise 2 on page 183.

SPEAKING

12 Work on your own. Using your own language, write a menu for a restaurant in your country. Have six to eight dishes including starters, main courses and desserts.

13 Work in pairs. Ask your partner to explain what the things on their menu are in English. Then decide what you would eat and who has the best menu.

A HEALTHY DIET

GRAMMAR

Explaining quantity

Some words that we use to show quantity go with both countable and uncountable nouns.

Other words only go with one of these kinds of nouns.

1 Look at the pictures and the sentences (1–5) that show quantity with an uncountable noun (*meat*). Match them to the sentences (a–e) that show the same quantities with a countable noun (*vegetables*).

1 I eat **a lot of** meat.

4 I don't eat **much** meat.

2 I eat **quite a lot of** meat.

5 I don't eat **any** meat.

3 I eat **some** meat.

a I eat **quite a lot of** vegetables.

b I don't eat **many** vegetables.

c I eat **a lot of** vegetables.

d I don't eat **any** vegetables.

e I eat **some** vegetables.

2 Work in pairs. Answer these questions.

1 Which words in Exercise 1 go with both countable and uncountable nouns?

2 Which word only goes with countable nouns?

3 Which word only goes with uncountable nouns?

4 Which words do we often use in negative sentences?

G Check your ideas on page 183 and do Exercise 1.

3 Complete the sentences with one word in each space.

1 I'm a vegetarian. I don't eat _____ meat or fish.

2 I don't eat _____ chocolate bars – maybe just one or two a month.

3 I had _____ biscuits half an hour ago, so I'm not very hungry.

4 Most days, I don't have _____ time to cook, so I just do something quick and easy.

5 A: Did you add _____ salt to this? I can't taste it.

 B: Oh no! I forgot.

6 A: Do you eat a _____ of pasta?

 B: Yeah, _____ a lot, but I sometimes have potatoes instead.

4 Work in groups. Tell each other how much / how many of these things you eat or drink. Follow the example below. Who has the best diet?

*I eat **a lot of** fruit – maybe three or four pieces a day.*

chicken	fish	red meat	sweets
coffee	fruit	soft drinks	vegetables

G For further practice, see Exercises 2 and 3 on page 183.

MY EATING HABITS

HANNA

I'm on a diet at the moment, so I'm eating a lot of cabbage soup. I'm quite bored of it, but I already weigh five kilos less than I did last month. In the past, I was quite unhealthy. I ate a lot of sweets and cake and things like that, but I've stopped completely. I feel great.

AGUSTIN

I'm from Argentina and we eat a lot of meat, especially beef. In fact, I read somewhere recently that Argentinians eat more meat per person than anyone else in the world! Maybe this is because we have the best steaks! Some people think we don't eat a lot of vegetables, but that's not true. We usually add them to the main dishes, though, instead of cooking them separately.

ROBIN

I don't eat any meat or fish. I also avoid animal products, so I don't eat any cheese or milk or butter. I don't wear leather either. I eat a lot of vegetables – fresh and raw usually – and quite a lot of nuts and beans. Recently, I've started eating a lot of papayas too. They're a kind of fruit. They're very good for you. They're full of vitamins.

SOPHIA

I'm pregnant at the moment and my eating habits have completely changed. I'm trying to eat healthy food – a lot of salads and fruit and vegetables – but sometimes I just really want a burger. Or two! I also want unusual combinations of food. For example, yesterday morning I had chocolate cake and cheese – for breakfast!

READING

5   Read the article about eating habits. Which of the four people do you think eats the healthiest food? Why?

6   Decide if the sentences are true (T) or false (F).

1   Hanna is trying to lose weight.

2   She doesn't eat a lot of sweets or cake.

3   Agustin thinks some excellent food comes from his country.

4   Argentinians don't eat many vegetables.

5   Robin eats some dairy products.

6   He doesn't usually cook his vegetables.

7   Sophia has recently had a baby.

8   She sometimes wants to eat some strange things.

7   Work in pairs. Discuss the questions.

• Which person is most similar to you? Why?

• Do you think it's good to go on a diet sometimes? Why? / Why not?

• Do you like raw food? If yes, what kind?

• Are your eating habits the same as they were in the past – or have they changed?

UNDERSTANDING VOCABULARY

Forming negatives by adding *un-*
We often form negatives of adjectives by adding the prefix *un-*.

healthy – **un**healthy

usual – **un**usual

8   Complete the sentences with either the adjectives in the box or their negative form.

employed	friendly	happy	popular
fair	forgettable	healthy	tidy

1   I don't eat any burgers or chocolate. I try to just eat _____ food like salads and fruit.

2   I spent two years working in a restaurant and hated it! It was a very _____ time in my life.

3   Luigi's is the most _____ restaurant in town. You have to book if you want to eat there.

4   I'm _____ at the moment, but I'm looking for a job.

5   I work part-time in a café. The people I work with are lovely. They're all very _____.

6   He's very _____. He always makes a terrible mess when he uses the kitchen.

7   The girls at my school learn to cook, but the boys don't. It's really _____.

8   My dad took me to an amazing restaurant for my birthday. It was an _____ experience.

9   Can you think of two more adjectives that you can add *un-* to?

10   Work in groups. Tell each other about:

1   two unusual things you've eaten / drunk.

2   an unforgettable meal you've had.

3   something that you know is unhealthy, but that you still love eating.

4   something that makes you unhappy.

5   something that you think is unfair.

SOUNDS AND VOCABULARY REVIEW

11   ▶ 82 Listen and repeat the sounds with /ɪə/, /eə/ and /ʌ/. Are any of them difficult for you to hear or say?

12   ▶ 83 Work in groups. Listen to eight sentences using these words. Together, try to write them down. Then listen again and finish writing them.

anywhere	blood	here	unusual
beer	dairy	nuts	vegetarian

G   For further revision, see Exercises 1–3 on page 184.

12 FEELINGS

1

2

5

6

7

11

12

13

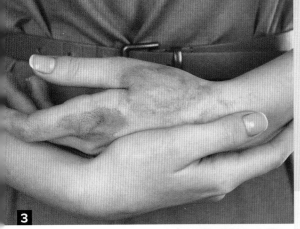

3

4

8

IN THIS UNIT YOU LEARN HOW TO:

- talk about health problems
- give advice
- say no to offers and advice
- talk about how you feel and why
- understand some news stories

WORDS FOR UNIT 12

1 **Work in pairs. Match the phrases to the photos. Which phrase does not match a photo?**

a big storm	protest against it
complain to the staff	put ice on it
fans celebrating	put on sun cream
get some fresh air	read the news
have a big smile	she's a bit upset
I burnt my hand	she's fallen asleep
it's badly damaged	stop infection
my stomach hurts	stop shouting!
not interested in politics	

2 ▶ 84 **Listen. Check your answers. Listen again. Repeat the words.**

3 **Work in pairs. Test each other. Cover the words.**

Student A: point to a photo.

Student B: say the words.

4 **Match each of the phrases above to a person you know. Then work in pairs and explain your choices.**

For example:

get some fresh air – my friend Karen. She lives in the countryside.

read the news – my dad. He reads the news a lot.

14

9

10

15

16

ARE YOU OK?

LISTENING

1   Find each of these parts of the body in the pictures. What problems do you think each person has? Why?

arm	foot	head	stomach
back	hand	leg	

2   ▶ 85 Listen to five conversations and match them to the pictures. There is one picture you don't need.

3   Work in pairs. Decide which pair of words goes with which conversation. Try to explain what they said.

a   sick / fresh air

b   doctor / a bad cough

c   hurts / lie down

d   play / warm up

e   broken / cancel

4   ▶ 85 Listen again and read the audio script on page 208 to check your ideas.

VOCABULARY Health problems

5 Complete the sentences with these words.

burnt	cough	headache	hurts	sick
cold	cut	hungry	infection	stiff

1 Do you have any aspirin? I have a _____.

2 Do you have a plaster? I've _____ my foot on a piece of broken glass.

3 You shouldn't carry that if your back _____.

4 That _____ sounds terrible. Maybe you should stop smoking.

5 I'm really _____. I haven't eaten all day.

6 I needed antibiotics to stop the _____.

7 I'm going to take the day off. I have a _____. I don't want anyone else to get it.

8 Can we go a bit slower? My legs are a bit _____ after my run yesterday.

9 I feel terrible. I think I'm going to be _____.

10 A: What's up? Why did you shout?

   B: I just _____ my hand on the hot frying pan. It's OK. I just need to put some ice on it.

6 Work in groups. Discuss these questions.

- Have you hurt / cut / burnt yourself recently? How?
- Have you ever broken a bone? Which one? How?
- When was the last time you had a cold / a cough / a headache – or were sick?
- Did you go to the doctor? If yes, what did they do?

GRAMMAR

should / shouldn't

We use should(n't) + infinitive to give advice.

Should shows we think it's a good idea to do the action.

Shouldn't shows we think it's a bad idea.

7 Complete the sentences with *should* or *shouldn't*.

1 A: That cough sounds terrible. Maybe you _____ stop smoking.

   B: I know, but that's easy for you to say!

2 A: You _____ carry that if you have a bad back. Let me take it.

   B: Oh, thanks.

3 A: You _____ sit in the sun. You can burn easily.

   B: It's fine. I've put on some sun cream.

4 A: That's a bad cough.

   B: I know. I _____ go to the doctor's.

5 A: He looks really tired.

   B: I know. He _____ work so hard.

   A: Yeah. He _____ take a holiday.

G Check your ideas on page 184 and do Exercise 1.

8 Work in pairs. Give two or three pieces of advice for each person in the pictures on page 106.

G For further practice, see Exercise 2 on page 184.

PRONUNCIATION

9 ▶ 86 Listen to six sentences with *should / shouldn't* – first fast, then slow. Notice that you sometimes don't hear the /d/ or /t/ at the end of the words.

10 ▶ 86 Listen again and repeat what you hear.

DEVELOPING CONVERSATIONS

Saying no

When we say no to offers and advice, we often give a reason. It's polite.

A: *Maybe you should lie down.*

B: *No, it's OK. I think I'm just hungry.*

A: *Are you sure?*

B: *Honestly, I'll be fine after I have something to eat.*

11 Write four similar conversations starting with sentences 1–4. Say no to the advice or offers. Give reasons. Use your own ideas, or phrases from the box below.

1 Maybe you should go to hospital.

2 Would you like any more to eat?

3 Maybe you should take the day off.

4 You shouldn't stay here on your own.

No, thanks.	I'm fine.
No, it's OK,	it's not serious.
Honestly,	it's just a small cut.
Really,	it's just a cold.
I just need to sit down.	
I just need to put some ice on it.	
I'll be OK in a few days.	
I'll be fine in a moment.	

12 Read out your conversations in pairs.

CONVERSATION PRACTICE

13 Have conversations with different students. Use the guide below to help you. For each new conversation, change partner and choose a different problem.

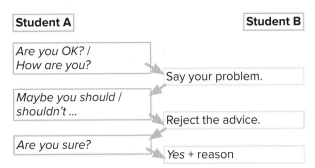

Student A   **Student B**

Are you OK? / How are you?

Say your problem.

Maybe you should / shouldn't ...

Reject the advice.

Are you sure?

Yes + reason

▶ 22 To watch the video and do the activities, see the DVD-ROM.

FEELING GOOD?

SPEAKING

1 Read the short text on page 109. Then work in groups and discuss the questions.
- Why do you think Switzerland was at the top of the list?
- Why do you think Syria was near the bottom?
- Why do you think the Texan women were happier with friends than with their children?
- What things make you happy?
- Do you think governments can improve people's happiness?

VOCABULARY Feelings

2 Decide if the words in the box describe positive or negative feelings.

angry	excited	relaxed	tired
annoyed	happy	stressed	upset

3 Complete the sentences with words from Exercise 2.

1 Some friends are getting divorced. I'm very _____ about it. I **cried** when I heard the news.

2 On my way to work yesterday, someone almost hit my car. We had an argument and I **shouted** at him. I was very _____!

3 I'm really _____. I passed my driving **test**.

4 I worked from six until seven today, so I was very _____ when I got home. I **fell asleep** watching TV.

5 I have to do a lot of work this week, and my boss isn't very patient, so I'm feeling very _____ at the moment.

6 I was a bit _____ because I had to wait for 20 minutes to pay the bill. I actually **complained** to the manager about it.

7 He's much more _____ now he's on holiday. He's actually started **smiling** and joking again! The last few months have been terrible for him.

8 I'm going to go to France with my school. I'm really _____ because it's my first time away without my parents. I'm really **looking forward** to it.

4 Work in pairs. Answer these questions about the words in bold from Exercise 3. Use a dictionary if you need to.
- Why might you cry?
- Why might you shout at someone?
- What other tests do people do?
- In what places do people often fall asleep?
- Why else might you complain in a restaurant?
- When might you smile?
- What other things might you look forward to?

5 Tell a partner about the last time you did four of the things in Exercise 4.

LISTENING

6 ▶ 87 Listen to a woman talking about what she did yesterday. For each of the nine things she talks about, choose how she felt.
1 tired / happy / annoyed
2 angry / upset / excited
3 stressed / tired / relaxed
4 happy / angry / bored
5 positive / annoyed / stressed
6 bored / angry / surprised
7 worried / happy / annoyed
8 excited / relaxed / tired
9 bored / tired / stressed

7 Work in pairs. Why did she have each feeling?

8 ▶ 87 Listen again and check.

GRAMMAR

because, so and *after*

We use *because, so* and *after* to join two parts of a sentence.

*She was upset **because** her boss shouted at her.*

*The bus was full, **so** I couldn't sit and read.*

***After** the meeting finished, I sat and thought about everything I had to do.*

***After** dinner, I watched the news on TV.*

9 Complete the rules with *because, so* or *after*.
1 _____ shows when a situation or action happens.
2 _____ shows why a situation or action happens.
3 _____ shows the result of a situation or action.
4 The phrases following _____ and *so* always have a verb, but _____ can start a phrase that only has a noun and no verb.

 Check your ideas on page 185 and do Exercise 1.

10 Complete the sentences with your own ideas.
- I'm really stressed because _____.
- I was stressed, so _____.
- I was really tired after _____.
- After work, _____.
- He cried _____.
- She shouted at me _____.

 For further practice, see Exercise 2 on page 185.

11 Work in groups. Think of a day and describe it to the group. Say what you did, where you went and who you met. Describe your feelings.

Happiness around the world

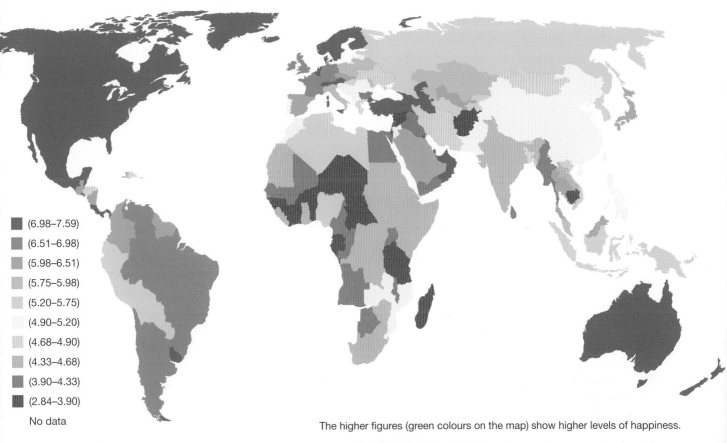

(6.98–7.59)
(6.51–6.98)
(5.98–6.51)
(5.75–5.98)
(5.20–5.75)
(4.90–5.20)
(4.68–4.90)
(4.33–4.68)
(3.90–4.33)
(2.84–3.90)
No data

The higher figures (green colours on the map) show higher levels of happiness.

In 2015, the *World Happiness Report* found that Switzerland was the happiest country in the world and Syria was one of the unhappiest. The report shows that money is not the only thing for a happy life. For example, Singapore was the third richest country in the world but only 24th on the list, and Costa Rica is twelfth in the list, and only the 68th richest country. Research by Daniel Kahneman found that this was also true for individual people. He asked some women in Texas to write down how they felt at different times in their day. Most of them were happy most of the time – rich and poor! The thing that made them happiest was spending time with friends and relatives. They enjoyed this more than looking after their children! They didn't like travelling to and from work.

Now some economists think that governments should do more to improve people's happiness and not only worry about the economy and money.

GOOD AND BAD NEWS

SPEAKING

1 Work in groups. Discuss the questions.

- How often do you read / watch / listen to the news?
- Where do you get your news from? Why?
- How do you feel about these different kinds of news? What kind do you read most?

business	entertainment	politics	sport
crime	foreign	science	weather

VOCABULARY In the news

2 Work in pairs. Decide if you think each headline describes good news or bad news.

1 PLANS TO BUILD 800 NEW HOMES

2 New supermarket opens in town centre

3 Teachers protest against pay cuts

4 PRIME MINISTER'S CAR HIT WITH EGGS

5 Bad weather causes delay at airport

6 Country celebrates Independence Day

7 FIRE DAMAGES FACTORY

8 EIGHT KILLED IN MOTORWAY ACCIDENT

3 Match 1–4 with a–d, then match 5–8 with e–h.

1 build	a a new restaurant / to the public
2 open	b the car in front / your head
3 protest	c against job cuts / against changes to working hours
4 hit	d a new stadium / more hospitals
5 cause	e the environment / your health
6 celebrate	f animals for sport / ten people
7 damage	g serious damage / a lot of problems
8 kill	h a win / your birthday

4 Work in pairs.

Student A: close your book.

Student B: say a verb.   *build*

Student A: say a phrase.   *build a new stadium*

5 Work in groups. Use the phrases in Exercise 3 to say true things about where you live.

For example:

The government building is sometimes open to the public.

There was a terrible accident last week. A bus killed three people.

READING

6 Read the four short newspaper articles on page 111. Decide in which article people felt:

a happy.

b excited.

c angry.

d upset.

7 Work in pairs. Compare your answers and explain your ideas.

8 Work in pairs. Say what you remember about these numbers from the article.

1 2,500

2 a small number

3 77

4 2–1

5 eleven

6 over 100

7 hundreds

8 six months

9 Read again and check your ideas.

SPEAKING

10 Think of a news story that made you feel happy, upset or angry. Spend two minutes planning how to explain the story. Use a dictionary if you need to. Then work in groups and share your stories. Do you all feel the same way about the stories?

SOUNDS AND VOCABULARY REVIEW

11 ▶ 88 Listen and repeat the sounds with /h/, /θ/ and /ð/. Are any of them difficult for you to hear or say?

12 ▶ 89 Work in groups. Listen to eight sentences using these words. Together, try to write them down. Then listen again and finish writing them.

birthday	headache	hospital	weather
hand	health	hungry	without

G For further revision, see Exercises 1–3 on page 185.

IN THE NEWS TODAY:

1 Police have stopped a protest by workers at the main national airline office. After yesterday's news that the company are planning to cut 2,500 jobs, workers met this morning to express their feelings. The police took action when a small number of people started throwing bottles.

2 Fans of the Black Bears are today still celebrating after their team won the King's Cup for the first time in 77 years. In the most exciting final in a long time, the Bears won 2–1. The winning goal came in the last minute of the game, and caused celebrations across the whole city.

3 Big storms in the Pacific Ocean have killed eleven people and caused serious damage to many parts of Vanuatu. In the capital, Port Vila, the bad weather destroyed over 100 houses. Families are now sleeping outside – and hoping that the government is going to send help.

4 Tickets for a concert by the pop group One Dimension went on sale today at the national stadium. Hundreds of fans queued through the night to get the best seats. This is going to be the group's only concert this year because singer Harry Payne is going to get married in the autumn and is planning to then take a break for six months.

1 Look at the photo and read the text to find out what *initiation* is.

Initiation is when someone does something to become part of a group. For example, it could be when:

- a child becomes an adult.
- a person joins a religion.
- a person joins an army or a gang.
- a person ends their education and begins work.

During the initiation, the person often has to do something difficult or show a skill. For example, they have to do something painful or kill something or concentrate for a long time. They also often change the way they look in some way. For example, someone cuts off all their hair or they have to wear special clothes or make-up. Initiation is often a celebration. People can dance and sing, eat nice food or drink something special and some people give presents or money.

2 Work in pairs. What examples of initiation can you think of? What happens?

3 🎦 **23** Watch part of a programme called *The Beast Hunter*. The presenter of the programme takes part in an initiation ceremony in a village. Which of the things in the text in Exercise 1 do you see? What feelings does he have?

4 🎦 **23** Complete the sentences from the video with the nouns in the box. Watch again to check.

| boat | gloves | pain | turn |
| dance | mind | trust | 24 hours |

1 The boy struggles not to show his _____.
2 After five minutes, the _____ come off.
3 All too soon, it's my _____.
4 The pain keeps building and it'll last for _____.
5 The _____ ends and I'm alone with my pain.
6 I had hoped that this ordeal would simply earn me some _____.
7 Here in a forest in Brazil, I'm losing my _____.
8 How did we get on the _____?

5 Work in groups. Discuss these questions.

- What do you think of the presenter and the programme?
- Would you like to do anything like this?
- Are you good with pain?
- What has been your best feeling ever?

UNDERSTANDING FAST SPEECH

6 🎦 **24** Read and listen to this extract from the video said fast, then slow. Stressed sounds are in CAPITALS.

when i PUT my HANDS in the ICE WAter, it's the BEST feeling on EARTH. It feels SO GOOD.

7 You try! Practise saying the extract with the same stressed sounds.

REVIEW 6

GRAMMAR

1 Complete the sentences with one word in each space.

1 A: I have a headache.

   B: Maybe you _____ lie down.

2 A: I hate carrots.

   B: Me _____. I never eat them.

   A: Me _____.

3 A: I've never tried spinach.

   B: I _____. I like it. It's good for you.

4 A: I thought the food was delicious.

   B: I _____. I thought it was awful.

5 I feel a bit sick. I need to get _____ fresh air.

6 There are too _____ cookery programmes on TV.

7 Do your homework _____ you finish dinner.

8 I can't buy it. I didn't bring _____ money with me.

2 Choose the correct option.

1 I need to send *a few* / *a bit of* emails.

2 There's not *many* / *much* risk of rain today.

3 You're pregnant. *I think you shouldn't* / *I don't think you should* eat that.

4 We don't use *a lot of* / *much* spices in our cooking.

5 I don't eat *any* / *much* pork because it's against my religion.

6 I had a headache *because* / *so* I drank too much coffee.

7 You're always late! You should get up *early* / *earlier* / *the earliest*.

8 There was an accident on the motorway, *so* / *because* / *after* there were big delays.

3 Correct the mistakes underlined in 1–6.

1 A: I don't drink wine or beer. B: <u>Me too</u>.

2 A: I don't like cheese.

   B: Really? <u>I like.</u> It's one of my favourite things.

3 We should leave some money <u>because</u> they know we liked the service.

4 The factories there cause <u>many</u> pollution.

5 We don't have <u>no</u> bread. Can you buy some?

6 I don't eat <u>many</u> pasta. I prefer potatoes.

4 ▶ 90 Listen and complete the sentences with one word in each space. Contractions (*I'm, don't,* etc.) are one word.

1 We eat _____ _____ _____ _____ rice and fish.

2 I was sick _____ _____ _____ _____ seafood.

3 There _____ _____ _____ _____ _____ eat near here.

4 _____ _____ _____ tell him _____ _____ stressed.

5 They didn't _____ _____ tables, _____ we _____ _____ there.

6 I _____ think _____ _____ pay _____ _____ _____ pounds for it.

VOCABULARY

5 Put the words into three groups – restaurants, health problems or news.

the bill	kill twelve people
build a new stadium	protest against cuts
cause delays	put a plaster on
dairy products	take antibiotics
include service	a terrible cough
an infection	a well-cooked steak

6 Complete the sentences with these adjectives.

annoyed	busy	excited	full	tired
bored	delicious	fried	healthy	unfair

1 The film was really slow and I got quite _____.

2 I can't eat anything else. I'm really _____.

3 For my main course, I'd like the _____ chicken.

4 I'm really _____ about the trip. It's going to be great!

5 How did you make this soup? It's _____!

6 I have quite a _____ diet.

7 I complained because I was _____ about the terrible service.

8 I was very _____ when I got home last night. I fell asleep on the sofa!

9 You should book a table before you go. They're usually very _____.

10 Male workers get more money than female workers. It's so _____!

7 Match the verbs in the box to the groups of words they go with in 1–8.

burn	celebrate	damage	open
cancel	cut	hit	order

1 ~ my foot on a piece of glass / ~ jobs / ~ some garlic

2 ~ my hand / ~ the dinner / ~ easily in the sun

3 ~ my head / ~ the car in front / ~ me in the face

4 ~ your health / ~ a building / ~ the environment

5 ~ to the public / ~ at nine o'clock / ~ a new store

6 ~ a starter / ~ online / Are you ready to ~?

7 ~ your birthday / ~ the win / ~ Independence Day

8 ~ the meeting / ~ my flight / ~ my credit card

8 Complete the text with one word in each space. The first letters are given.

I'm trying to keep my [1]we_____ under control. It's hard, because I love eating [2]de_____ like cake and ice [3]c_____! Now, though, I eat lots of fruit and [4]ve_____ and I don't eat red meat, because it has too much [5]f_____. I avoid [6]s_____ drinks and [7]sw_____ too, because they have too much [8]su_____ in them.

1

2

5

6

7

8

12

14

13

15

IN THIS UNIT YOU LEARN HOW TO:

- talk about the weather
- talk about possibilities in the future
- ask for more details
- talk about the countryside and the city
- talk about animals
- talk about duration

WORDS FOR UNIT 13

1   Work in pairs. Match the phrases to the photos.

a bit windy	an icy road
chase each other	it smells bad
check the forecast	jump off a mountain
climb a hill	pick up rubbish
a cloudy day	scared of spiders
a crowded street	the top of a wall
don't let it bite	surrounded by fields
an empty road	want attention
a farmer using chemicals	a warm summer's day

2   ▶ 91 Listen. Check your answers. Listen again. Repeat the words.

3   Work in pairs. Test each other. Cover the words.

Student A: point to a photo.

Student B: say the words.

4   Put the phrases into two groups: *My life* and *Not my life*. Then work in pairs and explain your choices.

WHAT'S THE FORECAST?

VOCABULARY Weather

1 Which words in the box can you use with each sentence starter (1–4)?

1 It's going to …

2 It's going to be …

3 There's going to be a lot of …

4 There's going to be a …

cloudy	dry	ice	snow	sunny	wet
cold	hot	rain	storm	warm	windy

2 Work in pairs. What's the weather forecast for today? For tomorrow? For the rest of the week?

3 Work in groups. Discuss these questions for your country. There is an example for the first question.

- What's the weather like in the spring? In the summer?

  In the spring, it's usually quite warm. Sometimes it's very sunny, but sometimes there are storms and it rains. Occasionally it snows and it's very cold.

- What's the weather like in the autumn? In the winter?

- Which season do you like most? Why?

- Which places have the best / worst weather? Why?

LISTENING

4 ▶ 92 Listen to three conversations in which people decide what to do. Complete the table.

	Forecast	They decide to …
1		
2		
3		

GRAMMAR *might* and *be going to*

5 Look at these extracts from the listening. Complete the rules in the Grammar box below.

1 *It's going to be quite hot. They said it might reach 35 degrees.*

2 *It might rain this morning, but it's going to be dry this afternoon.*

3 *I think it's going to be cold. They said it might snow.*

We use *might* + infinitive and *be going to* + infinitive to talk about the future.

¹_____ shows certainty.

²_____ shows possibility.

Ⓖ Check your ideas on page 186 and do Exercise 1.

6 Complete the sentences with *might* or the correct form of *be going to*.

1 A: Do you have any plans for later?

   B: I _____ go shopping, but I'm not sure.

2 A: What are they doing to that church?

   B: They're pulling it down. They _____ build some new flats there.

3 A: What are you going to do when you leave school?

   B: I'd like to continue studying, but I _____ have to get a job. My family needs the money.

4 A: What's the forecast for tomorrow?

   B: It _____ definitely _____ be cold – and they said it _____ possibly snow!

5 It said on the news it _____ continue raining for the next two days. There _____ possibly be some flooding.

PRONUNCIATION

7 ▶ **93** Listen to six sentences with *might*. Notice that you don't always hear the final *t*. Now listen again and write the sentences you hear.

8 ▶ **93** Listen again. Repeat what you hear.

9 Write four things you *might* do in the next week, month or year. Think about why they are just possibilities. Is it because of the weather, money, other people or some other reason?

10 Work in groups. Explain your ideas.

For example:

A: *I might go to Germany this summer. I'm not sure yet. I need to save some money first.*

B: *That sounds good. I might start learning Chinese this year. First, I want to learn more English, but maybe after that …*

G For further practice, see Exercise 2 on page 186.

DEVELOPING CONVERSATIONS

Short questions

In conversation, we often use short questions without verbs.

A: *Why don't we go to the swimming pool?*

B: *We could do.* **Which one?**

A: *The open-air one.*

11 Choose the best short question to complete each conversation.

1 A: Why don't we go and see *Insanity*? It's on at King Cinema.

   B: Yeah, maybe. *Where?* / *What film?* / *What time?*

   A: There's a showing at 8.40.

2 A: I might go for a walk later.

   B: Oh, OK. *Who with?* / *When exactly?* / *Where?*

   A: Just round town. Would you like to come?

3 A: Do you want to go into town later?

   B: Maybe. *How?* / *What for?* / *What time?*

   A: I don't know. To maybe have a drink or something.

4 A: Look, we're both stressed. Why don't we take a holiday?

   B: We could do. *How long for?* / *When?* / *Where?*

   A: Just a few days.

5 A: Why don't you invite some friends for dinner?

   B: *Who?* / *Why?* / *When?*

   A: Do you need a reason? It's just a nice thing to do!

6 A: It's nice and sunny. Why don't we go to the beach?

   B: Yeah. We could do. *Which one?* / *What time?* / *How?* Is there a bus?

   A: No, but I can borrow my friend's car.

12 Work in pairs. Practise reading out the conversations in Exercise 11.

13 Change partners.

Student A: say the first line of each conversation in Exercise 11.

Student B: ask a different short question.

Student A: give an answer.

CONVERSATION PRACTICE

14 You are going to have similar conversations to the ones you heard in Exercise 4. Work in pairs. Look at the guide below and spend two minutes thinking about what you are going to say.

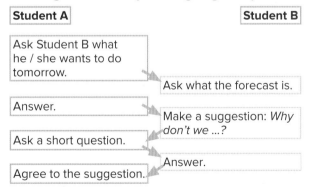

Student A	Student B
Ask Student B what he / she wants to do tomorrow.	
	Ask what the forecast is.
Answer.	
	Make a suggestion: *Why don't we …?*
Ask a short question.	
	Answer.
Agree to the suggestion.	

15 Now roleplay the conversation. Then change roles and have another conversation.

25 To watch the video and do the activities, see the DVD ROM.

COUNTRY GIRL?

VOCABULARY
The countryside and the city

1 **Work in pairs. For each category, decide two things for the city and two for the countryside.**

  1 the most common animals

  2 the main entertainment / activities outside the home

  3 things people are often scared of

  4 things people often complain about

2 **Compare your ideas with another pair. Did they have the same ideas as you?**

3 **Work in groups. Check you understand the words in bold. Decide if the descriptions are by people living in the countryside or the city.**

  1 We're **surrounded by** big blocks of flats.

  2 I live on a **farm**, so we're surrounded by **fields**.

  3 They **grow** a lot of rice in the area. It's hot and wet.

  4 It's very **flat** and the wind is always blowing.

  5 It's very quiet. We live on the edge of a big **forest**.

  6 We live on top of a **hill**, so we have a nice view.

  7 It's completely **empty**. There's just a few sheep.

  8 The smell is from the big chemical **factory** near here.

  9 There are a lot of empty houses and the roads are in **bad condition**.

  10 The streets are **crowded** and there's a lot of **pollution**.

  11 The water in the river has a lot of **chemicals** in it.

  12 It's **convenient** for shops and transport.

  13 It's very clean. You don't see any **rubbish** on the streets.

  14 It's dangerous. There are a lot of **violent gangs**.

4 **Work in pairs. For each sentence in Exercise 3, say:**

  • if you think it's a good environment to live in.

  • a place you know the sentence could describe.

READING

5 **You are going to read a post on a funny blog called *Six reasons not to …* . Read the introduction and complete the title of the post.**

SIX REASONS NOT TO _____.

I saw a programme on TV yesterday about a couple building their perfect house. It cost almost a million dollars and they built it in the countryside. They said they wanted to escape the city and the crime and pollution. They wanted fresh air and 'a good environment for their children'. I shouted at the TV, 'Are you crazy? Don't waste all that money – don't move to the *countryside*!!

6 **What do you think the six reasons might be?**

7 **Read the article and match the headings (a–f) to the paragraphs (1–6). Decide what the writer doesn't like about each thing.**

  a The jobs

  b The smell

  c The shops

  d The animals

  e The scenery

  f The clothes

8 **Read the article again and decide if these sentences are true (T) or false (F), according to the article.**

  1 Everything in the country is natural.

  2 A cow once hurt the writer.

  3 All the shops close early.

  4 It's difficult to keep your clothes clean.

  5 Most of the countryside looks the same.

  6 There's a good internet connection everywhere.

9 **Work in pairs. Discuss what you think of each of the six reasons not to live in the country. Do you agree or disagree with them? You might use some of these adjectives.**

funny	strange	true
sad	stupid	wrong

SPEAKING

10 **Work in pairs. Choose one of these tasks (a or b).**

  a Think of six reasons not to live in the city.

  b Discuss these questions based on the vocabulary in Exercise 3.

  • Do you think being a farmer is a good job in your country? What are the main things they grow or produce?

  • Are there any factories near you? What do they produce?

  • Are there any forests near where you live? Do you ever go there?

  • What hills or mountains are there near where you live? Have you been to the top of any of them?

  • Do you know any empty buildings in your town? Why are they empty?

  • Is your home in a convenient place?

  • How good is the water and air where you live?

1 People say the country has fresh air, but the country is full of animals: pigs, cows, horses. They're all dirty and they smell bad. And farmers put chemicals on the fields. The countryside doesn't smell fresh – it's horrible!

2 My parents took me on a walk once. In one field, a group of cows started following us. I didn't like the cows following me and looking at me with their big eyes. My parents said I shouldn't worry, but I didn't believe them. I ran and I climbed on a wall at the edge of the field and the cows came and looked at me with their big scary eyes and I cried. I hate cows now.

3 The country might be full of cows, but can you buy milk at eight o'clock in the evening? No chance! And if you want to buy anything during the day, you have to travel half an hour by car to get it!

4 You have to spend a lot of time outside in the wind or rain and your clothes and shoes get dirty from all the earth and grass. That's why people in the countryside wear big boots and old coats or jeans. I like fashion. You can't wear nice fashionable clothes in the country.

5 I like hills and mountains. I don't like climbing them, but I like looking at them. The problem is, there aren't enough hills and mountains. When you travel through the countryside by train, you look out of the window and what do you see? A field, another field and another field, a small forest, a field, a farmer in a field, field, field, cows (No!!!!), field, field. It's very flat and very boring!

6 And how do you earn money in the country? Let's be honest, the choice of work is very limited – be a farmer, work in a forest, work with cows (no thank you!). I know you can work on the internet these days, but where do you get cafés with nice cappuccino and wi-fi in the country?

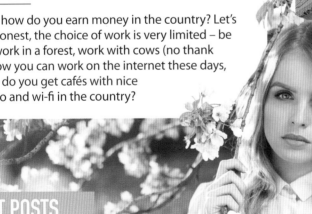

RECENT POSTS

Six reasons not to …

… have a boyfriend.

… watch sport.

… vote.

… drink beer.

… have a dog.

THEY'RE LOVELY ANIMALS!

VOCABULARY Animals

1 Label the photos with the words in the box.

cat	dog	horse	rat
cow	fox	pig	sheep

2 Work in groups. Look at the photos. Discuss the questions. There is an example for the first question.

- Which animals do you like? Are there any you don't like?

  I like horses. They're beautiful animals.

  I don't like pigs. I think they're really dirty.

- Can you say one good or bad thing about each animal?

- Does anyone you know own any of these animals?

3 Choose the two words that fit in each sentence (1–8). Cross out the word that doesn't fit. The first one is done for you.

1 They're very friendly. They sometimes *sit / jump / ~~ride~~* on you.

2 They need a lot of *exercise / noise / attention*.

3 I try to avoid them. They often *sit / smell / bite*.

4 They're very useful. They provide us with *disease / milk / leather*.

5 They're fun to *play with / ride / smell*.

6 They sometimes make a terrible *exercise / mess / noise*.

7 They sometimes *chase / jump / kill* other animals.

8 They can cause *attention / damage / disease*.

4 Work in pairs. Use the ideas in Exercise 3 to talk about the animals in the photos.

For example:

Cats are very friendly. They sometimes sit on you. My cat sits on me when I'm watching TV.

LISTENING

5 ▶ 94 Listen to three conversations about animals. Answer the questions.

a Which of the animals in Exercise 1 is each conversation about?

b Why are they talking about these animals?

c Have you had good or bad experiences with these animals?

6 Work in pairs. Decide what conversations these phrases came from. Explain your decisions.

a We need to pay someone to come in and kill them.

b Scary!

c How annoying!

d I found it outside the next day.

e He's huge!

f I see them quite a lot.

g I think they're a bit scared of her.

h We have more space now.

i I worry they'll bite the kids one day.

7 Work in groups. Have you ever had any good / bad experiences with any animals? Tell your stories.

GRAMMAR
Present perfect to say *how long*

8   Look at the extracts from the listening where people talk about duration (how long). Then choose the correct option to complete the rules in the Grammar box below.

1   B: *How long **have they been** there?*
    A: *For a few months, I guess.*

2   D: *How long **have you had** him?*
    C: *Five years.*

3   ***We've been** here a year now.*

---

1   We can use the present perfect to talk about the duration of something from ...

a   one time in the past to another time in the past.

b   a time in the past to now.

c   now to the future.

2   When we say the duration, we ...

a   always

b   sometimes

c   never

... use *for* at the start of the time phrase.

G   Check your ideas on page 186 and do Exercise 1.

9   Complete the questions using the present perfect form of the verbs in brackets.

1   How long _____ your cat? (you / have)

2   How long _____ together? (you / be)

3   How long _____ married? (they / be)

4   How long _____ each other? (they / know)

5   How long _____ in this house? (you / live)

6   How long _____ there? (she / work)

10   ▶ 95 Listen and check your ideas. Write the answers you hear to the questions.

11   Practise saying the questions and answers.

12   Work in groups. Find out:

•   who has had a pet the longest.

•   who has known their best friend the longest.

•   who has lived in their house / apartment the longest.

•   if anyone knows a couple who have been together for fifty years or more.

G   For further practice, see Exercise 2 on page 186.

SOUNDS AND VOCABULARY REVIEW

13   ▶ 96 Listen and repeat the sounds with /kr/, /dr/, /tr/ and /str/. Are any of them difficult to hear or say?

14   ▶ 97 Work in groups. Listen to eight sentences using these words. Together, try to write them down. Then listen again and finish writing them.

countryside	crowded	dry	streets
crime	drive	strange	transport

G   For further revision, see Exercises 1–3 on page 186.

14 OPINIONS

3

4 7

9

16

IN THIS UNIT YOU LEARN HOW TO:

- give your opinion about films, plays and musicals
- ask for descriptions and opinions
- discuss news and newspapers
- make predictions about the future
- talk about society and social issues

WORDS FOR UNIT 14

1   Work in pairs. Match the phrases to the photos. Which phrase does not match a photo?

the acting was bad	leader of a team
advert for a musical	lost the election
arrive at the border	more efficient
don't get on well	a scary film
extra wages	start peace talks
get treatment	a strong economy
go and see a play	support each other
have insurance	there's been a murder
injure herself	use violence

2   ▶ 98 Listen. Check your answers. Listen again. Repeat the words.

3   Work in pairs. Test each other. Cover the words.

Student A: point to a photo.

Student B: say the words.

10

11

17

WHAT WAS THE FILM LIKE?

SPEAKING

1 Work in pairs. Discuss these questions.

- When was the last time you saw:
  - a film?
  - a concert?
  - a play?
  - a musical?

- What did you see? What did you think of it?

- Have you seen any of the films in the posters? What did you think of them?

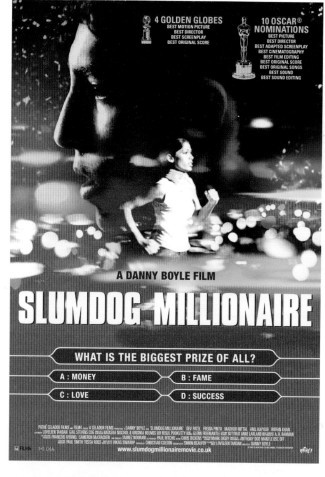

VOCABULARY
Describing films, plays and musicals

2 Complete the sentences with these adjectives.

brilliant	funny	scary	terrible
depressing	predictable	strange	violent
entertaining	sad		

1 It was _____. It really made me laugh.

2 It was really _____. I cried a lot at the ending.

3 It was very _____. There was a lot of killing and a lot of blood in it.

4 It was really _____. I spent half the time hiding behind the sofa.

5 It is very _____. After ten minutes, you know how it's going to end.

6 It was _____ – one of the best things I've ever seen in my life.

7 It was _____ – one of the worst things I've seen in a long time.

8 It was very _____ – very unusual.

9 It was very _____. I felt sad for days afterwards.

10 It was really _____. I really enjoyed it.

3 Work in pairs. Which of the descriptions in Exercise 2 do you think are positive and which are negative? Why?

LISTENING

4 ▶ 99 Listen to two conversations, one about a film and the other about a musical. Answer these questions about each conversation.

1 Have both people seen the film / musical?

2 What did they think of it?

3 Do you think the person who didn't see it would like it? Why? / Why not?

5 ▶ 99 Complete each of the sentences below with one word. Then work in pairs and compare your ideas. Then listen again and check.

Conversation 1

1 Have you ever seen a film _____ 28 Days Later?

2 I've heard _____ it, but I've never seen it.

3 What's it _____?

4 It _____ terrible!

5 No, it's great! _____!

Conversation 2

6 What did you think _____ it?

7 It was quite entertaining in _____, I suppose.

8 The _____ and the music were great.

9 But what about the _____?

10 I _____ it really sad.

6 Work in pairs. Discuss these questions.

• Would you like to see 28 Days Later or Dogs? Why? / Why not?

• Can you think of something you found: really scary? too violent? very predictable?

DEVELOPING CONVERSATIONS

> ## What's it like?
>
> If we want someone to describe something or someone, we often ask What is / was ... like?
>
> A: I've never seen it. What's it like?
>
> B: It's brilliant. It's really, really scary.

7 Match the questions (1–8) to the answers (a–h).

1 What was the film like?

2 What was the acting like?

3 What was the band like?

4 What was the ending like?

5 What's the food like there?

6 What's your boss like?

7 What're your parents like?

8 What was your holiday like?

a Very sad. I couldn't stop crying.

b She's great. She's very easy to talk to.

c Quite good. They played their roles very well.

d It started well, but I didn't like the ending.

e Oh, it was wonderful. It was very relaxing and we were very lucky with the weather.

f They were great. They played for two hours and did all their most famous songs.

g My mum's great, but I don't get on with my dad.

h Amazing! They do a delicious garlic chicken!

8 Work in pairs.

Student A: ask the questions in Exercise 7.

Student B: say the correct answer from a–h.

9 Change roles.

Student B: ask the questions in Exercise 7.

Student A: invent your own answers.

10 Write three What is / was ... like? questions. Then ask other students in the class your questions.

CONVERSATION PRACTICE

11 Make a list of six films, plays, concerts or musicals you have seen in the last few months.

12 Work in pairs. Take turns asking about the things on your list. Follow this model and continue the conversations for as long as you can.

A: Have you seen ...?

B: No, I haven't. What was it like?

or

Yes, I loved it! What did you think of it?

🎥 26 To watch the video and do the activities, see the DVD-ROM.

WHAT DO YOU THINK WILL HAPPEN?

LISTENING

1   Work in groups. What are the big news stories at the moment connected to each of the areas below? What do you think about each story? Explain your opinions.

sports news	international news
entertainment news	national news
business news	the weather forecast

2   Work in pairs. What order do the different kinds of news usually appear on news reports?

3   ▶ 100 Listen to a news report. Match each story (1–5) to an area of news in Exercise 1.

4   ▶ 100 Listen again. Tick (✓) the sentences that are true. Correct the sentences that aren't true.

1   Most people think that the Popular Front are going to win the election.

2   The final result is going to be sometime on Monday.

3   NBE lost nearly four hundred million dollars last year.

4   They're planning to close two factories and cut 500 jobs.

5   Adjikistan and Kamistan have started peace talks.

6   The problem is about where the two countries begin and end.

7   Shaneez has been with her boyfriend for a long time.

8   Her boyfriend is also a singer.

9   Florian Mendy hurt himself during the recent match against Brazil.

10   Mendy is definitely going to miss the rest of the World Cup.

5   Choose one of the following to talk about. Decide if you think the story was a good thing or a bad thing – and why. Spend a few minutes preparing what you want to say.

*   an important election result
*   a company with big problems
*   a war
*   a couple getting married
*   a player who got injured

6   Work in groups. Share your stories and explain your thoughts and feelings.

GRAMMAR

will / won't for predictions

In Units 8 and 13, you saw that we use *be (not) going to* + infinitive to say what we think is certain or probable in the future.

We can also use *will / won't* + infinitive to do this.

Tomorrow's general election **will** probably **be** the closest in many years.

There's a chance he **won't play** *in the rest of the competition.*

We often use the contraction of *will – 'll*.

8 Which of the comments in Exercise 7 are optimistic (= think good things will happen) and which are pessimistic (= think bad things will happen)?

9 Complete the sentences with *will* or *won't*.

1 I probably _____ come out with you tonight. I need to finish some work.

2 You can try and talk to her if you want, but it _____ make any difference.

3 I think he _____ be a very good leader.

4 They don't have a very good team. They _____ win the game.

5 The new law might help a bit, but it _____ completely solve the problem.

6 I don't expect I _____ pass the exam. I haven't done enough work for it.

7 We _____ probably arrive sometime in the evening. It depends on the traffic.

8 The company lost a lot of money this year. I hope we _____ lose our jobs.

PRONUNCIATION

10 ▶ **101** Listen and write the sentences you hear. Notice that *'ll* is pronounced /əl/ – and *won't* is pronounced /wəʊnt/.

11 ▶ **101** Listen again. Repeat what you hear.

7 Below are five comments from the chat room on the radio station's website. Match each comment to one of the five stories you heard in Exercise 3.

a
This will be terrible for the whole area. It'll have a really bad effect on local communities because people will have to move to find work.

b
It won't last. They'll probably be divorced by the end of the year.

c
This loss won't make any difference. They'll still have a very strong team tonight.

d
I don't think the situation will get any worse. They both have too much to lose. Their big neighbours will push for more talks, and they'll all find a solution to the problem.

e
It'll be better if there's no clear winner. It'll mean they all have to work together!

12 Work in pairs. Ask and answer the questions. Use the answers in the box below.

1 Do you think you'll ever speak perfect English?

2 Do you think you'll live to be 80?

3 Do you think your country will ever win the World Cup?

4 Do you think you'll ever live or work abroad?

5 Do you think you'll ever be really rich or famous?

6 Do you think we'll find life on other planets?

7 Do you think there'll ever be world peace?

8 Do you think we'll ever learn how to look after the environment?

- Yes, definitely.
- Yes, probably.
- Maybe.
- No.

13 Write two predictions of your own about what *will* / *won't* happen in the future. You might want to think about these areas:

| holidays | politics | relationships | sport | work |

14 Work in groups. Explain your ideas. Do your partners agree with you?

G For further practice, see Exercises 1 and 2 on page 187.

Agentur für Arbeit

A BETTER LIFE

VOCABULARY Life and society

1 Choose the sentence (a or b) that best matches each sentence 1–5.

1 **The economy** is quite weak.

a There's a lot of unemployment.

b Wages are high and it's easy to find work.

2 **Crime** is a huge problem.

a I have insurance, but I've never needed to use it.

b You see a lot of violence and murder on the news.

3 **The people** are very nice and friendly.

a I get on with my neighbours and we really support each other.

b People are polite but they don't talk to you much.

4 **The climate's** good.

a It's dry and warm all year round.

b It's really cold in winter and too hot in summer.

5 I'm unhappy with **the health system**.

a Treatment is expensive, so you need health insurance.

b Treatment is free and the service is quite efficient.

2 Spend two minutes remembering the sentences in Exercise 1. Then work in pairs and test each other.

Student A: keep your book open. Say the a or b sentence in 1–5.

Student B: close your book. Say the correct sentence (1–5) or the opposite.

For example:

A: *Wages are high and it's easy to find work.*

B: *The economy is strong.*

3 Work in pairs. Write one more sentence about each of the things in bold in Exercise 1.

4 Work in groups. Read your sentences. Can the rest of the group guess what each sentence is about?

For example:

A: *Everything is very expensive.*

B: *The economy.*

A: *Right.*

READING

5 Work in pairs. Discuss these questions.

- Are there many people from your country living abroad? Why? In which countries?
- Do you know anyone who has moved to another country or city? Why did they move?
- What other reasons are there to move to another country?

6 Work in groups of four: two As and two Bs. Read about two people who have moved to live in a different country.

Student As: read the text below.

Student Bs: read the text in File 6 on page 194.

Decide how the writer of your text would answer these questions.

1 How long have you lived here?
2 Why did you move here?
3 Do you like it here?
4 What do you think of the people?
5 What do you think of the climate?
6 What do you think of the health system?
7 How's the economy doing?
8 Is there much crime?
9 Do you think you'll ever go back home?

A NEW LIFE   Maja

I came here to work. It's really easy to get a job in computing because there are so many tech companies here and wages are high. I've lived here for five years now. I love it.

I don't miss anything about my country. People here are very relaxed and open and I get on very well with my neighbours. We don't have long, dark, cold winters here – it's warm all year round. But if I want snow, I can go to the mountains and I can still watch ice hockey here. The only problem is, it's difficult to find time to do those things because I work long hours.

Before I came here, I heard crime was bad and that the health system was expensive, but I haven't had any problems. In big cities, it can be dangerous to walk at night and there's gun violence, but in my small town I've never seen anything like that. I don't always lock my front door and no-one has ever stolen anything. As for the health system, the service is expensive, but my company provides health insurance, so I've had no problems when I've needed treatment.

7 Compare answers with the person in your group who read the same text. Which country do you think the writer is from and where do you think they are living?

8 Now work in pairs: one Student A and one Student B. Without looking at your texts, ask and answer the questions in Exercise 6 to find out about your partner's text.

9 With the same partner, discuss which of the two writers has a better quality of life.

GRAMMAR

Adjective + verb
We can use an adjective and a verb together.
*It's really **easy to get** a job in computing.*

10 Work in pairs. Look back at the texts and answer these questions.

Text A

1 What is difficult for the writer?
2 What is dangerous sometimes?

Text B

3 What was dangerous?
4 What is difficult?

Can you see the same pattern in the five different sentences?

 Check your ideas on page 187 and do Exercise 1.

11 Make true sentences about the place you live or work, using the pattern from Exercise 10.

1 It's easy _____.
2 It's important _____.
3 It's nice _____.
4 It's cheap _____.
5 It can be difficult _____.

For further practice, see Exercise 2 on page 187.

SPEAKING

12 Work in groups. Discuss what you think of the things in the box in your country or city. Do you think they are better or worse than other places?

crime	the health system	politics
the climate	the quality of life	work

SOUNDS AND VOCABULARY REVIEW

13 ▶ 102 Listen and repeat these common word endings: /əns/, /mənt / and /ʃən /. Are any of them difficult for you to hear or say?

14 ▶ 103 Work in groups. Listen to eight sentences using these words. Together, try to write them down. Then listen again and finish writing them.

differences	environment	situation	treatment
election	insurance	solution	violence

For further revision, see Exercises 1–3 on page 188.

VIDEO 7

NATIONAL SYMBOLS

1   **Work in groups. Look at the photos of different national symbols. Discuss these questions.**

- Do you know which countries these things are national symbols of?
- Do you know what connects the four countries?
- Why do you think these things became national symbols?

2   **Read the short text to find the answers to the questions in Exercise 1.**

3   **Work in groups. Discuss these questions.**

- Does your country have a national animal / bird / tree / flower?
- How much do you know about each one?
- Are there any other things that you think are national symbols of your country?

4   📹 **27 You are going to do a quiz. Work in teams. Watch the video and answer the ten questions.**

5   📹 **27 Watch the second part of the video (4.34–8.37) to find the answers. Write one new piece of information you hear about each answer. The winner is the team with the most correct answers and / or the most extra information.**

6   **Choose one of the things below to talk about. Spend two minutes planning what to say.**

- a time you went to one of the countries mentioned in the quiz
- the country that you would most like to visit
- three symbols of your town / city – and how you feel about them
- a good symbol for your family
- a good symbol for the class you're studying in

7   **Work in pairs. Share your ideas.**

The photos show national symbols of the four countries that make the United Kingdom. **The thistle** is the national flower of Scotland. For example, there's a thistle on the national rugby team shirt. An old story says that one night, Vikings tried to quietly enter Scotland from the sea, but one of them stepped on a thistle and screamed loudly. Scottish soldiers then woke up and won the fight.

The leek is a national symbol of Wales. An old story says Welsh soldiers once wore leeks when fighting to show who they were. Other stories say that hundreds of years ago, Welsh doctors used leeks to make all kinds of medicine.

The blue flax flower is a symbol of Northern Ireland. The country is famous for making cloth from flax. Northern Ireland is home to people of different religions – Protestants and Catholics – and there have been problems in the past, but both groups like the flower.

The only lions in England live in zoos, but **the lion** is still England's national animal – maybe because a famous English king, Richard I, was called Richard the Lionheart. The national football team wear three lions on their shirt, and there are also big statues of lions in Trafalgar Square, in London.

REVIEW 7

GRAMMAR

1 Complete the sentences with one word in each space.

A: What's the forecast for tomorrow?

B: It said it's ¹_____ to continue raining.

A: Oh no! When do you think it ²_____ stop?

B: It's difficult ³_____ say. It can sometimes rain for days. When are you going ⁴_____ go home?

A: I don't know now. I ⁵_____ go back early. It's horrible to ⁶_____ sightseeing in the rain.

B: No, stay. You haven't been here very ⁷_____ – and there's a ⁸_____ the weather will get better over the weekend.

2 Put the word(s) in bold in the correct place in the sentence.

1 They said it might be very cold next weekend. **not**

2 They said it's going to very cold and it snow tonight. **may**

3 How long you worked here? **have**

4 Let's go out somewhere. It's hot to stay in all day. **too**

5 I've had a cough a few days now. **for**

6 I don't think things will get worse. **any**

7 I haven't known him long. **very**

8 Do you think you'll move? **ever**

3 Rewrite the sentences as positive statements (+), negatives (-) or questions (?).

1 I'll do it before Friday. (-)

2 Is it easy to find work there? (+)

3 I might go to the party. (-)

4 I don't think they'll miss her. (+)

5 It's good to be scared at times like that. (-)

6 I think they'll win. (?)

4 ▶ 104 Listen and complete the sentences with one word in each space. Contractions (*I'm, don't,* etc.) are one word.

1 _____ lived _____ _____ _____ life.

2 How _____ _____ _____ known _____ this?

3 It's difficult _____ _____ worry _____ what _____ _____.

4 _____ _____ try, but I _____ _____ _____ change things.

5 _____ _____ _____ economy _____ _____ stronger next year.

6 They said _____ _____ _____ _____ hot and _____ _____ _____ a storm.

5 ▶ 104 Work in pairs. Compare your ideas. Listen again and check.

VOCABULARY

6 Choose the best adjective.

1 He's a very *famous / icy / convenient* writer.

2 The film was really *dangerous / violent / relaxing*.

3 Crime's a big problem there. It's *an efficient / a free / a scary* place to live.

4 The countryside there is very *warm / flat / brilliant* and boring.

5 The economy's very *weak / sad / high* at the moment.

6 Hospital treatment here is quite *polite / expensive / strange*.

7 It's *a predictable / a huge / an empty* country.

8 We've had some really *sunny / crowded / entertaining* weather.

7 Match the verbs in the box to the group of words they go with in 1–8.

check	find	have	need
fail	grow	make	vote

1 ~ the forecast / ~ with my wife / ~ the meaning

2 ~ for the Peace Party / ~ in a general election / ~ against the idea

3 ~ insurance / ~ long, cold winters / ~ problems

4 ~ rice / the economy ~s / ~ in the field

5 ~ a solution to the problem / ~ work / ~ time to do it

6 peace talks ~ / ~ an exam / ~ to win

7 ~ a big difference / ~ friends / ~ a terrible noise

8 ~ a lot of attention / ~ some help / ~ a lot of exercise

8 Put the words into three groups – weather, animals or society.

cause disease	provide leather
cloudy	reach 40 degrees
friendly neighbours	ride across the fields
a good climate	smell terrible
a lot of unemployment	wet and windy
low wages	win the election

9 Complete the text with one word in each space. The first letters are given.

I moved here from the city a few years ago. I prefer it. There were so many people in the city. The streets were always ¹cr_____ and there was always ²ru_____ everywhere as well. Once there was a ³mu_____ near my house. It was awful. It's safer here – and cleaner. There isn't any ⁴po_____ because there aren't any factories. I live on the ⁵e_____ of a big forest and I'm ⁶su_____ by fields. My house was in a bad ⁷co_____ when I bought it, but I've repaired it. I keep cows, and they ⁸pr_____ me with milk and meat.

15 TECHNOLOGY

1

2

5

6

7

10

11

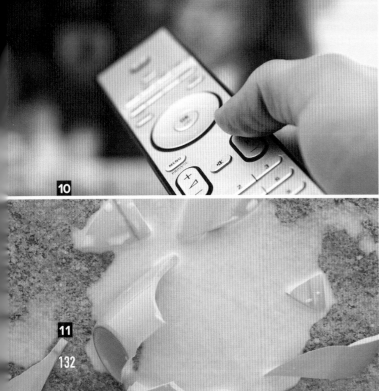

12

HOMEPAGE

LOGO

IMAGE BANNER

NAVIGATION

CONTENT

NEWS

BLOG

3

4

8

IN THIS UNIT YOU LEARN HOW TO:

- talk about useful machines
- find out how much people know
- talk about computers and the internet
- spell and give addresses
- explain what's good about apps and websites

WORDS FOR UNIT 15

1   Work in pairs. Match the phrases to the photos.

change the battery	produce electricity
design a website	read the instructions
do a search	save energy
I dropped it	shelves of food
install solar power	try to repair it
keep files	various apps
plug it in	very heavy
press the button	

2   ▶ 105 Listen. Check your answers. Listen again. Repeat the words.

3   Work in pairs. Test each other. Cover the words.

Student A: point to a photo.

Student B: say the words.

9

13

14

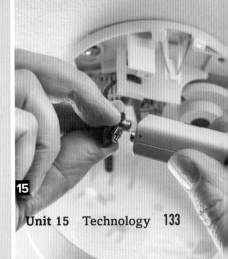

15

Unit 15   Technology   **133**

CAN YOU RECOMMEND ANYTHING?

VOCABULARY
Machines and technology

1 Label the pictures with the words in the box.

digital camera	laptop	vacuum cleaner
dishwasher	mobile phone	washing machine
hairdryer	tablet	

2 Work in groups. Discuss these questions.

- Which of the things in the photos do you have?
- Which brands do you have?
- Which is most useful? Why?
- What other machines or technology do you own?
- Are there any you don't have, but would like to get?

3 Check you understand the words in bold. Then work in pairs. Look at the photos again and point to:

1 a **screen**.
2 a **plug**.
3 a **keyboard**.
4 where you **turn** them **on** and turn them **off**.
5 where the **battery** goes.
6 **buttons** you can **press**.

LISTENING

4 ▶ 106 Listen to three conversations about technology. What kind of machine do they talk about in each one – and why?

5 ▶ 106 Listen again. Complete the table.

	Brand	What's good about it?
1	1_____	• Quite a lot of 2_____ • Not too heavy • The 3_____ lasts a long time.
2	Kotika	• They 4_____ great. • Nice and 5_____ • Huge 6_____ – great for playing 7_____ and watching videos
3	Bonny	• Quite strong, so hard to 8_____ • Takes great pictures – even when it's 9_____ • Not very 10_____

6 Work in pairs. Discuss these questions.

1 Do you think the things they recommend sound good or not? Why?

2 Is there anything else they should think about for each piece of technology?

3 How much does each thing cost in your country?

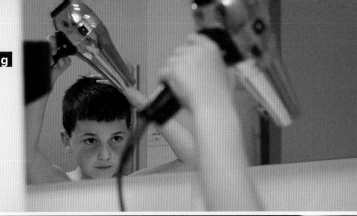

GRAMMAR

be thinking of + -ing

To talk about plans that we are not 100% sure about, we often use *be thinking of + -ing*.

I'm **thinking of** buy**ing** a laptop.

She's **thinking of** start**ing** her own internet company.

We're **thinking of** gett**ing** a new washing machine.

7 Complete the sentences with the correct form of *be thinking of* and the verbs in brackets.

1 I _____ my dad some new clothes, but I don't know any good shops. (buy)

2 My brother _____ an English course. (do)

3 We _____ to the cinema later. (go)

4 I _____ the mobile phone company I use. (change)

5 My parents _____ a new car. (buy)

6 They _____ to Japan for their holiday. (go)

7 I _____ a pet for my younger sister. (get)

8 My sister _____ Engineering at university. (study)

8 Work in pairs.

Student A: say each sentence in Exercise 7. Then ask *Can you recommend anything / anywhere?*

Student B: make recommendations.

Then change roles and repeat.

9 Write three sentences about things you – or people you know – are thinking of doing. Explain your ideas to a partner.

G For further practice, see Exercises 1 and 2 on page 188.

DEVELOPING CONVERSATIONS

Do you know much about …?

To find out how much people know about general topics, we often say *Do you know much about …?* To answer, say *No, not really. / A bit. / Yeah, quite a lot.*

A: **Do you know much about** computers?

B: **A bit.** Why?

10 You are going to find out how much people in your class know about the topics in the box. First, add two extra topics. These could be things you know a lot about – or things you want to learn about.

history	the moon	cows	_____
Australia	cars	tennis	_____
geography	computers		

11 Now find out how much other people in your class know about each of the topics.

CONVERSATION PRACTICE

12 Decide on two pieces of technology you're thinking of buying. Decide how much you want to spend on them.

13 Talk to some other students. Explain what you're thinking of buying – and why. Ask for and make recommendations.

14 Tell a partner who gave you the best advice.

📹 28 To watch the video and do the activities, see the DVD-ROM.

EMAIL ME THE LINK

VOCABULARY
Computers and the internet

1 Complete the dialogues with these pairs of nouns.

computer + memory stick	software + download
files + email	video + search
photo + email address	website + link

1 A: That's a lovely _____ of us.

   B: I know. I'll send it to you if you want. What's your _____?

2 A: Do you always save everything like that?

   B: I do, yeah. My old _____ died last year and I lost a lot of files, so now I keep copies of everything online and on this _____.

3 A: I read a great article about Lisbon on the Graddy _____ last night.

   B: Oh really? Can you send me the _____? I'd like to read that.

4 A: I don't know why it's working so slowly.

   B: You need the latest version of their _____. You don't need to pay for it – just _____ it from their website.

5 A: Did you get those _____ I sent you?

   B: I'm not sure, actually. I haven't checked my _____ today.

6 A: Have you seen that _____ of the singing dog – the one that everyone's talking about?

   B: No. What's that?

   A: Oh, just do a _____ for it. It's really funny!

2 Complete each group of collocations (1–5) with one noun from the box in Exercise 1.

1 send an ~
  check my ~
  get an ~
  delete an ~ by accident

2 buy a new ~
  check on the ~
  restart the ~
  my ~ died

3 design a ~
  build a ~
  visit our new ~
  have a look on their ~

4 create new ~
  open ~
  copy ~
  save all my ~ on a memory stick

5 write ~
  download ~
  use ~
  install ~

3 Work in pairs. Discuss these questions.

- Which websites do you visit most?
- Do you have a memory stick? If yes, what do you keep on it?
- How many email addresses do you have? Why?
- Can you remember the last search you did? Did you find what you wanted?
- How often do you install new software?

PRONUNCIATION

4 ▶ 107 Listen to each group of letters and repeat them.

1	/iː/	b, c, d, e, g, p, t, v
2	/e/	f, l, m, n, s, x, z
3	/eɪ/	a, h, j, k
4	/juː/	q, u, w
5	/aɪ/	i, y
6	/əʊ/	o
7	/ɑː/	r

5 Work in pairs. Take turns saying the letters of the alphabet in the correct order.

For example:

A: *a*

B: *b*

A: *c*

Which letters are the most difficult for you to say?

When we say website and email addresses, we say 'dot' for . and 'at' for @.

We usually say 'co', 'com', 'net', 'org', etc. as one word.

6 ▶ 108 Listen and write the three different addresses.

1   Her website address: _____

2   Her email address: _____

3   Her home address: _____

7 Write a website address, an email address and a home address. Then work in pairs. Say your addresses and spell them for your partner to write down.

LISTENING

8 You are going to listen to – and answer – a questionnaire about computers and technology. First, work in pairs and read the options in the questionnaire. Discuss what you think the questions are.

9 ▶ 109 Listen and check your ideas. Try to write the questions you hear. Then compare your ideas with your partner.

10 ▶ 110 Now listen to the whole questionnaire and tick (✔) the answers that are best for you.

11 Work in pairs. Compare your answers. Who do you think likes technology more?

12 Change partners. Tell your new partner about two people you know – one who loves technology and one who hates it. Give examples of how they love / hate it.

TECHNOLOGY – LOVE IT OR HATE IT?

1 _____
- a ☐ none   b ☐ one   c ☐ two or more

2 _____
- a ☐ Maybe an hour or two – if I turn it on.
- b ☐ Four or five hours. Most of the evening.
- c ☐ I never turn it off.

3 _____
- a ☐ Maybe once a day, maybe less.
- b ☐ Two or three times a day.
- c ☐ I check it all the time on my phone.

4 _____
- a ☐ 0–10   b ☐ 10–30   c ☐ 30–100

5 _____
- a ☐ The most basic pay-as-you-go phone.
- b ☐ An OK phone with quite a good camera. It does everything I need it to do.
- c ☐ The very best, latest model.

6 _____
- a ☐ What do you mean? Phoning people, of course!
- b ☐ I use the camera, I listen to music, and I sometimes play games.
- c ☐ Apart from the camera, I use the diary, Facebook, maps – all kinds of things. I can't list them all.

7 _____
- a ☐ Yes, I've deleted files on my computer by accident.
- b ☐ Yes. I sent an email to the wrong person once.
- c ☐ No, of course not.

8 _____
- a ☐ I ask someone to show me the very basic things.
- b ☐ I read the instructions and learn to do a few things. I'm not interested in the complicated things.
- c ☐ I just start playing about with it and teach myself. To find out more detailed things, I watch videos or look at the instructions or their website.

9 _____
- a ☐ Get angry, shout and jump up and down – until someone tells me I need to plug it in.
- b ☐ Check it's plugged in and, if it is, call someone to repair it.
- c ☐ Check everything is plugged in. Turn it off and on again – and if it still doesn't work, I repair it myself.

10 _____
- a ☐ Hardly ever. Why do I need it when my old things work?
- b ☐ Sometimes. Some things are better, and I change when my old things break.
- c ☐ All the time. I like to have all the latest things.

IT'LL SOLVE ALL OUR PROBLEMS

VOCABULARY What technology does

1 Match 1–4 with a–d and 5–8 with e–h.

1 It allows you to keep

2 It allows you to develop

3 It allows you to check

4 It allows you to produce

a electricity at home.

b your own apps quickly and easily.

c all your files in one safe place.

d your heart rate easily.

5 It allows you to create

6 It allows you to solve

7 It allows you to control

8 It allows you to save

e a lot of energy because it's so efficient.

f tests for the vocabulary you've learned.

g problems with the computer quickly.

h everything in your house from your phone.

2 Work in pairs. Discuss what you think each sentence in Exercise 1 might refer to.

a a mobile app or computer software

b a machine or some other piece of technology

READING

3 Work in pairs. You are going to read an article about technology. First, discuss these questions.

1 What do you think are the biggest problems in the world now?

2 Look at the title of the article on page 139. Do you think the writer is optimistic about the future, or not?

3 Look at the photos in the article. What do you think the technology is? What problems do you think it will solve?

4 Now read the article and find out what the writer thinks.

5 Work in pairs. Discuss why the writer mentions these things. Then read the article again to check your ideas.

1 the economy

2 Morocco

3 paint

4 offices

5 LED lights

6 a cupboard

7 chemicals

6 Work in pairs. Discuss if you agree or disagree with these statements.

- I'm also excited about the future and the possibilities of technology.
- I feel better about the future after reading about this technology.
- This technology might work well, but it won't solve the problem of unemployment.
- We should help more people install solar power in our country.
- I wouldn't want to eat food from a pink farm.
- I don't think these are the most important developments in technology now.

GRAMMAR

Adverbs

Adverbs can describe verbs – how we do things. The most common one is *well* (= good).

*This technology works really **well**.*

*A: How **well** do you speak English?*

*B: Not very **well**.*

7 Work in pairs. Ask each other these questions. Use the answers below.

1 How well do you speak English?

2 How well do you know your country?

3 How well can you draw?

4 How well can you use presentation software?

5 How well did you do in your last test / exam?

6 How well are your local football team doing?

Really well.	Not very well.
Quite well.	Not very well but better than before!

8 Work in pairs. Read the sentences and underline the adverbs and the verbs they describe. Then complete the rules in the box below.

1 The economy's doing quite badly, but our company is growing.

2 I had a problem, but the company solved it very quickly.

3 I have an app that allows me to check my heart rate easily.

4 Things in the digital world are changing very fast.

To make most descriptive adverbs, we add ¹_____ to an adjective. A few have the same form as the adjective, for example ²_____.

We can modify descriptive adverbs with *quite* and ³_____ the same way as adjectives.

G Check your ideas on page 188 and do Exercises 1 and 2

TECHNOLOGY CAN SAVE US

There are lots of problems in the world: in many places the economy's doing badly; there are too many people and the world doesn't produce enough jobs, food, or energy for all of them. It's easy to get depressed with all the bad news we hear, but I don't worry. In fact, I'm excited about the future, because I think technology will solve these problems. Here are just two amazing things that are already happening.

ELECTRICITY-PRODUCING HOMES

Only 1% of the world's electricity comes from solar power at the moment, but this is changing fast. Many countries, such as Morocco, are building huge solar farms, and some companies are developing very, very small solar cells for homes and offices. They have created some 'nano-cells' successfully, but the cells aren't very efficient and don't produce enough electricity yet. However, when they work more efficiently, the nano-cells could be used in windows and in paint to put on the outside of houses. Then, millions and millions of homes could become electricity producers and we'll have enough energy for all!

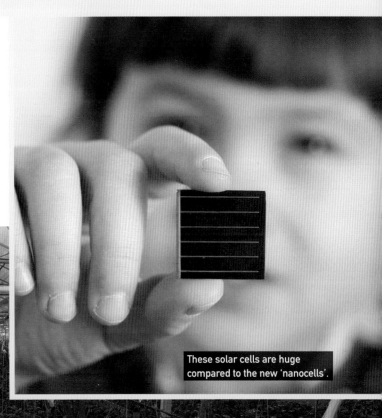

These solar cells are huge compared to the new 'nanocells'.

VERTICAL PINK FARMS

Plants need light to grow, but it's actually red and blue light that they need most. 'Pink farms' use red and blue LED lights that allow the plants to grow very quickly. LED lights are bright, last longer than other lights and don't get too hot, so the farms can work all year. The farms save space too, because the plants don't need earth and so they can be grown on shelves. And because conditions are always perfect, the farmer doesn't need to use chemicals to kill insects and diseases. Maybe one day, homes will have pink gardens: we won't just keep food in a cupboard, we'll *grow* it there!

Pink farms could feed the world.

SPEAKING

9   Think of a website, app or piece of software for each category below. Then work in groups and share your ideas.

1   I use it all the time.

2   I've recently found / started using it.

3   It's good fun.

4   I've tried it, but I don't like it.

5   I used it a lot in the past, but now don't.

6   It's good for learning English.

SOUNDS AND VOCABULARY REVIEW

10   ▶ 111 Listen and repeat the sounds for the letter 'a': /aː/, /æ/, /ɪ/, /ei/, /eə/, /ɒ/, /ə/, /ɔː/. Are any of them difficult for you to hear or say?

11   ▶ 112 Work in groups. Listen to eight sentences using these words. Together, try to write them down. Then listen again and finish writing them.

allows	change	installed	various
app	hard	language	washing

G For further revision, see Exercises 1–3 on page 189.

1

2

5

6

7

8

11

12

3

4

9

13

IN THIS UNIT YOU LEARN HOW TO:

- describe different events in relationships
- give news about relationships
- explain when and where you met people
- make promises

WORDS FOR UNIT 16

1 Work in pairs. Match the phrases to the photos. Which two phrases do not match a photo?

be in love	celebrate their anniversary
Don't slip!	encourage each other
go to a nightclub	hold the baby
I don't approve	I'm jealous!
I promise I will	knock at the door
make an appointment	musical instruments
negotiate the price	plant some flowers
remove the paint	protect your head

2 ▶ 113 Listen. Check your answers. Listen again. Repeat the words.

3 Work in pairs. Test each other. Cover the words.

Student A: point to a photo.

Student B: say the words.

4 Choose five of the photos. Write one more word or phrase to go with each photo. Then work in pairs and say your words or phrases. Can your partner guess the photo?

10

14

DID I TELL YOU MY NEWS?

VOCABULARY Love and marriage

1 Work in pairs. Discuss these questions.

1 What's the difference between a girlfriend, a wife and a partner?

2 What's the equivalent for men?

> We often say *partner* instead of *girlfriend / boyfriend* when the couple are older or have been together a long time. We can also use it when we don't know if a couple are married or not.

2 Work in pairs. Discuss which pairs of words in the box only refer to married couples, which refer to unmarried couples and which can refer to both.

married + wedding	broken up + getting on
a date + asked me out	divorced + jealous
saved + move	in-laws + approve
anniversary + together	pregnant + baby

3 Complete the sentences with the pairs of words in Exercise 2.

1 We're going to have a party for my parents' wedding _____ on Saturday. They've been _____ for 25 years.

2 My daughter is six months _____. She's due to have her _____ on Christmas Day!

3 We're getting _____ next summer. Would you like to come to the _____?

4 Sorry I can't go with you. I have _____ on Friday. This boy at school _____ and I've liked him for ages.

5 I'm pleased they're going to get _____. I never liked him. He was very _____ and controlled what she did.

6 We lived with my in-laws while we _____ enough money to _____ into our own place.

7 Sorry, but I'm a bit upset. I've _____ with Toni! To be honest, we weren't _____ very well. We argued quite a lot and now he's met someone else.

8 I get on with my _____ now, although they didn't _____ of our marriage at first.

4 Choose three or four sentences from Exercise 3 and imagine you are talking to the people who said them. Write what you would say in response.

For example:

A: *We're going to have a party for my parents' wedding anniversary on Saturday. They've been together for 25 years.*

B: *That's nice. Where are you going to have it?*

5 Work in pairs. Read out your conversations from Exercise 4 together. Try to continue each conversation.

LISTENING

6 ▶ 114 Listen to four short conversations where someone gives news about a relationship. Correct the wrong piece of information in each sentence below.

1 Owen has broken up with his girlfriend after around three months.

2 Her brother Gerrard Is going to get married to one of her friends.

3 Fiona and Kieran are getting divorced because Kieran met someone else.

4 She's going on a date with a guy from work. They're going to do karaoke.

7 ▶ 114 Choose the correct option. Then listen again and check your answers.

Conversation 1

1 How long *are they / have they been* together?

2 She's very *well-looking / good-looking*.

Conversation 2

3 A: When's the wedding?

B: Next May *sometimes / sometime*.

4 *What's / What does* his partner like?

Conversation 3

5 Did I *tell / say* you Fiona and Kieran are going to get divorced?

6 What a *shame / mistake*. They're both such nice people.

Conversation 4

7 He *sees / seems* very nice. He's quite quiet, but he's funny.

8 He's quite *high / tall* and he has lovely eyes.

8 Work in groups. Discuss these questions.

- Do you know anyone who moved in with a partner / got married after only being together a short time?

- Does anyone you know have a partner you don't like?

- What divorces have you heard of in the news recently? What was the cause?

- Do you think karaoke is a good thing for a first date? Why? / Why not? What might be better?

DEVELOPING CONVERSATIONS

Did I tell you ...?

We often introduce news we want to give by asking *Did I tell you ...?* The news might be about the future, past or present, so we use different tenses.

Did I tell you my brother Gerrard is going to get married? (future)

Did I tell you Fiona and Kieran have got divorced? (present perfect)

Did I tell you I saw Maria and Colin last weekend? (past simple)

Did I tell you my sister's pregnant? (present)

9 Complete the *Did I tell you ...?* questions using the correct tense and the verb in brackets.

1 A: Did I tell you Mena and me _____ travelling next year? (go)

B: Really? That's exciting. How long are you going to go for?

2 A: Did I tell you Rebecca _____ a new boyfriend? (have)

B: No. Have you met him yet?

3 A: Did I tell you I _____ Martin's parents last week? (meet)

B: No. How did it go?

4 A: Did I tell you Lucia and Marc _____? (break up)

B: No, but it doesn't surprise me. When did that happen?

5 A: Did I tell you we _____ finally _____ a flat? (find)

B: No. That's great! Where is it?

6 A: Did I tell you we _____ a party for our anniversary? (have)

B: No! Is that an invitation?

10 Work in pairs. Practise reading out the dialogues in Exercise 9. In each dialogue, answer the second question.

CONVERSATION PRACTICE

11 Write a piece of news about a relationship starting *Did I tell you ...?* Your news can be true or invented. Look at the audio script for Track 114 on page 213 if you need to, and underline the questions the people use to continue the conversations.

12 Have conversations with other students in the class. Tell them your piece of news, starting *Did I tell you ...?* They should ask questions to continue the conversation.

▶ 29 To watch the video and do the activities, see the DVD-ROM.

a
b

LOVE AT FIRST SIGHT

SPEAKING

1 Work in groups. Discuss these questions.

- What do you think *love at first sight* means?
- Have you ever heard any stories about love at first sight? Do you believe them?
- Do you think it's possible to fall in love with things or places – as well as people – at first sight?
- Can you give any examples?

LISTENING

2 Work in pairs. Look at the photos. Discuss how each photo might be connected to the idea of love at first sight.

For example:

Maybe two people met in this house and when they met it was love at first sight.

3 ▶ 115 Listen to three people talking about their experiences of love at first sight. Match each person to a photo and check your ideas from Exercise 2.

4 ▶ 115 Listen again. Tick (✔) the sentences that are true.

1 a They needed to move quickly because they planned to start a family.

   b They didn't have an appointment to visit the house they bought.

   c They tried to negotiate a better price.

2 a His first guitar was a present.

   b His uncle was a very important person in his life.

   c He now plays music for a living.

3 a Second Life is an online dating company.

   b The speaker met her future husband in a nightclub.

   c The speaker isn't actually married yet.

5 Work in pairs. Discuss these questions.

- Where would your dream house be? What would it be like?
- Can you play any musical instruments? How well?
- Which people have had a big influence on you?
- Have you heard of Second Life before?
- What do you think is good / bad about it?

GRAMMAR Past continuous

6 Look at these sentences from the listening. Underline one example of the past continuous and one example of the past simple in each sentence. Then complete the rules in the Grammar box below.

1 *I was working in a Second Life nightclub when one night, I met my future husband.*

2 *We were driving home from another appointment when we suddenly saw it – the house of our dreams!*

3 *We weren't getting on very well, so I started spending a lot of time online.*

To make the past continuous, we use *was* / ¹_____ + *(not)* + the *-ing* form of the verb.

We often use the past continuous and the past simple in the same sentence. We use the past ²_____ to show one action started and was in progress at the time that a past ³_____ action happened.

To link the two actions together, we often use the words ⁴_____ and *so*.

G Check your ideas on page 189 and do Exercise 1.

7 Complete the sentences with the correct past continuous form of the verbs in the box.

do	have	stay	walk
fly	listen	take	watch

1 We _____ dinner in a restaurant when she came in and sat at the next table.

2 I _____ in a hotel in Singapore when one day he got in the same lift as me.

3 I _____ the underground across town when she got on and sat opposite me.

4 We _____ to Vienna to visit some friends when we saw him at the airport.

5 I _____ through a street market one day when I saw it on a table.

6 I _____ some shopping in town when I saw it in one of the shops. It was love at first sight!

7 I _____ TV one night when an advert for it came on and I just thought it looked amazing.

8 I _____ to the radio one day when this song came on and I just fell in love with it.

PRONUNCIATION

8 Work in pairs. Practise reading out the sentences below. The stressed sounds are in bold. Note that in positive past continuous sentences, *was* and *were* aren't usually stressed. Instead, we use the weak forms /wəz/ and /wə/. In negative past continuous sentences, *was* and *were* are stressed.

1 I was **do**ing some **sho**pping when I **met** an **old friend**.

2 She was **ru**nning for the **bus** when she **fell**.

3 They were **wor**king in **Greece** when it **ha**ppened.

4 I **was**n't en**joy**ing it, so I **left**.

5 She **was**n't **fee**ling very **well**, so she **went home**.

6 We **were**n't **get**ting **on**, so we **bro**ke **up**.

9 ▶ 116 Listen and check. Repeat the sentences.

G For further practice, see Exercise 2 on page 190.

SPEAKING

10 Choose one of these topics to talk about. Spend two minutes planning what to say. Describe what happened and say where the people were and what they were doing. Try to use the past continuous.

- something you saw or heard – and fell in love with
- any famous people you have met / seen
- how and when you first met your best friends
- how and when some couples you know first met

11 Work in groups. Share your ideas.

I PROMISE

SPEAKING

1 Work in groups. Discuss these questions.

- Which of these ideas do you prefer? Why?

  a *Promise little, do a lot.*

  b *It's better to break a promise than never to make one.*

- Do you ever make promises? Who to?

- What's the last promise you made? For example:

  I promised to take my son to the cinema.

GRAMMAR

will / won't for promises

To make promises, we usually use *will / won't*. We sometimes add *I promise*.

A: *Dad, can we go to the cinema today?*

B: *Sorry, I'm too busy. **I'll take** you next week, **I promise**.*

2 Work in pairs. Make promises using *will / won't* and these ideas.

1 Promise to call later.

2 Promise not to tell anyone.

3 Promise to try harder.

4 Promise not to be late.

5 Promise not to make a mess.

We often promise something by using *will / won't* as a short response.

A: *Call me later.*   A: *Don't be late.*

B: *I will.*   B: *I won't.*

3 Work in pairs. Take turns to say and respond to the sentences. Respond using *I will. / I won't.*

1 Don't start before I get back.

2 You need to pay me back tomorrow.

3 Remember to go to the bank.

4 Don't forget to call your grandmother to thank her.

5 Be careful.

6 I don't want you to miss the train.

 For further practice, see Exercises 1 and 2 on page 190.

READING

4 You are going to read some poems based on promises. First, discuss these questions.

- Who are the most famous poets in your country?

- Did you study them at school? Did you like them?

- Do you read poems now? By which poets?

- Have you ever written a poem? When? What about?

5 Match the words in the box with the meanings (1–8). Use a dictionary to help you.

double	fade	remain	trust
encourage	let go	trouble	weeds

1 stop holding something

2 two times

3 help someone do well by saying positive things

4 become less strong (of a colour, sound or memory)

5 plants / flowers that you don't want in your garden

6 stay

7 believe someone is honest

8 problems or difficulties

6 Read the poems and match them to these titles. Then work in groups and check your ideas.

In memory   Breaking up

New born   A threat kept

7 Decide who is making the promises in each poem – and who to.

8 Work in groups. Discuss these questions.

- Which poem did you like most?

- Were there any lines you didn't understand? Can your partners explain them?

SPEAKING

9 Work in pairs. Think of promises (or threats) that these people might make.

1 a couple who are in love

2 a child to a parent

3 a student to a teacher

4 a teacher

5 a boss

6 a politician

10 Now choose one of the people in Exercise 9 – or use your own ideas – and write a short poem.

11 Read out your poems and vote for the best one.

SOUNDS AND VOCABULARY REVIEW

12 ▶ **117** Listen and repeat the sounds for the letter 'o': /aʊ/, /ʌ/, /ɔː/, /ɒ/, /ʊ/, /uː/, /əʊ/, /ə/. Are any of them difficult for you to hear or say?

13 ▶ **118** Work in groups. Listen to eight sentences using these words. Together, try to write them down. Then listen again and finish writing them.

born	flowers	knock	love
control	hold	looking	remove

 For further revision, see Exercises 1–3 on page 190.

1 _____

This I promise.

I'll try to be a person you want to love.

I'll try to encourage and not to complain –

Try to ask, not to tell.

I'll protect you and be there to hold you,

But I promise I'll let go –

Let you grow.

2 _____

I'm sorry.

How could you?

I'll be better; I'll be stronger.

How can I know?

I'll be here; I won't slip and fall.

How can I trust you?

Because I'll love you.

And you didn't before?

3 _____

I'll look after your garden.

I'll remove the weeds that may cover it.

I'll plant new flowers when others die.

I won't let it fade.

I'll keep it alive.

And you'll remain –

In my heart.

4 _____

I'll pay you back.

I've asked before.

I'll pay you double.

I've given you chances,

said there'd be trouble.

I'll do what you want.

I've waited,

but I'll wait no more.

VIDEO 8

SNOW MAGIC!

1 Work in groups. Discuss the questions.

- Can you think of three kinds of business that do well when the weather is hot and sunny?
- Can you think of three kinds of business that do well when it's cold and it snows?
- What do you think the photo above shows?
- Why do you think people use machines like this?

2 ▶ 30 Watch the first part of the video (0.00–1.25). Answer these questions.

1 Where does Dan Raedeke live?

2 What business does he run?

3 How can weather be a problem for him?

4 What did he study?

3 ▶ 30 Watch the next part of the video (1.26–2.30). Complete the summary below.

The person making the snow has to watch the ¹_____, the air temperature and the direction of the ²_____. Snow guns are always quite tall to allow the water to ³_____ before it hits the ground. Real snow is drier, softer and is ⁴_____ for skiing, but man-made snow ⁵_____ longer.

Dan Raedeke's newest machines are called water ⁶_____. They can produce a lot of snow ⁷_____. The snow is very ⁸_____. It's almost as good as snow from the sky. These machines can cover a trail in one ⁹_____ and they use them on ¹⁰_____ of the trails on Wild Mountain.

4 ▶ 30 Watch the final part of the video (2.31–4.10). Choose the correct option.

1 *Six / Sixteen / Sixty* pumps control the water that go through all the pipes.

2 If a pipe freezes, it's useless *for the next day / for a week or two / for the rest of the winter*.

3 The reservoir on top of the mountain provides 3,000 gallons of water *a minute / an hour / a day*.

4 Dan Raedeke *sometimes / often / always* spends all day and most of the night checking the system.

5 If there's *not enough / the right amount of / too much* water, the snow gets soft.

5 Work in pairs. Discuss the questions.

- Have you ever been skiing? If yes, when? Where? Did you enjoy it?
- If no, would you like to? Why? / Why not?
- What other things do you like to do when it snows?
- Would you like to have a business like Dan Raedeke's? Why? / Why not?
- What are your five most important machines?

UNDERSTANDING FAST SPEECH

6 ▶ 31 Read and listen to this extract from the video said fast, then slow. Stressed sounds are in CAPITALS.

they make VEry SOFT snow, and it's ALmost, ALmost as GOOD as SNOW from the SKY, and in ONE NIGHT we can COver this enTIRE TRAIL. They're GREAT.

7 You try! Practise saying the extract with the same stressed sounds.

REVIEW 8

GRAMMAR

1 Complete the conversation with one word in each space. Contractions (*won't*, *weren't*, etc. are one word).

A: What ¹_____ you doing last night? I called you, but you didn't answer.

B: Yeah, sorry. My phone was turned off and I saw your message too ²_____ to call.

A: Don't worry. I ³_____ doing anything special. I just thought you might like to go out.

B: Actually, I was with Simon. He asked me to marry him!

A: Really! ⁴_____ you say yes?

B: Of course!

A: That's great news. When are ⁵_____ thinking of having the wedding?

B: ⁶_____ thinking of August next year, but I ⁷_____ let you know! Obviously, you're invited!

A: Great. I promise I'll ⁸_____ there.

2 Complete the sentences with the correct form of the verb *be*.

1 I _____ thinking of going to the cinema later.

2 I broke my leg when I _____ playing football.

3 We met when we _____ working for a local company.

4 They _____ thinking of moving house. They want somewhere smaller.

5 What _____ you thinking of doing this evening?

6 I saw Mariah Carey once when she _____ coming out of a hotel.

3 Add the adverb form of the adjective in brackets in the correct place in the sentence.

1 I can't run very because I have a bad leg. (quick)

2 He works too. (hard)

3 How can you swim? (good)

4 I didn't do in my exam. (bad)

5 We arrived so that we could get a seat. (early)

6 It only worked for a while. (successful)

4 ▶ 119 Listen and complete the sentences with one word in each space. Contractions (*I'm*, *don't*, etc.) are one word.

1 We met _____ _____ _____ _____ studying _____ Germany.

2 _____ _____ _____ asking _____ _____ marry me.

3 _____ _____ do _____ without talking _____ _____ first.

4 I saw _____ _____ I _____ _____ _____ New York.

5 He crashed _____ _____ _____ _____ _____ fast.

6 _____ tell _____ when _____ _____ _____ news.

5 ▶ 119 Work in pairs. Compare your ideas. Listen again and check.

VOCABULARY

6 Complete the description with the words in the box.

allows	creates	fast	help	rate
app	energy	fit	improve	saves

I like keeping ¹_____ and I recently got a new ²_____ for my phone to ³_____ me. It tells me how far I've run and how ⁴_____ I've done it. I also have a special watch that ⁵_____ me to check my heart ⁶_____ and how much ⁷_____ I'm using when I'm doing exercise. Then the app ⁸_____ all these details on the phone and ⁹_____ a programme of activities to show me how I can ¹⁰_____. It's amazing.

7 Put the words into three groups – computers, the internet or love.

anniversary	download	laptop	screen
battery	jealous	link	search
button	in-laws	plug	tablet
date	keyboard	pregnant	website

8 Match the verbs in the box to the groups of words they go with in 1–8.

produce	delete	develop	join
knock	hold	keep	send

1 ~ an email / ~ a package / ~ me the link

2 ~ the file / ~ my old emails / ~ it by mistake

3 ~ electricity / ~ apple juice / ~ energy

4 ~ an app / ~ your ideas / ~ it successfully

5 ~ on the door / ~ hard / ~ loudly

6 ~ my hand / ~ the door open / ~ the baby

7 ~ a gym / ~ a chat group / ~ the army

8 ~ it safely / ~ him alive / ~ it in a cupboard

9 Choose the correct option.

1 The guy *promised* / *threatened* to shoot us if we didn't give him the money, but we persuaded him to *let go* / *fall* of the gun.

2 I don't *trust* / *honest* him. He's *broken* / *damaged* his promises too many times.

3 We often *argued* / *jumped* about who should do the washing-up, so we bought a *dishwasher* / *washing machine*.

4 I tried to *turn* / *make* on the computer, but nothing happened. Then I saw someone had pulled the *plug* / *keyboard* out.

5 I didn't read the *instructions* / *rules*, so I *put* / *pressed* the wrong button and it stopped working.

1 WRITING Forms

VOCABULARY Common questions

1 Complete the conversation below with the questions in the box.

- What's your surname?
- Do you have a middle name?
- Where do you live?
- What's your email address?
- What's your first name?
- What's your telephone number?
- Where are you from?
- When were you born?

A: I need to ask you some questions so we can complete this form.

B: OK.

A: Right, [1]_____

B: David.

A: And [2]_____

B: Abbott – that's a–double b–o–double t.

A: OK. I've got it. And [3]_____

B: Yes, it's Sebastian.

A: OK and [4]_____

B: Canada. I'm Canadian.

A: Oh, OK. Right. And [5]_____

B: In Dublin. 25 Cook Street.

A: And [6]_____

B: It's 07791–773–119.

A: And [7]_____

B: It's david abbott at shotmail dot com.

A: OK – nearly finished. One more question: [8]_____

B: 1987. October the fourth.

A: OK. Great. That's everything. Thanks.

2 Work in pairs. Take turns to ask and answer the eight questions in the conversation above.

WRITING Completing forms

3 Complete the form for the person in the conversation in Exercise 1. The first answer is given.

VOCABULARY Nationalities

4 Complete the table.

Country	Nationality
	Canadian
the United States	
Ireland	
India	
	Scottish
England	
	Australian
China	
	Thai
	Japanese
France	
Germany	
	Italian
	Polish
Russia	
	Spanish
Brazil	
	Mexican
Turkey	
	Egyptian

SURNAME	Abbott_____
FIRST NAME	_____
MIDDLE NAME	_____
GENDER	Male Female
NATIONALITY	_____

DATE OF BIRTH	_____
ADDRESS	_____
	_____
TELEPHONE NUMBER	_____
EMAIL ADDRESS	_____

The nationality words in Exercise 4 are adjectives. We can use them to describe food, people, etc.

*I love **Mexican** food.*

*I live with two **Australian** women and a **Polish** man.*

*I watch a lot of **Italian** football.*

5 Work in pairs. Discuss what you can see in the photos.

For example:

A: *Is that the Spanish football team?*

B: *No. They wear red.*

6 Work in groups. Discuss these questions.

- Can you think of famous people from each of the countries in Exercise 4?
- Do you have any friends from any of these countries? If yes, who?
- What do you know about the different kinds of food from each country?
- Do you know any other famous things from each country?

PRACTICE

7 Complete the form with your own information.

SURNAME	
FIRST NAME	
MIDDLE NAME	
GENDER	Male ☐ Female ☐
NATIONALITY	
DATE OF BIRTH	
ADDRESS	
TELEPHONE NUMBER	
EMAIL ADDRESS	

2 WRITING Pen friends

SPEAKING

1   **Work in groups. Discuss these questions.**
- Which people in the photos like doing the same things as you?
- How often do you do these things?
- Are you good at them?
- Are there any activities in the photos you really don't like doing? Why not?

WRITING

2 Complete the internet profile with the words in the box.

brothers	first	full	parents	student
evenings	foreign	meeting	playing	usually

HOME | MY PROFILE | FIND FRIENDS | LOG OUT

Hi,

My name's Tiiu (pronounced Tee-you). Well, that's my [1]_____ name. My [2]_____ name is Tiiu Lipping, but people [3]_____ just call me T! I'm from Estonia, in the north of Europe – it's next to Russia and above Latvia – and I want to write to someone in a [4]_____ country. It's a good way to practise my English.

I live in the capital city, Tallinn. I'm a [5]_____ at Tallinn University. I'm studying Medicine. I want to be a doctor in the future. I also work in a shop three [6]_____ a week. I enjoy it because I like [7]_____ people and the money's OK.

I like swimming, [8]_____ tennis and reading. I live with my mum and dad and my three [9]_____. It's OK. I really want to have my own flat, but my [10]_____ say I'm too young – I'm 19.

Anyway, if you want to write to someone from Estonia, try me! Tell me about yourself.

Tiiu

3 Work in pairs. Discuss how you are similar to Tiiu and how you are different.

For example:

She likes swimming, and I like it too.

She lives with her parents, but I live on my own.

KEY WORDS FOR WRITING

and

And is a linking word. We use *and* to join words and phrases together.

I live with my mum and dad. I live with my three brothers.

= *I live with my mum and dad* **and** ~~I live with~~ *my three brothers.*

Note that here we don't need to repeat *I live with.*

When more than two words or phrases are connected, we only use *and* between the last two.

I like swimming. I like playing tennis. I like reading.

= *I like swimming,* ~~I like~~ *playing tennis* **and** *reading.*

Note that here we don't need to repeat *I like.*

4 Connect these sentences using *and*. Don't repeat any words that you don't need to repeat.

1 I play volleyball. I play golf.

_____.

2 Bangkok is really crowded. It's polluted.

_____.

3 I like reading. I like learning languages. I like computers.

_____.

4 My brother lives in Dubai. My sister lives in Istanbul.

_____.

5 I live with my mum and dad. I live with my sister. I live with my aunt. I live with my grandfather.

_____.

PRACTICE

5 Write a reply to Tiiu. Use some of phrases in the box and tell her:

- where you are from and where you live.
- what you do.
- what you like doing.
- who you live with.

- My full name is _____, but people usually call me _____.
- I'm from _____ and I live in _____.
- I live with _____ / I live on my own.
- I like _____, _____ and _____.

3 WRITING Cards

SPEAKING

1   Match the cards in the box to the pictures.

a birthday card	a Valentine card	a Christmas card
a get well soon card	a Mother's Day card	a wedding card

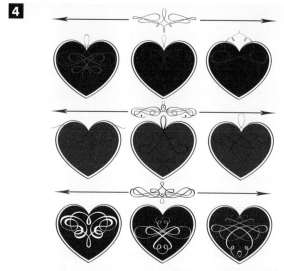

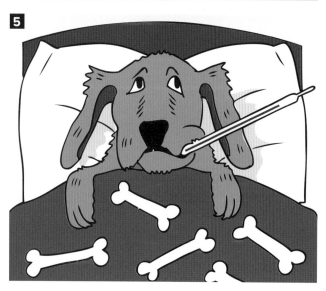

2 Work in groups. Discuss these questions.

- Do you ever send cards or e-cards? Who to? When? Why?
- Can you remember the last card you sent?
- Can you remember the last card you received?
- What kind of thing is good to write in the different kinds of cards in the box?

VOCABULARY

Beginning and ending cards

To show who a card is for, we usually write *Dear* + first name. For example:

Dear Yoichi,

Dear Tom and Susanna,

We usually finish with one of these expressions and then our first name.

Regards,	(for people we don't know very well)
Best wishes,	(for friends)
All the best,	
Lots of love,	(for family members and old friends)
Love,	

3 Cover the information box above. Complete the cards with one word in each space.

---

1 _____ Sally,

Happy birthday!

I hope you have a great day.

2 _____ wishes,

Trini

Dear Maria 3 _____
Miguel,

Congratulations on your new baby boy.

I hope you are all well.

Lots of 4 _____,

Rebecca

Dear Aaron,

Good luck with your new job.

I hope everything goes well.

All the 5 _____,

Suzie

KEY WORDS FOR WRITING

hope

We use *hope* to show what we want to be true now – or what we want to happen in the future.

I **hope** you are all well.	(= now / at the moment)
I **hope** everything goes well.	(= in the future)

When we use *hope* to talk about the future, we usually use a verb in the present simple form after it.

4 Match the sentences with the follow-up comments.

1 Sorry to hear you were ill.

2 Sorry to hear about your computer.

3 Good luck with your exams next week.

4 Good luck with your interview.

5 Happy birthday.

6 Happy Christmas and New Year.

a I hope you have a fantastic day.

b I hope you get the job.

c I hope it isn't too expensive to replace.

d I hope you're feeling better now.

e I hope you enjoy your holiday.

f I hope you pass them all.

5 Work in pairs. Discuss why people hope the things in the sentences below. There is an example for the first sentence.

1 I hope it doesn't rain.

A: *Maybe the person wants to go to the beach.*

B: *Yes, or maybe they want to play football in the park.*

2 I hope it's open tonight.

3 I hope she got home OK.

4 I hope you like it.

5 I hope they lose!

6 I hope it doesn't take too long.

6 Think of two things you hope are true – or that you hope happen in the future. Then tell your partner your ideas.

PRACTICE

7 Write three cards to different people. They can be birthday cards, cards wishing someone good luck, wedding cards, etc. Use some language from these pages.

SPEAKING

1 Work in groups. Discuss these questions.

- Where are the most popular meeting places in your town / city?
- Where do you usually meet your friends?
- Do you usually arrive before, at or after the time you agree to meet? Why?
- What are good meeting places for these different kinds of people:
  - parents with children?
  - teenagers?
  - older people?
  - people going on a date?

WRITING

2 Complete the email with the words in the box.

four	me	that	what	where

To   melkent@shoemail.gb
Subject   Tomorrow

Hi Mel,

Let me know ¹_____ time you want to meet tomorrow – and ²_____. My class finishes at ³_____, so any time after ⁴_____ is fine with ⁵_____.

All the best,

Emma

3 Complete Mel's reply with the words in the box.

can	easy	from	on	near

To   emma2001jenkins@shoemail.gb
Subject   Re: Tomorrow

Hi Emma,

I don't finish work until about five tomorrow. Maybe we can meet somewhere ¹_____ my office. There's a café near there called Café Blue. It's quite nice. They do good food there if you want to have something to eat.

It's ²_____ Clarendon Street, which is off Bedford Road. When you come out of the station, turn right and walk down Bedford Road. Clarendon Street is the first on the left. The café is two minutes' walk ³_____ there. It's ⁴_____ to find. It's a big place with chairs and tables outside. You ⁵_____ always phone me on your mobile if you can't find it.

See you,

Mel

4 Match the names of the places from Mel's email to a–d on the map. Then work in pairs and compare your ideas.

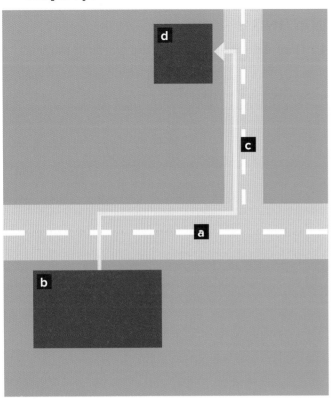

GRAMMAR

Present simple to talk about the future

We use the present simple to talk about timetables in the future – trains, planes, buses, classes, work, films, etc.

My class finishes at four.

I don't finish work until about five tomorrow.

5 Complete the sentences with the present simple form of the verbs in brackets.

1 What time _____ you _____ work tomorrow? (finish)

2 What time _____ your flight on Sunday? (be)

3 I _____ work until twelve tomorrow, so we can meet in the morning. (not / start)

4 I don't want to miss the last bus. It _____ at 11.30. (leave)

5 The shop _____ until ten, so let's meet at around half past nine. (not / open)

6 My train _____ at eight. We can meet after that. (arrive)

7 The café _____ at eight, so we need to get there before then. (close)

8 I think the film _____ at about ten. (end)

6 Work in pairs. Discuss these questions.

• What time does your class finish today?

• When is your next English class? What time does it start and finish?

• What time do you start work / school tomorrow?

KEY WORDS FOR WRITING

when

We use *when* to join two actions in a sentence. The *when* part of the sentence happens first.

When you come *out of the station, turn right and walk down Bedford Road.*

(= First, come out of the station. Second, turn right and walk down Bedford Road.)

*Call me **when you're ready**.*

(= First, be ready. Second, call me.)

Note that we use the present simple after *when* to talk about the future.

When I have *my next holiday, **I'm going to** watch every episode of Breaking Bad.*

7 Decide which action happens first in each pair (1–5). Then write a sentence and connect the ideas with *when*.

1 you can see the hotel / you come out of the station

2 you get to the end of Main Street / turn right

3 take a bus to the centre of town / you come out of the airport

4 call me / you get to the station

5 I'm going to go out and celebrate / I finish my exams

8 Work in pairs. Give directions from where you are now to where you live – or another place you know well.

For example:

When you leave *this building, take the 29 bus. Stay on the bus for about half an hour. **When you get to** St Ann's Road, get off the bus. Walk down Green Lanes. **When you get to** Seymour Road, turn left. I live there.*

9 Work in groups. Take turns to complete each sentence in different ways. Use *going to*. How many different sentences can you make?

1 When I have my next holiday, _____.

2 When my English is really good, _____.

3 When I become President, _____!

PRACTICE

10 Write your own reply to Emma's email in Exercise 2. Arrange what time to meet – and where. Use Mel's email to help you.

5 WRITING Visiting friends

SPEAKING

1 **Work in groups. Discuss these questions.**

- Do you have any friends or relatives in other towns, cities or countries?
- Where do they live? What do they do there?
- Have you ever visited them? If yes, when? How long for? Did you have a good time?
- Have they ever visited you? If yes, when? How long for? Did you take them anywhere special?

VOCABULARY Places to visit

2 **Match the words in the box to the photos.**

beach	church	island	mosque	waterfall
castle	gallery	lake	tower	

3 **Work in pairs. Discuss these questions.**

- Which of the places in the box do you have near where you live?
- Do you ever visit these places? How often?
- Which places do you recommend the most? Why?

WRITING 1

4 **Complete the email with the words in the box.**

can	like	planning	when	where

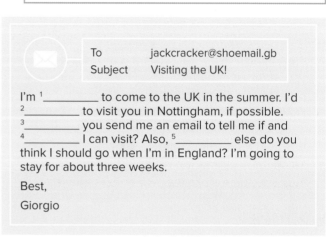

To   jackcracker@shoemail.gb
Subject   Visiting the UK!

I'm ¹_____ to come to the UK in the summer. I'd
²_____ to visit you in Nottingham, if possible.
³_____ you send me an email to tell me if and
⁴_____ I can visit? Also, ⁵_____ else do you
think I should go when I'm in England? I'm going to
stay for about three weeks.

Best,

Giorgio

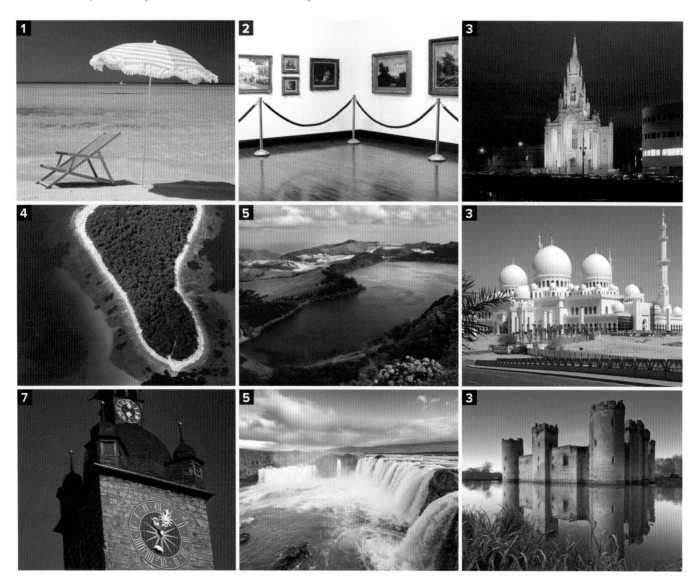

5 Look at this email. Underline everything that is the same as in Giorgio's email.

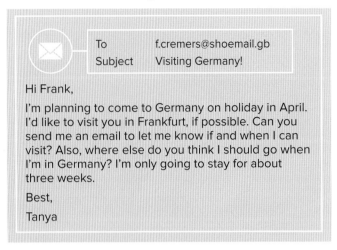

To f.cremers@shoemail.gb
Subject Visiting Germany!

Hi Frank,

I'm planning to come to Germany on holiday in April. I'd like to visit you in Frankfurt, if possible. Can you send me an email to let me know if and when I can visit? Also, where else do you think I should go when I'm in Germany? I'm only going to stay for about three weeks.

Best,

Tanya

6 Write an email to a friend in another country. Use language from the two emails above.

WRITING 2

7 Below is a reply to one of the emails from Writing 1. Complete it with the words in the box.

your plans	your email	a spare room
cities	the weather	the countryside

To t.tucker@shoemail.gb
Subject Re: Visiting Germany!

Hi Tanya,

Thanks for ¹_____. It was really nice to hear from you again. I'm really pleased to hear you're planning to come to Germany in April. If you like, you can stay at my flat. I have ²_____. I'm afraid it's not very big, but you can sleep there, if that's OK with you.

You asked about places to visit. Well, it depends what you want to do. If you like ³_____, you should go to Berlin. It's great, and there are lots of things to do there. It's also good if you're interested in history. If you prefer ⁴_____, you should go to the Allgäu, in the south. It's a really lovely place to go if ⁵_____'s nice. There are lots of rivers and lakes, and some amazing old castles.

Anyway, write to me again when ⁶_____ are clearer. I'm really looking forward to seeing you again.

Best,

Frank

8 Which place sounds better to you – Berlin or the Allgäu? Why?

KEY WORDS FOR WRITING

if

We often make suggestions using *If you ..., you should ...* .
If you like cities, **you should go** to Berlin.
If you prefer the countryside, **you should go** to the Allgäu.

9 Match the two parts of the sentences.

1 If you like tennis,
2 If you like the countryside,
3 If you like the sea,
4 If you like shopping,
5 If you're interested in history,

a you should go to the Komensky Museum.
b you should go to Wangfujing Street. That's where the big department stores are.
c you should go to Albufeira. It has some great beaches.
d you should watch some games at Wimbledon.
e you should go to Brittany. It's really beautiful.

10 Write three similar sentences about your own country.

If you _____, you should _____.

If you _____, you should _____.

If you _____, you should _____.

We use lots of other expressions with *if*.
I'm afraid the room's not very big, but you can sleep there, **if that's OK with you.**

11 Complete the *if*-expressions with the words in the box.

like	necessary	OK	possible	weather

1 You can stay at our house, if you _____.
2 I'd like to come and visit you when I'm in London, if _____.
3 I really need some help. I can pay someone, if _____.
4 Taking a boat down the river's great if the _____'s nice.
5 I'm going to arrive at your house at around six o'clock, if that's _____ with you.

12 Translate the five expressions with *if* from Exercise 11 into your language.

PRACTICE

13 Write to a foreign friend who is planning to visit your country. Before you write, underline any language in Frank's email that you want to use.

6 WRITING Describing food

SPEAKING

1 Work in groups. Discuss the questions. Use some of the expressions in bold in the box below.

- What do you know about each of the different kinds of food in the photos?

- Which have you tried? Where did you have it? Did you like it?

- What other different kinds of food have you tried? When? Where? What did you have?

> **I think it's** a Japanese dish.
>
> **It's called** *tagine*.
>
> **It's made from** beetroot.
>
> **It's quite** spicy.
>
> **It looks** really nice.
>
> I **cook it sometimes**.
>
> **I had it when** I was in England.

WRITING

2 Complete the email with the words in the box.

grill	heard	pork	share
healthy	pasta	red	typical

> To pshaw@shoemail.gb
> Subject Food!
>
> Hi again,
>
> How're you? I hope you're well. You asked me about ¹_____ Argentinean food. Well, let me tell you about it. In Argentina, we eat a lot of ²_____ meat. Some people say we eat *too much* meat and it's not very ³_____, but I love it. I think we have the best beef in the world. Our cows are free to run around in the countryside! We usually ⁴_____ the beef on a barbecue, and we cook lots of other meat like this too – lamb, ⁵_____ and chicken. We usually eat the meat with salad or chips.
>
> We also eat a lot of pizza and ⁶_____ because there are lots of Italians living here. We have great ice cream, too!
>
> Oh, I nearly forgot, we have a special drink called *mate*, which is very important here too. Have you ⁷_____ of it? It's a kind of tea and we ⁸_____ it with friends. It's very nice.
>
> Anyway, write and tell me about the food in your country.
>
> All the best,
>
> Héctor

3 Work in pairs. Discuss these questions.

- Have you ever tried Argentinean beef – or any other Argentinean food?
- From Héctor's email, do you think Argentinean food sounds good? Why? / Why not?
- What sounds best to you?
- Have you ever heard of *mate*?
- What kinds of food / drinks do you usually share with friends?

KEY WORDS FOR WRITING

too

Too has two main uses:

a Before adjectives, adverbs or *much / many* to show something is bad because it's more than we want.

*Some people say we eat **too much** meat.*

*I don't like Indian food. It's **too spicy**.*

b At the end of a sentence or clause to mean *also*.

*We have great ice cream **too**!*

*We cook lots of other meat like this **too** – lamb, pork, chicken.*

4 Read the explanation box and decide if *too* has meaning *a* or meaning *b* in each of these sentences.

1 I mainly eat vegetarian food, but I eat some seafood too.

2 I think people use too much salt in their food here.

3 Baklava is a typical dessert in Turkey but I find it a bit too sweet.

4 I love cooking. I make a lot of nice pasta dishes and I do good pizzas too.

5 There are a lot of Chinese restaurants in the city and there are quite a few other Asian places too – Thai, Indian, Korean.

5 Put *too* in the correct place in these sentences.

1 I tasted the soup but it was hot and I burnt my mouth!

2 We have the best beef in the world and the lamb we produce is really good.

3 I make dinner at home most days, but my husband and son cook.

4 I don't eat out round here because the restaurants are expensive.

5 He drinks a lot of cola and he eats many sweets. It's not healthy.

PRACTICE

6 Choose the words that are true for you and your country.

1 We *eat a lot of / don't eat much* red meat.

2 We usually *grill / fry / roast* meat.

3 We *eat a lot of / don't eat much* fish and seafood.

4 We *eat a lot of / don't eat much* fresh fruit and vegetables.

5 We eat quite a lot of *potatoes / pasta / rice*.

6 The food here is *quite / isn't very* spicy.

7 *I think / I don't think* we eat very healthily.

8 *I think / I don't think* our food is the best food in the world!

7 Now write an email to Héctor in Argentina. Tell him about the food in your country. Use language from Exercise 6 and from Héctor's email. Start like this:

Dear Héctor,

Hi, how're you? Thanks for your last email. It was really interesting. So let me tell you about the food in … .

7 WRITING Describing photos

SPEAKING

1   Work in groups. Discuss these questions.

- Do you like taking photos? Are you good at it?
- What do you take photos of?
- Do you share photos on the internet? On which websites?
- Do you often look at other people's photos?
- Do you like seeing photos of yourself? Why? / Why not?
- Have you got any photos on your mobile phone? What of?

WRITING

2   You are going to read two descriptions of the photos on this page. First, look at the photos. Which words in the box do you think go with each photo?

her tail	protected	forest
cheer up	wolves	cute

3   Now read the texts and see if you were right.

1

This is a photo of me with my new cat, Twinky. I've been ill, so my parents bought her to cheer me up. And it worked! She looks so cute and she's really funny – especially when she chases her tail! She makes me laugh. She's seven months old now and she runs around and plays all the time. I love her. I'm feeling a lot better now, so I might go back to school next week or the week after.

2

This is a photo of me and my friends walking in Great Bear Forest. It's near where I live in Vancouver, so we often go there – sometimes just for the day and sometimes longer. As you can see, the scenery is amazing with the mountains and rivers and trees. The area is protected because some of the trees are 1,000 years old and there are animals like bears and wolves – oh, and there are salmon too. It's sunny sometimes, but the day we took this photo, it rained all day. We decided to walk across the river because we were already so wet! Luckily, it was also a warm day, so we didn't get cold. I know I don't look happy, but we really had a good time!

4   Work in pairs. Discuss these questions.

- Which photo do you like best? Why?
- Do the photos and text:
  - make you want to have a cat? Why? / Why not?
  - make you want to go to Great Bear Forest? Why? / Why not?
- Has anyone ever bought you something to cheer you up? What? Why were you sad in the first place?
- Have you ever been for a walk in the rain? Where? Why did you go?

KEY WORDS FOR WRITING

> *SO*
>
> a We use *so* to link a reason to an action.
>
>   reason   action
>
>   <u>I've been ill,</u> *so* <u>my parents bought her to cheer me up.</u>
>
> b We also use *so* to mean *very*.
>
>   She looks **so** cute.

5 Find an example of each use of *so* in text 2.

6 Put *so* in the correct place in the sentences.

  1 I look strange in this photo.

  2 It was his birthday I made him a cake.

  3 It rained a lot we spent most of the holiday indoors.

  4 I was happy when I opened the present.

  5 You can't see her very well in the photo because it was dark.

  6 We missed our plane we had to wait in the airport for six hours.

7 Rewrite these sentences with *so*.

  1 You look very young there!

  2 We didn't go because it snowed.

  3 I took a photo because I wanted to show you my dog.

  4 You look very bored. Were you?

GRAMMAR

> ### Linking verbs
>
> Linking verbs like *be* and *look* can be followed by an adjective.
>
> She **looks so cute**.
>
> I know I **don't look happy**, but we had a good time.
>
> Other linking verbs are: *get, feel, seem, sound* and *taste*.

8 Complete the sentences with the correct form of the verb and the adjective in brackets.

  1 I hate this photo. I _____ in it. (look / stupid)

  2 This is a photo of me when I was trying the local tea – it _____. (taste / horrible)

  3 I didn't have a jersey with me, so I _____. (get / really cold)

  4 I didn't speak to her very much, but she _____. (seem / nice).

  5 This is a photo of the band I went to see. It's a shame you can't hear their music – they _____. (sound / great)

  6 You can see my brother at the back of the photo. It's the man who _____. (look / bored)

PRACTICE

9 You are going to write about a photo. Work in pairs. Choose one of the photos on this page or one of your own. Talk about:

- where the photo was taken.
- who the people are.
- what they are doing.
- the weather.
- how they look, feel, etc.
- anything that happened before or after the photo was taken.

10 Write a short description of between 40 and 100 words.

8 WRITING Messages

SPEAKING

1 **Work in pairs. Discuss how you share news about yourself and give messages.**

- Which of these are most common / least common for you?
  - post a public update on social media (Facebook, Twitter, etc.)
  - send a private message through social media
  - send a text
  - send an email
  - write a note / a letter / a card
  - phone and speak to someone
  - wait to speak face-to-face
- Does the way you share news depend on the kind of news / message?
- Have you shared any news or written any messages recently? What about?

WRITING

2 **Read the different messages. Complete the texts with one word in each space.**

Thanks	Very sadly	Back	In fact
Lovely	Great news	Sorry	Listen

3 **Work in pairs. How would you give each message? Use the ideas in Exercise 1.**

1 _____ for helping us move into the flat last week. We really needed the support! We're still organising everything, but when we finish, come for lunch. I'll call you.

2 _____ – can't come for the meal. Not feeling well. Will call you next week. Hope you all have a nice time. xxx

3 I can't come to the cinema with you tonight. I have too much work to do. _____, I don't think we should continue seeing each other. It's not you – it's me. I'm not ready for a serious relationship. I have too many other things to think about.

4 _____ about your new job. Congratulations. Want to meet for a drink sometime soon to celebrate?

5 _____ to see you at the weekend. Really enjoyed it. Send us the photos you took when you get the chance. Thanks. N.

6 Hi Andrew. I'm sorry I haven't been in contact for a long time. _____, my father died three months ago. As you can imagine, it was a big shock and it's been very difficult for me. I am very slowly trying to get back to my normal life. It would be really great to hear from you. Love J xx

7 Gone to town. _____ about 8. Text me if you want anything from the shops. XX

8 Bill. _____, I'm going to be in Boston next Tuesday. Could I come and stay with you? I have some work there. I'll be with you for three days. I really hope I can!

GRAMMAR

Shortening messages

We often write messages in note form by leaving out some grammar words:

- pronouns (*I, it, you*, etc.) if it is obvious who we are referring to
- auxiliary verbs (*am, have*, etc.), if the time is obvious
- articles (*a / the*)

Sorry – can't come to the meal.

(= **I'm** sorry. **I** can't come to the meal.)

Want to meet for a drink sometime soon?

(= **Do you** want to meet for a drink sometime soon?)

We also often use imperatives instead of *can / could you ...?* if we know the person well.

Send us *the photos you took.*

(= Could you send us the photos you took?)

4 Look at the messages in Exercise 2. Which ones use note form and which ones don't? Why do you think that is?

5 Write the full grammatical messages where note forms are used.

6 Write these messages in note form.

1 Can you go to the shops? We need some milk and a packet of pasta.

2 I had to go out. Your dinner is in the fridge. I'll be back at eleven.

3 I'm going to be late. There's a lot of traffic. I'll hopefully be there at 9.30.

KEY WORDS FOR WRITING

prepositions

We often use specific prepositions with certain words or expressions.

Thanks for *helping us.*

You must **come for lunch**.

Great news about *your job.*

Lovely to see you **at the weekend**.

I'm sorry I haven't been **in contact** *for a long time.*

7 Choose the correct preposition.

1 That's awful news *about / with* your dad. I'm so sorry.

2 Thanks to everyone *about / for* all your messages of support. They were really helpful.

3 Sorry I haven't been *for / in* contact recently. I've been very busy

4 Do you want to meet *about / for* a drink later tonight?

5 I was thinking *about / on* you yesterday. I hope the exam went well.

6 We're all ready *for / of* your visit and really looking forward *at / to* seeing you.

7 Would you like to come *at / for* dinner *at / on* the weekend?

8 Gone *to / for* the gym. Will be back *at / on* 6.

8 Complete each sentence in two ways.

1 Thanks _____.

2 Great news _____.

3 Would you like to come _____?

4 Gone _____. Will be back _____.

PRACTICE

9 Work in pairs. Write two messages to your partner. Choose from the ideas below. Use language from these pages.

- Share some good news.
- Share some bad news.
- Thank them for something.
- Say sorry for something.
- Invite them to do something.
- Offer to do something.
- Ask them to do something.

10 Exchange your messages. Write a reply.

GRAMMAR REFERENCE

1 PEOPLE AND PLACES

BE
*Hello. **I'm** Bruce.* (= I am)
__You're__ late! (= You are)
__He's__ a doctor. (= He is)
__She's__ 21. (= She is)
__It's__ cold today. (= It is)
__We're__ from Venezuela. (= We are)
__They're__ our friends. (= They are)
In normal spoken English, we usually use the short forms.

Negatives
__I'm not__ hungry. (= I am not)
__You're not__ in the right class. (= You are not)
__He's not__ French. (= He is not)
__She's not__ very interesting. (= She is not)
__It's not__ cheap. (= It is not)
__We're not__ happy about it. (= We are not)
__They're not__ married. (= They are not)

DID YOU KNOW?
We also use the negative short forms *isn't* and *aren't*. Choose the one you like!
*My dad **isn't** from here. They **aren't** married.*

Questions

__Am I__ next?	*Where __am I__ on the map?*
__Are you__ OK?	*How __are you__?*
__Is he__ happy here?	*Where __is he__ from?*
__Is she__ ill today?	*Who __is she__?*
__Is it__ cold outside?	*What time __is it__?*
__Are we__ late?	*Why __are we__ here?*
__Are they__ good?	*What __are their names__?*

Exercise 1
Complete the conversation with the correct form of *be.*
I: Hi. Come in. Sit down. How ¹_____ you?
M: Fine.
I: I'm Ivy. What ²_____ your name?
M: Miguel Hernandez.
I   And where ³_____ you from, Miguel? Spain?
M: No. I ⁴_____ from Mexico.
I: Which part?
M: Chihuahua. It ⁵_____ a city in the north.
I: ⁶_____ it nice?
M: Yeah. Some things ⁷_____ nice.
I: ⁸_____ it hot?
M: Now? No, it ⁹_____ not. In June, it's very hot. 30, 35.
I: OK. And what do you do?
M: Oh, I'm police.
I: Really? You ¹⁰_____ a police officer?
M: Yes.

DID YOU KNOW?
When we answer *Are you / Is it ...?* questions, we usually only say *yes* or *no*. Sometimes we add *I am / it is,* etc.
A: *Are you from here?*
B: *Yes, **I am**. / No, **I'm not**.*
A: *Is it cold outside?*
B: *Yes, **it is**. / No, **it isn't**.*
There is more practice on this in Unit 7.

Exercise 2
Put the words in the correct order.
1 teacher / a / French / I'm / .
2 where / from / you / are / ?
3 it / time / is / what / ?
4 not / sure / I'm / .
5 the / they / airport / are / at / .
6 big / it / is / a / not / place / .
7 are / grandparents / old / how / your / ?
8 winter / it / is / cold / in / ?

PRESENT SIMPLE

__I / you / we / they__
The present simple form is the same as the infinitive.
*I **go** swimming every day.*
*You **drink** a lot of coffee!*
*We **live** in the north of the country.*
*They **work** at the University of Salamanca.*

__it / he / she__
Add *-s* to the infinitive form.
*It rain**s** a lot in the winter. He like**s** swimming.*
*She want**s** to be a doctor.*

Look at these spelling changes for *he / she / it* forms.

*have – ha**s***	*do – do**es***	*try – tr**ies***
	*go – go**es***	*cry – cr**ies***

Negatives
I / you / we / they + __don't__ + infinitive
*I **don't like** the town very much.* (= do not)
*You **don't know** my town, I'm sure.*
*We **don't go** there a lot.*
*They **don't visit** us very often.*

he / she / it + __doesn't__ + infinitive
*He **doesn't have** any brothers or sisters.* (= does not)
*She **doesn't feel** safe.*
*It **doesn't snow** here.*

Questions
Do + I / you / we / they + infinitive
*Where **do I go** now?*
*Where **do you live**?*
*How **do we go there**?*
__Do they have__ any children?

Does + she / it / he / they + infinitive
*Where **does she work**?*
*When **does it start**? What **does he do**?*

Exercise 1
Choose the correct option.
1 She *work / works* for a big company.
2 Does he *like / likes* his job?
3 We *get up / gets up* at five every morning.
4 What time do *you / he* finish work?
5 Where *do / does* your grandparents live?
6 He's 40 and he *live / lives* with his mum.
7 I *doesn't / don't* like football.
8 My brother *have / has* three children.
9 It *don't / doesn't* rain a lot there.
10 How many cars do *he / they* have?

Exercise 2
Complete the questions.
1 Where _____ your parents live?
2 When _____ she finish work?
3 How many hours _____ your mum work every day?
4 What music _____ you like?
5 What _____ your father do?
6 Why _____ they like him? He's awful!

DID YOU KNOW?
When we answer *Do you / Does she ...?* questions, we usually only say *yes* or *no*.
Sometimes we add *I do / you don't / she doesn't*, etc.
A: *Do you enjoy your job?*
B: *Yes, **I do.** / No, **I don't.***

A: *Does he work with you?*
B: *Yes, **he does.** / No, **he doesn't.***
There is more practice on this in Unit 7.

Exercise 3
Complete the questions and answers with **do, does, don't** or **doesn't**.
1 A: What _____ you do?
  B: I'm a cleaner.
2 A: What _____ he do?
  B: I _____ know.
3 A: Where _____ your mother work?
  B: She _____ have a job at the moment.
4 A: Where _____ your parents live?
  B: Halifax.
5 A: _____ you enjoy working there?
  B: No, I _____.
6 A: We _____ live near my office, so I take the train to work.
  B: So what time _____ you leave home?
7 A: _____ they have any kids?
  B: Yes, they _____. Two, I think.

THERE IS ... / THERE ARE ...

With singular nouns

There	's	a / an	cinema. great museum. old church near here.
	isn't		park near here.
Is	there	a / an	café near here? airport?

With plural nouns

There	are	two some a lot of	cinemas. parks near here. shops in town.
	aren't	any a lot of	places for kids. shops.
Are	there	any	shops near here? people there?

Notice: *any* in questions and negatives, but *some* in positive sentences
You will learn more about *there is / there are* in Unit 2, Unit 3 and Unit 7.

Exercise 1
Choose the correct option.
1 *There's / There are* a cinema in the town.
2 It's nice. *There's / There are* a lot of trees and parks.
3 *There's / There are* a lot of hotels near the station.
4 *There's / There are* a beautiful river near here. I sometimes go swimming there.
5 It's not a bad place to live. *There's / There are* a nice feel to the area.
6 It's a nice city, but *there's / there are* a lot of cars!
7 *There's / There are* some nice shops and restaurants near here.
8 It's OK. *There's / There are* a nice beach and *there's / there are* a few cafés.

Exercise 2
Correct the mistake in each sentence.
1 Not there are any jobs here.
2 Have a lovely river in the town.
3 There are a lot expensive houses in this area.
4 There aren't good shops here.
5 Is a nice place to eat near here?
6 There is not cheap hotels in the centre.

REVISION

Exercise 1
Rewrite the sentences as negatives.
1 I like French food. _____ .
2 I'm hungry. _____ .
3 She works here. _____ .
4 They're from this country. _____ .
5 I work at the weekends. _____ .
6 He's in the office today. _____ .
7 They live together. _____ .
8 It's cold today. _____ .
9 There are some shops in the village. _____ .
10 There's a hotel near the airport. _____ .

Exercise 2
Complete the sentences with the present simple form of the verbs. Use short forms where possible.
1 She _____ sport. (not / like)
2 There _____ any nice shops near there. (not / be)
3 What time _____ you usually _____ your house in the morning? (leave)
4 There _____ a bank in the village. (not / be)
5 We _____ English. We _____ Scottish. (not / be, be)
6 _____ there a post office near here? (be)
7 My father _____ a new job. (have)
8 _____ they open today? (be)
9 I'm sorry. I _____. (not / understand)
10 Where _____ she _____? (live)

Exercise 3
Complete the sentences with one word in each space.
1 Where _____ you from?
2 Where _____ you work?
3 My sister _____ two children.
4 I _____ 26 and my sister _____ 33.
5 It's a nice house, but it _____ have a garden.
6 I _____ like shopping, but my wife loves it!
7 My boyfriend _____ a teacher. He _____ in a school in Graz.
8 _____ your mother work?

2 FREE TIME

VERB PATTERNS

A Some verbs are often followed by -ing.

I **love** play**ing** tennis.

He really **likes** swimm**ing**.

I **enjoy** work**ing** on my own.

I **hate** liv**ing** in the city.

Notice the spelling changes.

dan**ce** – dan**cing**	chat – cha**tting**
ha**ve** – ha**ving**	run – ru**nning**
li**ve** – li**ving**	swim – swi**mming**

B Some verbs are often followed by to + verb.

I don't **want to live** in an old building.

I want to **learn to drive**.

I **need to go** now.

Try to use the words you learn.

DID YOU KNOW?

These verbs can also be followed by nouns.

I **love** Mexico.

I **don't like** the traffic in my city.

Do you **want a drink**?

Try the food. It's great.

Exercise 1

Complete the sentences with the correct form of the verbs in brackets.

1 I don't like _swimming_ much. (swim)
2 Do you want _____ later? (go out)
3 I try _____ running every day. (go)
4 I hate _____ and I'm very bad at it. (dance)
5 How do you learn _____ a teacher? (be)
6 They really enjoy _____ music together. (play)
7 My dad loves _____ tennis. (play)
8 We need _____ where to have lunch. (decide)

DID YOU KNOW?

We also use -ing forms after prepositions such as at.

He's really good at learn**ing** languages.

I'm really bad at remember**ing** names.

Exercise 2

Correct the mistake in each sentence.

1 My brother really likes read.
2 I hate sing. I'm really bad at it.
3 My parents want have more free time.
4 I don't really enjoy to work in an office.
5 I always try go to bed before eleven.
6 I need finishing my homework before I go out.
7 I'm not very good at play the guitar.
8 She's bad at draw, but she enjoys doing it.

ADVERBS OF FREQUENCY

I	100%	always	
We		usually / normally	have a coffee after lunch.
They		often	
		sometimes	
He		occasionally	
She		hardly ever	has a coffee after lunch.
	0%	never	

Negatives

We use usually and often in negative sentences.

I **don't usually drink** coffee after six in the evening.

I **don't often go out**. / I **don't go out very often**.

Questions

Look at the adverbs we use to ask questions about frequency.

A: Where do you **usually** go out at night?

B: I normally go into town, but I sometimes go to the beach.

A: What do you **normally** do at the weekend?

B: I usually go to the countryside with my family.

We use ever to ask about habits. It means at any time.

A: Do you **ever** go to the theatre?

B: No, never.

A: Do you **ever** go swimming?

B: Occasionally, but not very often.

Exercise 1

Choose the best adverb.

1 I usually read novels, but I sometimes / normally read history books.
2 I don't earn much money, so I hardly ever / sometimes go out for dinner.
3 I really like football, but I never / often go and watch matches at the stadium.
4 My mum usually / always finishes work at six, but she sometimes works late – until eight or nine.
5 I never / occasionally drink coffee. I hate the taste and I think it's bad for your health.
6 I love cooking. I always / occasionally make dinner for my family.

Exercise 2

Put the adverb in the correct place in each sentence.

1 I sleep until twelve on Sunday mornings. (often)
2 My parents do sport. (hardly ever)
3 I don't go shopping. (very often)
4 I decide what to do in my family. (never)
5 A: Do you go out dancing? (ever)
   B: Yes, sometimes. With friends.
6 A: What time do you get up? (usually)
   B: At seven o'clock during the week.

COUNTABLE AND UNCOUNTABLE NOUNS

Countable nouns

+	I need I work in	a an	pencil. office.
	I need There are	some a lot of	new pens. cafés near here.
-	I don't need There isn't	a an	dictionary. airport near here.
	They don't have There aren't There aren't	any many a lot of	kids. places to sit. shops.
?	Do you have	a	sister?
	Are there Do you want	any some	places to eat near here? chips?

Uncountable nouns

+	There's There's	some a lot of	nice countryside near here. traffic today.
-	I don't have It's not There isn't	any much a lot of	money. homework. traffic.
?	Do you have Do you want	any some	paper? water?

Some other words which are often uncountable:
fish, food, fruit, help, news, time, paper, water

Exercise 1

Choose the correct option.

1 Do you have *some / a* dictionary?
2 Do you need *a / some* help?
3 A: Is it a good place to live?
   B: It's great. There are *a lot of / any* parks and trees, and there's not *much / many* traffic.
4 A: Do you want to take *any / a* break?
   B: No. We don't have *much / some* time.
5 A: Do you have *any / a* paper?
   B: Yes. How *much / many* do you want?
6 A: Do you want *a / any* fruit?
   B: Yes, please. Do you have *an / any* oranges?

DID YOU KNOW?

Liquids are usually uncountable, but in cafés, etc. we talk about drinks as countable.

A coffee and three hot chocolates.

Here's some coffee.

one and some

When we answer questions about nouns, we don't usually say the noun again. Instead, we replace singular nouns with *one* – and plural / uncountable nouns with *some*.

A: *Is there a bank near here?*
B: *Yes – there's **one** on the next road.*

A: *Do you have any tissues?*
B: *Yes – there are **some** on the table there.*

Exercise 2

Complete the answers with *one* or *some*.

1 A: Do you have a pen?
   B: I think there's _____ on the table.
2 A: Do you have any money with you?
   B: Yeah, I have _____ . How much do you need?
3 A: Does Jessica want a cup of coffee?
   B: No, she has _____ already.
4 A: Do you have any water?
   B: No, sorry. I think Gary has _____.
5 A: Do you have any tissues?
   B: No, but you can get _____ from the bathroom.

Don't worry if you are still not sure about this grammar. There are lots more examples in the book and there's more practice in Unit 3, Unit 6 and Unit 10.

REVISION

Exercise 1

Complete the sentences with these pairs of words. You might need to change the order.

want + very often	often + like
love + usually	hate + always
hate + never	hardly ever + need

1 I _____ doing sport. I _____ do something – swimming or running or tennis – every day.
2 I'm not very fit because I _____ do any exercise. I _____ to join a gym or something.
3 I _____ to have more free time. I don't go out _____.
4 I _____ cook dinner for my parents. I _____ doing it.
5 I _____ getting up early. I _____ get up before eleven at the weekends.
6 I _____ being late. I _____ get to school early.

Exercise 2

Put the words in the correct order to make sentences.

1 new / like / I / meeting / people / .
2 I / to / game / buy / a / want / computer / .
3 to / do / you / music / listening / like / ?
4 go / I / cinema / to / the / hardly / ever / .
5 chat / sometimes / on / I / internet / the / .
6 I / Wednesdays / play / on / tennis / usually / .
7 get / usually / what / time / you / home / do / ?
8 you / dancing / go / do / out / ever / ?

Exercise 3

Write questions with *a / an / any*.

1 you / have / white paper?
2 he / have / job / at the moment?
3 you / want / tissue?
4 you / need / alarm clock?
5 you / have / scissors?
6 you / need / help?

3 HOME

PREPOSITIONS OF PLACE

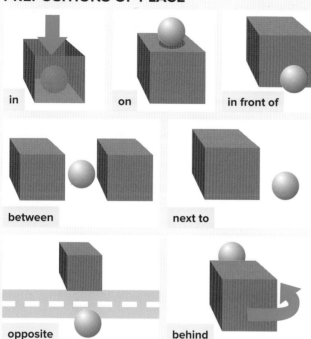

in   **on**   **in front of**

between   **next to**

opposite   **behind**

Many languages do not have different words for *in* and *on* or *to* and *at*. A good way to learn these is by learning phrases.

on
It's **on the left.**   It's **on the right.**
There's a café **on the corner of** *Fairfax Road.*
I live **on this street** / **on Broad Road.**

in
He's **in his bedroom** *playing computer games.*
Let's sit **in the kitchen.**
I work **in a department store.**
There's a bus stop **in front of** the hotel.

at
It's **at the end of the road.**
He's not here. He's **at work.**
Wait **at the bus stop.**

to
There's a bookshop **next to** the school.

Exercise 1
Complete the sentences with one word in each space.

1 There's a big car park _____ the end of this road.
2 He spends a lot of time _____ his room.
3 My house is number 53. It's _____ the left.
4 There's a new supermarket _____ the corner of Station Road and Queens Road.
5 My sister lives _____ the next street.
6 My office is _____ to the big bank in town.
7 There's a good café _____ this road.
8 There are lots of places to eat _____ the area.
9 It's small. It's _____ two restaurants – a fast food place on one side and a French place on the other.
10 There's a bank with a cash machine _____ Blackstock Road – _____ the right.

DID YOU KNOW?
We often say *I'll meet you* when arranging where to meet.
A: **I'll meet you** *in the restaurant at nine.*
B: *OK.*

Exercise 2
Write sentences beginning *I'll meet you* using the pictures and your own ideas.

PRONOUNS, POSSESSIVE ADJECTIVES AND 'S

Subject	Object	Possessive
I	*me*	*my book*
you	*you*	*your book*
he	*him*	*his book*
she	*her*	*her book*
it	*it*	*its food*
we	*us*	*our book*
they	*them*	*their book*

Possessive adjective + noun
her family   his car   their problem

Do you like **my jacket**? *It's new.*
Our house *is very near here.*

Name or noun + 's + noun
Maria's family   NOT   ~~the family of Maria~~
my dad's car   NOT   ~~the car of my dad~~
the school's problem NOT   ~~the problem of the school~~

Plural noun + ' + noun
my friends' house   his parents' wedding

Exercise 1
Choose the correct option.

1 *You / Your* house is really nice.
2 *Their / Them* house is next to the sea.
3 *She / Her* shares a flat with a friend.
4 Come and visit *we / us* soon.
5 *My parents' car / My car's parents* is very old.
6 I really like Andrew's flat. *Its / It's* really big.
7 The woman in the photo is my aunt. She's my *mum's / mums'* sister.
8 *They / them* are late. Can you drive *they / them* to the station?

DID YOU KNOW?

We can use a noun or name + *'s / s'* without a noun.

A: *Is this your book?*

B: *No, it's **Kenji's**.* (= Kenji's book)

A: *Is that your car?*

B: *No it's my **parents'**.* (= my parents' car)

Exercise 2

Correct the mistakes in the underlined phrases.

1 Where do <u>yours parents</u> live?
2 <u>My dads' part</u> of the family are from Malta.
3 What's <u>they address</u>?
4 <u>The sister of my boyfriend</u> lives with us.
5 It's not my money; it's <u>of Andrew</u>.
6 I don't like the <u>government ideas</u>.

CAN / CAN'T

Can and *can't* have the same form for all persons.
Can and *can't* are followed by the infinitive.

- If something is possible, use *can*.
  *I can **drive** you to the station.*
  *You can **sit** where you want.*
  *He / she can **start** tomorrow.*

- If something is not possible, use *can't*.
  *I can't **do** the exercise.*
  *He / She can't **hear** it.*
  *We / They can't **come** to the class.*

- To ask (someone) to do something, use *can* (I / you).
  *Can I **stay** here?*
  *Can you **open** the window?*

Look at these common answers to questions with *can*.

+	–
Yeah, of course.	*No. Sorry.*
Sure.	*I'm afraid not.*
Go ahead.	*Sorry, you / I can't.*

Exercise 1

Write questions with *Can I …?* or *Can you …?* and the words in brackets.

1 A: I can't see the TV. (move)
   B: Yeah, of course. There. Is that better?
2 A: I need to do some shopping. (take me in the car)
   B: I'm afraid not. I'm busy.
3 A: I can't speak now. (phone you later)
   B: Yes, of course. Call me after six.
4 A: Dinner's ready. (set the table)
   B: Sure.
5 A: I'm hot. (open the window)
   B: Yes, of course. Go ahead.
6 A: I need to eat something. (make a sandwich)
   B: No, I'm afraid not. I don't have any bread. Sorry.

Exercise 2

Complete sentences about the pictures using *can* or *can't*.

1 You _____ watch it. You're only sixteen.
2 You _____ smoke in here.
3 Sorry, but you _____ use your mobile phone in here.
4 You _____ pay here. You need to go over there.
5 We _____ eat over there. They have a picnic area.
6 You _____ use this telephone if you want to.

REVISION

Exercise 1

Complete the sentences with one word in each space.

1 A: Is _____ a post office near here?
   B: Yes, there's _____ at the end of the road, _____ the church.
2 A: Is there a restaurant _____ the village?
   B: No, but there's a pub _____ this road, _____ to the shop.
3 A: Where's the bus stop to go to town?
   B: _____'s just there – in _____ of the café _____ the right.

Exercise 2

Complete the second sentence using *'s, s'* or a possessive adjective. The first two are done for you.

1 The car belongs to me. It's ___*my*___ car.
2 My parents own it. It's *my parents'*.
3 That jacket belongs to him. It's _____ jacket.
4 The shoes belong to Steve. They're _____ shoes.
5 The chairs belong to them. They're _____ chairs.
6 The computer belongs to the school. It's the _____ computer.
7 My brothers own the flat. It's my _____ flat.
8 Does that book belong to you? Is that _____ book?
9 We own the house. It's _____ house.
10 The sofa belongs to her. It's _____ sofa.

Exercise 3

Choose the correct option.

1 A: I *can / can't* find my notebook.
   B: It's *on / in* the table, *between / opposite* the dictionary and the black book. I put it there.
   A: Oh right. *Can / Do* you pass it to me?
   B: Sure.
2 A: Who are the two boys in the photo?
   B: The one *on / in* the left is *my / me* son, and the other boy is one of *her / his / he* friends.
   A: Is that your *son's / sons'* guitar?
   B: Yes, but he *can / can't* play it.

4 HOLIDAYS

PAST SIMPLE

be

I / He / She / It	**was**	late.
You / We / They	**were**	here.

There	**was**	a cinema here before. a lot of traffic.
There	**were**	lots of people. ten students here yesterday.

Regular verbs

Add -*ed* to the infinitive form of the verb.
Add -*d* when the infinitive form ends in -*e*.
I **played** tennis and really **loved** it.
I **cooked** dinner and then **watched** TV.
I **stayed** with a friend. She **showed** me the town.

Notice these spellings.

try	try + **-ied**	> tried
like	like + **d**	> liked
chat	chat + **t** + **-ed**	> chatted
stop	stop + **p** + **-ed**	> stopped

Irregular verbs

Infinitive form	Past simple form
be	was / were
buy	bought
come	came
do	did
get	got
go	went
have	had
read	read
see	saw
spend	spent
take	took

To learn more irregular past simple forms, see page 191.

Time phrases often used with the past simple

yesterday	yesterday morning	last night
two days ago	last week	a few weeks ago
last year	five years ago	when I was 16

Exercise 1
Underline the irregular past forms and write the infinitive form of the verbs at the end of the sentence. The first one is done for you.

1 I felt ill, so I went home.
   feel, go
2 I went shopping and got some new boots.
3 I was lucky. I found €20 on the pavement.
4 I slept badly because I drank too much coffee.
5 We met at school. I sat next to her in class.
6 I spent three years in Japan. I taught English there.
7 I saw her yesterday and she said hello to you.
8 My son made dinner for us yesterday. It wasn't great, but I ate it.
9 She told me she swam five miles last Saturday.

Exercise 2
Complete the story with the past simple form of the verbs in brackets.

This summer, I [1]_____ (go) to the beach with some friends and we [2]_____ (make) a fire. We [3]_____ (sit) round the fire all night and [4]_____ (eat) lots of food, [5]_____ (talk), [6]_____ (tell) jokes and [7]_____ (laugh) a lot. At six in the morning, we [8]_____ (watch) the sun coming up. It [9]_____ (be) beautiful. We really [10]_____ (love) it. Then we [11]_____ (swim) in the sea. We [12]_____ (be) very cold afterwards! I [13]_____ (get) home at nine o'clock in the morning. I [14]_____ (have) breakfast and then I [15]_____ (sleep) until five in the afternoon!

PAST SIMPLE NEGATIVES

be

I / He / She / It	**wasn't**	very warm. in Moscow at that time.
You / We / They	**weren't**	happy about it.

There	**wasn't**	time to do it.
There	**weren't**	many cars on the road.

Other verbs

I		**go** out for dinner.
You		**try** very hard.
He / She	**didn't**	**come** yesterday.
We		**go** shopping.
They		**want** to talk about it.

Exercise 1
Complete the sentences with *didn't*, *wasn't* or *weren't*.

1 Sorry. I _____ hear you. Can you say it again?
2 Sorry I _____ clear. It was my mistake.
3 Sorry I _____ buy you a present.
4 Sorry there _____ more people at the party.
5 Sorry I _____ there. I was at work that night.
6 Sorry I _____ see you on Friday. I left early.
7 Sorry I _____ do my homework. I was busy.
8 Sorry there _____ anyone at the airport to meet you.
9 Sorry to hear you _____ well last week. Are you OK now?
10 Sorry I _____ call you yesterday. I forgot.

any

We use *any* + noun in negative sentences (and questions).
There wasn't **any traffic**.
They didn't have **any oranges**. Sorry.
Did the teacher give us **any homework**?

We also use *anyone*, *anywhere* and *anything* in negative sentences and questions.

anyone = any people
anywhere = any places
anything = any things

Exercise 2

Add *any*, *anyone*, *anything* or *anywhere* in the correct place in each sentence.

1 There weren't cheap hotels in the old town, so we stayed outside the city.
2 I was only in Cairo for two days. I didn't have time to see.
3 I didn't email or phone for two weeks! It was good to relax.
4 I was very tired, so I didn't do last night.
5 I didn't go on Sunday. I just stayed at home and relaxed.
6 We stayed in the mountains. We didn't see for almost a week.
7 I looked in ten different shops, but I couldn't find wine.
8 He didn't try local food. He just ate burgers all week.

DID YOU KNOW?

We often use *not very* + adjective / adverb.
It was**n't very** warm.
We did**n't** go **very** far.

Exercise 3

Replace the words in italics using *not* + *very* + the words in brackets.

1 The hotel *was a long way from* the sea.
  The hotel wasn't very near the sea.
2 We *went* to bed *early*. (late)
3 The hotel *was expensive*. (cheap)
4 I *had a quiet* weekend. (busy)
5 People *were unfriendly*. (friendly)
6 We *stayed a short* time. (long)
7 My parents *were annoyed*. (happy)
8 The water in the room *was cold*. (hot)

PAST SIMPLE QUESTIONS

be

	Was	it / he / she	OK?
How Where What time	**was**	the holiday? the hotel? the flight?	
	Were	you / they	OK?
When Who	**were**	you they?	there?

Other verbs

	Did	I you	**tell** you? **ask** him?
What time How long Who Where How	**did**	he it she we they	**get** home? **rain** for? **go** with? **meet** you before? **get back**?

any

We often use *any* + noun, *anything*, *anyone* or *anywhere* in questions.
*Were there **any** nice **beaches** there?*
*Did you go **anywhere** nice for your holiday?*
*Did you go with **anyone**?*
*Did you buy **anything** nice?*

Exercise 1

Put the words in the correct order to make questions.

1 did / what / last / do / you / night / ?
2 see / you / what / did / film / ?
3 it / good / was / ?
4 did / go / who / with / you / ?
5 where / you / your / buy / shoes / did / ?
6 they / very / were / expensive / ?
7 get / did / you / else / anything / ?
8 there / you / do / usually / go / shopping / ?

Exercise 2

Match the answers a–h to the questions in Exercise 1.

a *Four Seasons.* It's a love story.
b No, not really. They were €50.
c No, I didn't have any more money.
d Yes, it was really good.
e No, I don't. That was the first time.
f I went to the cinema.
g I went on my own, actually.
h In Jenson's, the department store in town.

When we answer *Were you ...? Did you ...?* questions, we usually only say *yes* or *no*.
Sometimes we add *I was / wasn't* or *I did / didn't*.
A: *Were you late?*
B: *Yes,* **I was**. / **No, I wasn't.**

A: *Did you go out yesterday?*
B: *Yes,* **I did**. *I went to the park / No,* **I didn't**. *I was tired.*

There is more practice on this in Unit 7.

REVISION

Exercise 1

Write the past forms of the verbs.

1 work	6 stay	11 see
2 meet	7 put	12 walk
3 make	8 sit	13 play
4 move	9 stop	14 study
5 want	10 try	15 can

Exercise 2

Complete the pairs of sentences with a past and a present form of the verbs in the box.

be	have	get	know
go	leave	feel	sleep

1 a They usually _____ to the cinema at the weekend.
  b We _____ walking in the mountains yesterday.
2 a I'm sure I _____ my keys here a moment ago.
  b _____ your things there on the table.
3 a Can I go? I _____ ill.
  b She _____ ill in the class and went home.
4 a We _____ a party for my son last night.
  b _____ a nice day!
5 a It _____ really wet when we were on holiday.
  b It _____ lovely weather today!
6 a I normally _____ home at seven.
  b I _____ home at five this morning.
7 a Put your hand up if you _____ the answer.
  b I _____ him well at school, but that was years ago.
8 a He usually _____ very well, but last night he didn't.
  b She was really tired, so she _____ during the flight.

Exercise 3
Write the full conversation using the notes.

1 A: Where / you / go / on holiday?
2 B: We / go / to the Czech Republic.
3 A: you / stay / in Prague?
4 B: No / we / not. We / rent / an apartment / in the mountains.
5 A: it / nice?
6 B: Yes, it / be. We / have / a great time.
7 A: What / you / do?
8 B: We / not do / much. We / read, / we / swim / in the lake / – just relax.
9 A: you / like / the food?
10 B: Yes / we / love / it! We / eat out / a lot.
11 A: How long / you / be / there?
12 B: Two weeks. We / arrive / back yesterday.

5 SHOPS

THAT / THIS / THESE / THOSE

1 This apple is nice.

2 That cake looks good.

3 I like these ones.

4 Those jeans are expensive.

Singular and uncountable nouns	
This	*is OK.* **orange** *is very sweet.* **music** *is good.* **one** *is nice*
That	*'s my book!* **T-shirt** *looks good on you.* **coffee** *was nice.* **one**, *please.*

Plural nouns	
These	**are** *fine.* **jeans** *feel good.* **ones** *are quite cheap.*
Those	**are** *my shoes!* **people** *didn't do anything.* **ones** *look OK.*

DID YOU KNOW?
After *this / these*, etc. we often replace the noun with *one* or *ones*.

Exercise 1
Choose the correct option.

1 *That / Those* jacket's nice. Is it leather?
2 Do you like *this / these* dress?
3 How much *is / are* those jeans? The black ones at the back.
4 These *one / ones* are fine for me. Thanks.
5 These *is / are* very big.
6 Can you pass me *this / that* pen on the table?
7 Did you know all *these / those* people at the party?
8 Here, listen to *this / that* song. I love it.

one / ones
We use *one / ones* instead of a noun. We often describe the noun using an adjectives before *one / ones*.
*I don't like the **red T-shirt**. I prefer the **blue one**.*
A: *Which **cakes** do you want? These **ones**?*
B: *No, those small **ones there**.*

Exercise 2
Replace the nouns in 1–6 with *one / ones*, where possible.

1 A: Which cake do you want?
   B: The cake with pink stuff on top.
2 A: Those jeans look OK, but I prefer the other jeans you tried on before.
   B: What about these black jeans?
   A: Yeah – they're nice as well. Which jeans are cheaper?
3 A: How much are the apples?
   B: The red apples are five euros a kilo and the green apples are 4.50.
4 A: Excuse me. You see these jumpers – do you have this jumper in a medium?
   B: No. Sorry. There are only extra large jumpers or the small size. That's why they're in the sale!

PRESENT CONTINUOUS
The present continuous uses a form of *be + -ing*.

I	**am**		**working** *very hard.*
She / He / It	**is**	*not*	**trying**.
You / We / They	**are**		**improving**.

Am	*I*	**improving** *at all?*
Are	*you / they*	**working** *hard?*
Is	*she / he* *it*	**getting** *tired?* **snowing**?

We often use contractions – *I'm / she's / they're / who's*, etc. You can also use the negatives *aren't* and *isn't*.
I'm *working.*   **What's** *he doing?*
*She **isn't** staying.*   *We **aren't** doing anything.*
*The shops in town **aren't having** any sales at the moment.*

Notice these spelling changes.
*have – hav**ing**   improve – improv**ing***
*give – giv**ing**   leave – leav**ing***
Some verbs double the final letter.
*get – ge**tt**ing   stop – sto**pp**ing*
*set – se**tt**ing   run – ru**nn**ing*

at the moment
At the moment shows actions or situations are temporary and not finished, so it usually goes with the present continuous. We often also use *now*.

Exercise 1

Make present continuous sentences using the notes.

1 Can you come back later? I / make / dinner.
2 Where / he / go / now?
3 you / look for / something?
4 She / talk / to her mother on the phone.
5 They / build / some apartments opposite my house.
6 Shhh! The baby / sleep.
7 He's not ready. He / get / dressed.
8 I / not go / outside now. It / rain.

PRESENT SIMPLE / PRESENT CONTINUOUS

Present simple

- for habits
  I usually / often / sometimes / hardly ever / never do it.
- for things in your life you see as permanent
  *I'm an English teacher. I **work** in a secondary school in Prague.*
- with some verbs: *know, think, want, like, hate,* etc. to show our opinions
  *I **like** helping people to find nice clothes.*
  *I **don't really know** what I **want** to do in the future.*
- with *have* for possessions
  *I **don't have** a car.*

Present continuous

- if an action or situation is temporary and not finished
  I'm looking for a job at the moment.
  Can you be quiet? I'm working!

Exercise 2

Choose the present simple or the present continuous form.

1 A: What *do you do / are you doing*?
   B: I'm a manager of a shop.
2 A: *Do your parents live / Are your parents living* near here?
   B: Yes – their house is on the next street!
3 A: Can you help me?
   B: Yeah, just a minute. *I write / I'm writing* an email.
4 A: I can't see you.
   B: Look to your left. *I sit / I'm sitting* by the window.
5 A: What *do you look / are you looking* for?
   B: My mobile phone. *I think / I'm thinking* I left it here.
6 A: Where's Tommy?
   B: *He just brushes / He's just brushing* his teeth. *Do you want / Are you wanting* a drink before we go?
   A: OK. Maybe some water. I am quite thirsty.

There is more practice on present continuous and differences with present simple in Unit 6, Unit 8 and Unit 15.

REVISION

Exercise 1

Complete the dialogues with one word in each space.

1 A: Where are you?
   B: I _____ waiting for you! I'm in the café _____ the second floor.
   A: Oh, OK. I'm _____ now!
2 A: I bought you a coffee.
   B: OK – Is it this _____ with milk?
   A: Yeah. And do you want one of _____ biscuits?
   B: Oh – no, thanks. I'm fine.
3 A: So where _____ we going now?
   B: _____ you want to go and look at the coats? _____ one I'm wearing is so old!
   A: Yeah, OK. Did you see _____ ones in the window?

Exercise 2

Add the correct form of *be* in the sentences. The first one is done for you.

1 What you trying to do?
   *What **are** you trying to do?*
2 Who Tamara talking to?
3 I looking for a job at the moment.
4 I not feeling very well.
5 you waiting for someone?
6 You making a mess. Clean the table when you finish.
7 He went into town. He doing some shopping.
8 Henry and Terry not coming, so we can start the meeting now.

Exercise 3

Correct the mistake in each sentence.

1 We're stay in the Grand Hotel.
2 I not am working at the moment.
3 Who are that people over there?
4 What she's doing in Australia?
5 They're haveing a meeting.
6 Can I have that one red?

6 STUDYING

MODIFIERS

Modifiers go before adjectives.

It's They're	**very / really** *good.* *good.* **quite** *good.* **not very** *good.*	👍 (= great) ↓ 👎 (= bad)

Exercise 1

Add the modifier in brackets in the correct place.

1 It's cold in here. Can we turn on the heating? (quite)
2 Thanks for inviting us. We had a great time. (really)
3 It isn't interesting. We always do the same things. (very)
4 He's OK, I guess, but he's strange! (quite)
5 He's good at sciences. He gets A grades. (really)
6 My teachers were helpful, so that made the course easier. (very)

DID YOU KNOW?

With adjectives that have a negative meaning, we can use *a bit* instead of *quite*.
*It's **a bit** / **quite** expensive.*
*It's ~~a bit~~ **quite** good.*

Exercise 2

Decide where you can use *a bit* instead of *quite*.

1 I found the course quite interesting. We did a lot of different things.
2 The exam was quite long – and quite difficult. I don't think I passed.
3 The college building is quite modern.
4 I know some people enjoyed it, but I found it quite boring.
5 He's quite nice, but he's quite lazy too!
6 It's quite important for me to pass the exam.
7 It's a good course. It's quite popular.
8 She's a good teacher, but quite strange sometimes.

COMPARATIVES

To compare two things, use a comparative adjective + *than*.

He's **taller than** his brother.

English is **easier than** Russian.

Bilinguals are **more creative** than other people.

I think History is **better than** Geography.

-er

Add *-er* to short adjectives (one syllable).

cheap – cheap**er**   hard – hard**er**

tall – tall**er**

Notice these spellings.

nic**e** – nic**er**   strang**e** – strang**er**

Some adjectives double the final letter.

ho**t** – ho**tt**er   bi**g** – bi**gg**er

-ier

For adjectives ending in *-y*, change *-y* to *-ier*.

easy – eas**ier**   lazy – laz**ier**

friendly – friendl**ier**

more

For longer adjectives (two or more syllables) use *more*.

interesting   **more** interesting

expensive   **more** expensive

popular   **more** popular

boring   **more** boring

Irregular comparatives

good – better   bad – worse   far – further

Exercise 1

Complete the sentences with the comparative form of the adjectives in brackets.

1 I think English is _____ to learn than German. (easy)
2 My brother's a bit _____ than me. (short)
3 Basketball is _____ than football in my country. (popular)
4 I think the people in the south are _____ than the people in the north. (friendly)
5 The weather is _____ in my country than here. It's _____. (bad, cold)
6 The TV is _____ here. The programmes are much _____. (good, interesting)
7 It's _____ to pass exams now. (difficult)

DID YOU KNOW?

We use *much* (= a lot) or *a bit* (= a little) with comparatives.

It's **much better**.   It's **a bit easier**.

Exercise 2

Complete the sentences with the comparative form of the adjective in brackets.

1 My English is getting much _____. (good)
2 The climate is becoming _____. (warm)
3 The situation is getting much _____. (bad)
4 Apartments are becoming a bit _____. (expensive)
5 The population is getting _____. (big)

REVISION

Exercise 1

Rewrite the sentences with an adjective in the box + *not very*.

interesting	warm	big	good

1 The film's quite bad.
2 The class was a bit boring.
3 The school's quite small.
4 I'm quite cold.

Rewrite the sentences 5–8 with an adjective in the box + *quite*.

cheap	difficult	low	near

5 The exam wasn't very easy.
6 The rent for my flat isn't very expensive.
7 The school I work for isn't very far from here.
8 He didn't get very high grades.

Exercise 2

Make comparisons using the verb *be* and a comparative form. The first one is done for you.

1 He / messy / me
    He's messier than me.
2 Your class / a high level / mine
3 You / good at sciences / me
4 Chinese / useful / French
5 My daughter / tall / my son
6 My dad / tidy / my mum
7 This year / difficult / last year
8 My exam results / bad / yours

Exercise 3

Complete the conversation with one word in each space.

A: How's your course going? You said you found it ¹_____ hard last year.

B: It ²_____ getting easier. It's still a ³_____ difficult, but my teachers are much better ⁴_____ last year. Last year, the teachers weren't ⁵_____ patient, but this year they are ⁶_____ helpful.

7 PEOPLE I KNOW

AUXILIARY VERBS

We can use auxiliary verbs in short answers. They help us avoid repeating information.

Are you over 18?	Yes, I **am**. / No, I**'m not**.
Is he staying with you?	Yes, he **is**. / No, he **isn't**.
Do you live near here?	Yes, I **do**. / No, I **don't**.
Did you get the tickets?	Yes, I **did**. / No, I **didn't**.
Can you see the board?	Yes, I **can**. / No, I **can't**.

We can also use auxiliary verbs when comparing things using *but* and *so* / *too*.
My brother went to the party, **but** I **didn't**.
I can drive, **but** my husband **can't**.
I'm quite tall, and my sister **is too**.
I speak French and **so does** my son, **but** my husband **doesn't**.

Exercise 1
Choose the correct option.

1 A: Can you take me to the airport later?
 B: I'm sorry, but I *can* / *can't*. I'm busy.
2 A: Did you see the film on Channel Six last night?
 B: Yes, *I saw the film* / *I did*. It was really good.
3 A: Do you two like football?
 B: I *did* / *do*, yes, but Jack *don't* / *doesn't*.
4 A: Are you feeling OK?
 B: No, *I aren't* / *I'm not*, actually. I've got a bad headache.
5 A: Do your children still live at home with you?
 B: My son *lives* / *does* / *do*, yes, but my daughter left home last year.
6 I stayed till the end of the party, but Tom *don't* / *didn't*.
7 Thanks for the present. I love it and the kids *do* / *love* too.
8 If he can become president, then so *can* / *do* I.

We can also use auxiliaries to correct information when we reply to something we think is wrong.
A: *I'm sure they have children.*
B: They **don't** ~~have children~~!

A: *He just doesn't like me very much.*
B: He **does** ~~like you~~. He's just not very good at showing his feelings.

Exercise 2
Complete the replies with the correct form of *be*, *do* or *can*.

1 A: I'm sure Russ isn't from New Zealand.
 B: He _____. He was born there. He told me!
2 A: She doesn't know what she's doing.
 B: She _____! You just need to give her more time.
3 A: I'm sure we saw that film together before.
 B: No, we _____. I don't remember anything about it!
4 A: We can't sit here.
 B: We _____. I mean, there's nothing to say we _____!
5 A: That's a really bad idea!
 B: No it _____! It's good.
6 A: You didn't put the milk back in the fridge last night.
 B: Yes, I _____. Maybe someone else took it out after me.

HAVE TO / DON'T HAVE TO

Have to / *has to* shows it's necessary to do something.
We have a dishwasher and I **have to fill** it and empty it.
My son Travis brings the kids to my house three days a week – when **he has to work**.

Don't have to / *doesn't have to* shows it's not necessary to do something. It means you can choose to do it.
My friends don't have to do jobs in the home.
I'm happy that she has a job and **doesn't have to** stay at home all the time.

Make questions like this:
Do you / I / we **have to do** it?   **Does** she / he **have to go**?

Exercise 1
Choose the correct option.

1 I can't come to the cinema with you. I *have to* / *don't have to* pick up my little brother from school.
2 It's your dog, so you *have to* / *don't have to* feed it and take it for walks.
3 My dad sometimes *has to* / *doesn't have to* work really long hours.
4 I set the table this morning. You *have to* / *don't have to* do it now. It's your turn.
5 Tell Simon he *has to* / *doesn't have to* pick me up. I already got a taxi.
6 I'm afraid I can't repair it. You *have to* / *don't have to* take it to a shop.
7 We *have to* / *don't have to* play computer games if you don't want to. We can do something else.
8 He's very ill. He *has to* / *doesn't have to* go to hospital.
9 I love spending time with my sister's kids. I tell them stories and we *sing* / *have to sing* songs together. It's fun.
10 It's good that we eat together as a family. We chat and *have to tell* / *tell* jokes to each other. It's nice.

Exercise 2
Complete the sentences with the correct form of *have to* or *don't have to* and the verbs in the box.

do	go	leave	wait	work

1 It's late. I _____ now. I don't want to miss my bus.
2 Start eating. You _____ for me.
3 My son _____ a lot of homework. He says it's hard.
4 Tomorrow is a public holiday, but our boss said we all _____. It's not fair.
5 She _____ to school tomorrow. It's a public holiday.

REVISION

Exercise 1
A Match the questions (1–6) to the answers (a–f).

1 Is your cousin working here?
2 Were you angry about it?
3 Are they very similar?
4 Can you speak French?
5 Does she have a boyfriend at the moment?
6 Did she have a good time?

a No, she doesn't.
b No, I can't.
c Yes, she is.
d Yes, she did.
e No, they aren't really.
f Yes, I was.

B Now write opposite answers for questions 1–6.

Exercise 2

Replace the words in italics with *do*, *does* or *did*. The first one is done for you.

1 I studied marketing at university and my brother *did* ~~studied marketing~~ too.
2 My father doesn't like sweet things, but I *like sweet things*.
3 We don't usually eat together during the week, but we always *eat together* on Sunday.
4 I didn't write any notes, but Juan *wrote some notes*.
5 I don't have any money, but my sister *has some money*.
6 You went to Hill School! I *went to Hill School* too!

Exercise 3

Write the second sentence using the words in brackets and the correct form of *have to* or *don't have to*.

1 Sorry, I can't talk now. (I / go.)
2 Johan says sorry he can't come. (He / work late.)
3 Is it an important exam? (you / pass it?)
4 She's lucky. (She / travel far to get to work.)
5 I'm bored. (we / stay?)
6 We can stay quite late. (We / get up early tomorrow.)

8 PLANS

GOING TO

We use the present form of the verb *be* + *going to* + infinitive to talk about the future – especially the plans we have.

I	am		start work this week.
You We They	are	(not) going to	work with me. stay in a hotel. arrive tomorrow night.
He She It	is		finish school this year. study Fashion. take a very long time.

We usually use contractions – *I'm, you're, she's, it's, we're, they're*, etc. You can also use the negatives *aren't* / *isn't*.

Questions

Am I		see you later?
Are you Are we Are they	going to	stay here? eat later? meet us?
Is he Is she Is it		come with us? get a taxi there? be expensive?

Exercise 1

Match the questions (1–6) to the answers (a–f).

1 What are you going to do later?
2 What time are you going to leave?
3 Where are you going to stay?
4 How are you going to get there?
5 How long are you going to stay?
6 Why aren't you going to come?

a I think we're going to get a taxi.
b Nothing. I'm going to go to bed early. I'm very tired.
c Three weeks. I'm going to come back on the 30th.
d We're going to be at a friend's for a week, then in Rome.
e I'm not going to be here. I'm going to go to Zurich that day.
f The flight is at seven so the taxi's going to collect us at four.

Look at these future time words and phrases we use with *going to*.

in a minute	*soon*	*tonight*	*next week*
in an hour	*later*	*tomorrow*	*next year*

Exercise 2

Complete the sentences with the correct form of *going to*.

1 We _____ (go) for a run in the park later.
2 My grandparents _____ (celebrate) 50 years together next month.
3 I think I _____ (get) a taxi home.
4 He _____ (not / like) your decision.
5 Where _____ (your cousins / stay)?
6 How long _____ (it / take)?
7 Where _____ (you / meet) Abdul?
8 I _____ (miss) you. I _____ (not / see) you for a long time.

Exercise 3

Correct each sentence by adding one word.

1 I'm not to do anything special tonight.
2 How are you going get home?
3 Where they going to go on holiday this year?
4 What your sister going to study?
5 How much it going to cost?
6 I going to have dinner with my parents tonight.

WOULD LIKE TO + INFINITIVE

We use *would like* (or *love*) *to* + infinitive to talk about things we want – or hope – to do in the future.
He'd like to / *love to spend less time working.*
I wouldn't like to be him!

With *would like to* we often use time phrases like *one day, sometime in the future, sometime in the next few years*.
We'd like to move to a bigger house sometime in the next few years.
Would you like to have dinner with me tomorrow night?

Exercise 1

Complete the sentences with the pairs of words in the box.

get + lose	leave + get	save + buy
learn + go	retire + relax	start + become

1 I'd like to _____ fitter and maybe _____ some weight.
2 I'd like to _____ sometime in the next ten years and then I'd just like to _____ more.
3 I'd like to _____ Arabic and _____ to Egypt.
4 I'd like to _____ my own business and _____ a successful businessperson.
5 I'd like to _____ home and _____ my own apartment.
6 I'd really like to _____ some money and _____ a car.

DID YOU KNOW?

We can offer people things using *would you like* + a noun. It means the same as *do you want* ..., but it is more polite.

Exercise 2

A Rewrite the questions using *would like*.

1 Do you want a cup of tea? _____?
2 Do you want a seat? _____?
3 Do you want a cigarette? _____?
4 Do you want a drink? _____?
5 Do you want some more cake? _____?
6 Do you want milk in your coffee? _____?

B Match the answers a–f to the questions in A.

a No, thanks. I don't smoke.
b I prefer coffee if you have any.
c No, thanks. I can't. I have to drive later.
d No, thanks. I can't. I'm full.
e No thanks. I like it black.
f Oh, thank you. That's very kind of you. Now I can rest my legs!

REVISION

Exercise 1

Complete the sentences with one word in each space.

1 Where _____ your brother going to study?
2 I'd really like _____ learn Spanish.
3 It's an OK city, but I wouldn't _____ to live there.
4 We _____ going to have a party on Friday.
5 What _____ you like to eat tonight?
6 I'm just going _____ go home and sleep.
7 When _____ your parents going to arrive?
8 I'm _____ going to tell you again!

Exercise 2

Choose the correct option.

1 *I wouldn't like to / I'm not going to* come to the meeting tomorrow. I have to be somewhere else.
2 *I'd like to / I'm going to* learn to drive, but I don't have enough money.
3 *I'd like to / I'm going to* go to the concert tomorrow. A friend bought me a ticket.
4 *I wouldn't like to / I'm not going to* be her!
5 *Would you like to / Are you going to* see my holiday photos?
6 Sorry. I can't come to the class tomorrow. *I'd like to / I'm going to* go to the dentist.

Exercise 3

Put the underlined words in the correct order to make time phrases.

1 I'm going to see my grandparents *weekend this*.
2 I'm going to have a meeting about it *afternoon later this*.
3 I'd like to study abroad *the sometime in future*.
4 Unfortunately, I'm not going to have a holiday *summer this*.
5 I'm going to do it *next weeks in sometime few the*.
6 I'm going to be busy *this later evening*.
7 The government would like to change the education system *years the next in few*.
8 I hope we're going to move *the three months in sometime next or four*.

9 EXPERIENCES

PRESENT PERFECT

We use the present perfect to talk about actions before now, when we feel they're connected to the present situation.

We can use the present perfect to ask if someone has experience of something.

Have you been to London before?

A friend of mine is going to move to Istanbul. Have you been there?

We'd like to maybe go to Turkey on holiday this year. Have you ever been there?

There's a new Turkish place near here. Have you tried Turkish food?

To make the present perfect, use a form of the verb *have* + a past participle.

Regular past participles are the same as regular past simple forms: we add *-ed* to the infinitive.
Remember these spellings.

arrive – arrived	*change – changed*
plan – planned	*stop – stopped*
try – tried	*study – studied*

Some past participles are irregular, for example *be – been*.

You learn more about irregular past participles on page 180.

DID YOU KNOW?

In questions, we sometimes add *ever* to mean 'at any time in your life'.

Have	*we / you / they*		*visited Paris?*
		(ever)	*tried sushi?*
Has	*she / he*		*been to India?*

Answer with *Yes, I have. / No, never. / No, I haven't. / No, but I'd like to.*

Exercise 1

Complete the dialogues with one word in each space.

1 A: _____ your friend been _____ Mexico before?
   B: No, never.
2 A: Have you ever _____ to Cairo in Egypt?
   B: No, never, but I'd really _____ to one day.
3 A: Have you _____ tried German food?
   B: Yes, I _____ . Have _____?
   A: No. Is it good?
   B: It's not bad.
4 A: Have you ever _____ Russian food?
   B: No, I _____. Have you?
5 A: Have you _____ Poland before?
   B: No, never. This is my first time.

Statements

I / You / We / They	**have (not / never)**	**been** *there.*
He / She	**has (not / never)**	**tried** *it.*

Common mistakes

We don't use the present perfect with past time expressions. To give – or ask about – details of the action, we use the past simple.

~~Have you seen~~ **Did you see** the film **yesterday**?

~~I've been~~ **I went** to the supermarket **a few days ago**.

Exercise 2

Complete the sentences using the correct form of the verb in brackets (present perfect or past simple).

1 A: I'm going to go to Tokyo for work next week.
B: Wow! _____ (you / go) there before?
A: Yes, I have, actually. I _____ (go) there last year on holiday.

2 A: Is this your first time in Moscow?
B: No, I _____ (be) here before, actually. I _____ (come) here a few years ago.
A: Oh really? Where _____ (you / stay)?
B: With friends.

3 A: So when _____ (you / arrive) here?
B: Last Friday.
A: And _____ (you / go) to the cathedral?
B: Yes, _____ (we / go) yesterday. We _____ (love) it!

4 A: It's a lovely city. I'm really enjoying it.
B: _____ (you / try) the local food?
A: No, I haven't.
B: Oh, you should try it! A friend _____ (take) me to his favourite restaurant last night and it _____ (be) great.

5 A: I'm planning to go to Krakow for a few days next month.
B: Nice! _____ (you / visit) the city before?
A: No, never. Have you?
B: Yes. I _____ (be) there a few times, actually. The last time I _____ (go) was maybe three or four years ago.
A: OK. And _____ (you / like) it?
B: Yeah. Very much.

PAST PARTICIPLES

The present perfect is *have / has* + past participle. Past participles usually have the same form as the past simple, but some are different.

Regular		Irregular		
present	**past simple / past participle**	**present**	**past simple**	**past participle**
arrive	arrived	be	was/were	been
change	changed	break	broke	broken
check	checked	come	came	come
happen	happened	cut	cut	cut
miss	missed	do	did	done
plan	planned	fall	fell	fallen
stop	stopped	feel	felt	felt
study	studied	find	found	found
try	tried	forget	forgot	forgotten
visit	visited	go	went	gone
		have	had	had
		hurt	hurt	hurt
		leave	left	left
		lose	lost	lost
		make	made	made
		see	saw	seen
		take	took	taken
		throw	threw	thrown

For a full list of verbs forms, see page 191.

Exercise 1

Put the irregular verbs in the box above into groups that you think follow the same pattern.

cut / hurt   They don't change (cut-cut-cut and hurt-hurt-hurt).

Exercise 2

Decide if the past participles in the sentences are correct or not. Change the ones that are wrong.

1 Have you saw my wallet?
2 I need to go home. I've forget to bring my travel card.
3 Where have you been? We were worried.
4 I'm sorry I can't drive you there. My wife's took the car today.
5 I'm sorry. We've done everything we can. We can't do any more.
6 I'm sorry. We've make a mistake. We've charged you too much.
7 The government's done a lot to help poor people.
8 Things here are quite difficult because the government's cutted a lot of services.

Remember that we use the present perfect to talk about an action before now – because it's connected to the present situation. We don't use the present perfect with past time expressions.

We use the past simple to give details.

A: *Have you seen Karina?*
B: *Yes – I have seen saw her ten minutes ago. She was in her office.*

Exercise 3

Choose the correct option.

1 A: Have you seen any good films recently?
B: Yeah. I *saw / have seen* 'Big Storm' last week. *Have you seen / Did you see* it?
A: No, but I'd like to.
B: You should. It's great.

2 A: *Did you lose / Have you lost* something?
B: Yeah. I think I *left / have left* my book in the classroom last night.
A: Oh no! Hey, maybe someone else *took / has taken* it with them after the lesson.

3 A: You look tired.
B: Yes, I am – and I'm hungry. I *got up / have got up* late this morning and I *missed / have missed* breakfast.
A: Oh no.
B: And I *didn't stop / haven't stopped* all day. I *didn't eat / haven't eaten* anything.
A: Well, sit down. Dinner's almost ready.

REVISION

Exercise 1

Complete the set of forms for each verb (present, past simple, past participle).

1 buy – bought – _____
2 _____ – chose – chosen
3 come – came – _____
4 cut – _____ – cut
5 do – did – _____
6 drive – _____ – driven
7 _____ – felt – felt
8 get – got – _____
9 know – knew – _____
10 _____ – left – left
11 put – put – _____
12 _____ – sold – sold
13 steal – _____ – stolen
14 take – _____ – taken

Exercise 2

Match the questions (1–8) with the answers (a–h).

1 Have you ever been to the King Hotel restaurant?
2 Have you ever read *War and Peace*?
3 Have you ever met anyone famous?
4 Have you ever eaten oysters?
5 Have you ever lived abroad?
6 Have you ever seen a dead body?
7 Have you done kung fu before?
8 Have you played this game before?

a No, but I've played something similar.
b Yes, I have. I worked in Dubai for two years.
c No, I've never read anything by Tolstoy.
d Yes. I had some once, but I didn't really like them.
e No, but I once saw Al Pacino in a pizza place in New York.
f No, never, but I did karate when I was little.
g I studied Medicine, so we saw them as part of our degree.
h Yes. I took my wife there once. It was very romantic.

Exercise 3

Complete the questions using the present perfect or past simple.

A: ¹_____ London before? (visit)
B: No, this is our first time.
A: When ²_____? (arrive)
B: Two days ago. We're really enjoying it.
A: Where ³_____? (be)
B: Well, on Sunday we went to Buckingham Palace and Hyde Park, and yesterday we went on the London Eye.
A: ⁴_____ it? (enjoy)
B: Yeah, it was great. You get a great view from the top.
A: Yes. ⁵_____ round any of the museums? (look)
B: No, but we're going to the British Museum tomorrow.

10 TRAVEL

TOO MUCH, TOO MANY AND NOT ENOUGH

too much

Too much only goes with uncountable nouns.
*There **is too much crime**. The government needs to do more.*
*You can't ride a bike here. There**'s too much traffic**.*

too many

Too many only goes with plural nouns.
*You can't sit on the bus. There are **too many people**.*
*There **are too many cars**. I can't park.*

not enough

Not enough can go with uncountable nouns or plurals.
*There **isn't enough help** for old people on public transport.*
*There **aren't enough places to park**.*

Remember to use *there is* with uncountable nouns – and *there are* with plural nouns.

Exercise 1

Complete the sentences with *is* or *are*.

1 There _____ too much traffic on my street.
2 There _____ too many accidents on our roads.
3 There _____n't enough cheap seats on the trains.
4 Sorry, there _____ not enough space for all those bags in my car.
5 There _____ too many people in our city.
6 The government says there _____ not enough money to repair the roads.

too + adjective / adverb

You can also use *too* with an adjective when you're not happy with something.
*I don't like going on the bus. It's **too slow**.*
*I can't take everyone in my car. It's **too small**.*

Exercise 2

Complete the sentences with *too*, *enough*, *too much* or *too many*.

1 There are _____ trucks on the motorways.
2 I don't drive into town. It's _____ difficult to park.
3 The local government is going to cut some bus services because it costs _____ money.
4 People are complaining because they say they're paying _____ tax.
5 Taxi drivers find it difficult to make money. There are _____ taxis, so there's _____ competition.
6 The government says there aren't _____ flights coming here because the airport is _____ small.

DID YOU KNOW?

If we feel happy / OK about something, we don't use *too*. Use *lots of* / *very*.
*It's good. There are ~~too many~~ **lots of trains**.*
*The train is ~~too~~ **very fast**. It only takes ten minutes.*

SUPERLATIVES

To compare more than two things, use *the* + a superlative adjective.

-est

Add *-est* to short adjectives (one syllable).
*cheap – the cheap**est***	*fast – the fast**est***
*small – the small**est***	

Notice these spellings.
*strang**e** – the strang**est***	*nice – the nic**est***

Some adjectives double the final letter.
*ho**t** – the ho**tt**est*	*bi**g** – the bi**gg**est*

-iest

For adjectives ending in *-y*, change to *-iest*.
*earl**y** – the earl**iest***	*laz**y** – the laz**iest***

the most + adjective

For longer adjectives (two or more syllables), use *the most* + adjective.
boring	***the most** boring*
interesting	***the most** interesting*

Irregular superlative adjectives
good – the best	*bad – the worst*	*far – the furthest*

Exercise 1

Choose the correct option.

1 Yesterday was *hottest / the hottest* day of the year.
2 That was the *more / most* difficult exam I've ever taken.
3 They were the *loudest / most loud* band I've ever heard!
4 I live in one of the *busyiest / busiest* streets in town.
5 It was the *worse / worst* day of my life!
6 The *easiest / most easy* way to get around is on foot.
7 They were the *most nice / nicest* people I've ever met.
8 I'm the *tallest / most tallest* person in my class.

DID YOU KNOW?

We often use superlatives with the present perfect.
*That was **the funniest** film **I've (ever) seen**.*
*It's **the best** holiday **I've (ever) had**.*

We also often use this pattern with superlatives:
*It was **one of the worst meals** I've (ever) had.*
*He's **one of the most creative people** I know.*

Exercise 2

Complete the sentences with either a comparative or superlative form of the adjectives in brackets.

1 She's one of _____ teachers I've had. She's _____ than my last teacher, that's for sure. (good)
2 October is the _____ time of year in Zambia, so it was much _____ than it is here. (hot)
3 Moussa is _____. He's six years _____ than my daughter, Mariam. She's seven – and Salif is _____. He's only four. (old, old, young)
4 He's changed! For a long time, he was one of _____ people I know – and now he's _____ than me! (quiet, loud)
5 Berlin is actually _____ than my city. I'm from Jakarta, one of the _____ cities in the world! (small, big)
6 That was one of _____ things I've ever seen! Her last film was much _____! (boring, good)

REVISION

Exercise 1

Correct the underlined mistake in each sentence.

1 There are <u>too cars</u> parked on my road.
2 There were too <u>much people</u> on the train.
3 Getting the bus is <u>easyest way</u> to get here.
4 There is <u>too many rubbish</u> on public transport.
5 It's bad because there are <u>too many</u> buses at night and taxis are expensive.
6 The <u>most fast</u> train you can get only takes three hours.

Exercise 2

Complete the sentences with the superlative form of the adjective in brackets.

1 It's the _____ restaurant in the area. (cheap)
2 The _____ way to get here is on the motorway. (quick)
3 What's the _____ film you've ever seen? (funny)
4 The _____ chapter in the book was the one about the war. (interesting)
5 Where's the _____ metro station? (near)
6 That was the _____ day of my life! (exciting)
7 The _____ time of the year is July. (hot)
8 The _____ way to travel is by bicycle. (nice)

Exercise 3

Complete the text with one word in each space.

I love New York. I think it's [1]_____ greatest city in the world. It has every kind of shop and museum and restaurant. There's almost too [2]_____ choice because I can't decide what to do!

The transport system is really good. I don't drive because there aren't [3]_____ cheap places to park, but I really don't need a car anyway. The subway is quite cheap and reliable and there are [4]_____ of buses and taxis, but [5]_____ best way get around is on foot. That way, you can see all the fantastic buildings and feel the great atmosphere. It's [6]_____ nice.

There aren't many things I don't like here, but the [7]_____ thing for me is the weather in the summer. It's terrible. It's often over 35°C in August. It's [8]_____ hot for me and I find it difficult to work.

11 FOOD

ME TOO, ME NEITHER AND AUXILIARIES

me neither

We use *me neither* to agree with a statement with *not* or *never*.

A: *I can't decide.*
B: ***Me neither***. *It all looks so delicious.*

A: *I don't like lamb.*
B: ***Me neither***.

A: *I've **never** had Mexican food before.*
B: ***Me neither***, *but this is really good, isn't it?*
A: *Yeah, great.*

me too

We use *me too* to agree with a positive statement.

A: *I hate tomatoes.*
B: ***Me too***.
A: *I'm going to go to the cinema later.*
B: *Oh, **me too**! What are you going to see?*
A: *I've been there several times.*
B: *Yeah, **me too**. It's great.*

I do / don't

To disagree with a statement in the present simple, we often use *I do* or *I don't*.

Statement	Reply – disagree
A: *I don't eat much meat.* A: *I don't like reading.*	B: *Oh, I **do**. I have it every day.* B: *Really? I **do**.*
A: *I love seafood.* A: *I work near my home.*	B: *Really? I **don't**.* B: *Oh, I **don't**. You're lucky!*

We use *did / didn't* to disagree with a statement in the past simple.

Other auxiliary verbs

We sometimes use other auxiliary verbs like *have, would, can, be*, etc. to disagree. We use the same auxiliary verb as the one in the statement we disagree with.

Statement	Reply – disagree
have	
A: *I **haven't** had Mexican food.* A: *I've been there before.*	B: *I **have**. It 's nice.* B: *I **haven't**. What's it like?*
would	
A: *I **wouldn't** like to try it.* A: *I'd like to go there.*	B: *Oh, I **would**!* B: *Really? I **wouldn't**.*
can	
A: *I **can't** see him.* A: *I **can** cook quite well.*	B: *I **can**. He's over there.* B: *That's good, because I **can't**!*
be	
A: *I'm not going to go.* A: *I'm hungry.*	B: *Why not? I **am**.* B: *I'm **not**. Can you wait?*

For other uses of auxiliaries see Unit 7.

Exercise 1

Replace the words in brackets with a phrase for agreeing or disagreeing, using *me too*, *me neither* or an auxiliary verb.

1 A: I love cheese.
   B: (I love cheese.) What's your favourite?
2 A: I don't like seafood.
   B: (I don't like seafood.) It makes me feel ill.
3 A: I drink too much coffee.
   B: Really? (I don't drink too much coffee). I hate coffee!
4 A: I don't drink enough water.
   B: (I drink enough water.) I always have a bottle with me.
5 A: I'd like to learn to drive.
   B: Really? (I wouldn't like to learn to drive.) It's too expensive and I prefer to cycle.
   A: (I prefer not to cycle.) It's too dangerous with all the cars on the roads!
6 A: I've never been abroad.
   B: (I've never been abroad.) I'm scared of flying.
   A: (I'm not scared of flying.) I just haven't had the chance.

Exercise 2

Complete the dialogues with one word in each space. Contractions (*don't*, *can't*, etc.) are one word.

1 Ann: Are you going to go to Jean's birthday dinner next week?
   Ben: No, I can't.
   Ann: No, me _____, but I want to get him something.
   Ben: Me _____. Let's put our money together.
2 Ann: The writing's too small. I can't read the instructions.
   Ben: I _____. Let me have a look.
   Ann: I need to get my eyes tested.
   Ben: Me _____, actually! I was wrong. I can't read them either!
3 Ann: What are you going to have?
   Ben: I haven't decided.
   Ann: _____ _____. There's too much choice.
   Cal: Well, I think I'm going to have the cheese bake.
   Ann: Really? I hate cheese.
   Ben: Oh, _____ _____. I love it.
   Cal: _____ _____. How can anyone not like cheese?
   Ann: I don't know. I just don't.

EXPLAINING QUANTITY

- *(Quite) a lot of*, *some* and *any* go with both uncountable (singular) nouns and countable (plural) nouns.
- We use *many* with countable (plural) nouns.
- We use *much* with uncountable (singular) nouns.
- We often use *much*, *many* and *any* in negative sentences and questions.

	Uncountable nouns	Plural nouns
Do you eat	**much** *meat?* **any** *fruit?*	**many** *chips?* **any** *vegetables?*
I eat	**a lot of** *ice cream.* **quite a lot of** *sugar.* **some** *fish.*	**a lot of** *biscuits.* **quite a lot of** *sweets.* **some** *beans.*
I don't eat	**much** *rice.* **any** *cheese.*	**many** *cakes.* **any** *eggs.*

Exercise 1

Decide if both options are possible, or only one.

1 I usually use *much / a lot of* onions when I cook.
2 I try not to eat *many / any* meat. It's better for the environment.
3 I drink *a lot of / quite a lot of* coffee!
4 I eat quite *a lot of / some* meat, but I don't eat *many / any* pork. It's against my religion.
5 We don't really drink *much / some* wine – just a glass once or twice a month.
6 I don't drink *any / many* soft drinks like Cola. They have *a lot of / much* sugar in.
7 A: Do you eat *many / any* dairy products?
   B: *No, not many / Yes, quite a lot.*
8 A: Did you use *much / many* cream in the sauce?
   B: Yeah, *some / quite a lot.*

DID YOU KNOW?

We often say *not a lot of* instead of *not much / not many*.
*I don't eat **much / a lot of** rice.*
*I don't eat **many / a lot of** cakes.*
Instead of *some*, we can use *a bit of* with uncountable nouns and *a few* with countable nouns.
*I eat **some / a bit of** fish. I have it maybe two or three times a month.*
*I usually add **some / a few** beans to the soup, but today I forgot.*

Exercise 2

Replace the words in italics with *much*, *many*, *a bit of* or *a few*.

1 I don't eat *a lot of* sweet things.
2 I eat *some* foreign food, but I mainly eat things from my country.
3 I like *some* of their songs.
4 He doesn't eat *a lot of* meat.
5 Do you eat *a lot of* fruit?
6 We had *some* drinks.
7 I'm about 90% vegetarian, but I eat *some* fish sometimes.
8 Do you use *a lot of* spices when you're cooking?

Exercise 3

Both options in each sentence (1–6) are correct. Decide if the words in italics show the same quantity or a different quantity. If the quantities are different, which quantity is less?

1 I use *a lot of / a bit of* salt in my cooking.
2 I don't put *much / any* sugar in my coffee.
3 Do you eat *any / many* sweets?
4 I have *some / a bit of* fat in my diet, but not much.
5 I don't drink *a lot of / many* cups of coffee a day.
6 I eat quite *a lot of / some* eggs.

REVISION

Exercise 1

Choose the correct option.

1 I ate *a lot of / a few* chocolate and I feel a bit sick now.
2 I only have tea in the house, I'm afraid. I don't have *any / much* coffee.
3 I used *quite a lot of / quite much* chilli, so it's spicy.
4 Have you seen *much / any* good films recently?
5 I watch *a lot of / any* comedies, but not *many / some* dramas.
6 A: What vegetables would you like?
   B: Just *some / any* potatoes and *a bit of / a few* carrots, please.

Exercise 2

Decide if the words in italics are correct or not. Correct the wrong ones.

A: I'd like ¹*any* coffee, please.
B: ²*I* too.
C: Do you take sugar?
A: No, thanks.
B: I ³*take*. One for me, please.
A: I think we eat too ⁴*much* sugar.
B: It's fine. I only have it in coffee and a ⁵*few* sugar every day is fine. Or do you think it's bad to have ⁶*any* sugar?
A: No, but I'd like to be thinner.
B: I ⁷*don't*. I'm happy as I am. And you look fine too.
A: I don't think so.
B: Well, I ⁸*too*!

Exercise 3

Complete the text with one word in each space.

I love cooking. I started when I was eight or nine. I made ¹_____ chocolate biscuits with my mum. I really enjoyed it. After that, we made a ²_____ of cakes together. My poor dad had to eat them all and he put on ³_____ lot of weight!

Now I cook other kinds of food. I make the dinner a ⁴_____ times a week. Tonight I'm going to do steak with ⁵_____ bit of sauce and some chips. I actually don't cook ⁶_____ meat. I prefer doing fish, but my dad bought the steak.

12 FEELINGS

SHOULD / SHOULDN'T

We use *should(n't)* + infinitive to suggest actions.
Should shows we think it's a good idea to do the action.
Shouldn't shows we think it's a bad idea to do the action.

I You He / She We They		
I You He / She	**should**	stop smoking. go to the doctor. have a holiday.
We They	**shouldn't**	sit in the sun so long. work so hard.

DID YOU KNOW?

We often add *maybe*. It makes the advice sound less strong.
***Maybe** you should lose some weight.*

Exercise 1

Complete the sentences with a pronoun + *should / shouldn't*.

1 A: I feel a bit sick.
   B: Maybe _____ _____ lie down.
2 A: My stomach hurts and I think I'm going to be sick.
   B: Maybe _____ _____ have any more to eat today.
3 A: He says he's really stressed and has no energy.
   B: Maybe _____ _____ take some time off work.
4 A: Hurry up! We're late.
   B: Perhaps _____ _____ take a taxi.
5 A: The kids are always tired in the morning.
   B: Perhaps _____ _____ stay up so late.
6 A: She often says her back's stiff and it hurts a lot.
   B: Maybe _____ _____ go and see someone about it.

We often use a comparative with *should*.
*You should go to bed **earlier**.*
*She's so thin! She should **eat more**.*
*I think the government should spend **more money** on health.*
*I think they should spend **less money** on the army.*

Exercise 2

Complete the sentences with the word in brackets and a comparative, or a comparative form of the word in brackets. The first one is done for you.

1 I shouldn't spend so much money eating out. I should _____. (cook)
   I shouldn't spend so much money eating out. I should cook more.
2 I think people should work _____ before they retire. (long)
3 I think the government should _____ to improve the health service. (do)
4 I should do _____. I'm getting fat. (exercise)
3 Maybe you should eat _____. (sugar)
4 My son is getting bad grades at school. He should study _____. (hard)
5 He shouldn't try to do everything so quickly. He should take his time and _____. (concentrate)
6 Maybe he should spend _____ complaining and _____ working. (time, time)

BECAUSE, SO AND AFTER

We use *because*, *so* and *after* to join two parts of a sentence.

after

After shows when a situation or action happens. The phrase with *after* can have a verb.

After the meeting finished, *I sat and thought about everything I had to do.*

After I did some shopping, *I went home.*

*My dad sold his business **after he retired**.*

After is often used as a preposition. It can go with a phrase that has a noun and no verb.

After dinner, *I watched the news on TV.*

After work, *I often meet friends for a drink.*

*He started his business **after the war**.*

*He was off work for six weeks **after the accident**.*

because

Because shows why a situation or action happens. The phrase following *because* always has a verb.

*She was upset **because her boss shouted at her**.*

*I was upset **because he didn't call**.*

*I stayed at home last night **because I was tired**.*

so

So shows the result of a situation or action. The phrase following *so* always has a verb.

*The bus was full, **so I couldn't sit and read**.*

*I was tired, **so I stayed at home last night**.*

*I passed my driving test, **so I went out and celebrated**.*

Exercise 1

Complete the sentences with *because*, *so* or *after*.

1 I had a headache, _____ I went home early.
2 _____ I had lunch, I felt a bit sick.
3 She can't come with us _____ she's broken her leg.
4 _____ the war, my parents decided to stay here.
5 Our flight was delayed for hours _____ the weather was so bad.
6 They told him he's going to lose his job, _____ he's quite upset.
7 My back was quite stiff _____ the match yesterday.
8 I was quite annoyed _____ my brother took my house keys.

Exercise 2

Join the pairs of sentences using the words in brackets. You may need to change the order. The first one is done for you.

1 I'm really happy. I passed all my exams. (so)
  I passed all my exams, so I'm really happy.
2 I'm very stressed. I have my final exams soon. (because)
3 He's quite upset. He really wanted the job, but he didn't get it. (so)
4 They lost the final. He sat on the sofa and cried for an hour! (after)
5 I really love opera. I'm really looking forward to going to see *La Traviata*. (so)
6 I moved to London. Then I met my wife. (after)
7 I'm going to go on holiday next week. I'm happy. (because)

REVISION

Exercise 1

Complete each sentence with *should* or *shouldn't* and one of these verbs.

be	carry	drive	eat	see	take

1 A: That's a bad cough.
   B: I know. I've had it for a week. Maybe I _____ a doctor about it.
2 A: I feel really strange.
   B: Well, you _____ home. Would you like me to call a taxi instead?
3 A: I cut my finger playing with a knife.
   B: That was stupid! You _____ more careful in future.
4 A: I've got a really bad headache.
   B: Really? Maybe you _____ a couple of aspirin.
5 A: The doctor said I need to lose weight.
   B: Well, maybe you _____ so many sweets!
6 A: My back hurts.
   B: Really? Well, you _____ those boxes.

Exercise 2

Rewrite the sentences using the words in bold. The first one is done for you.

1 I finished work and then I went to the cinema. **after**
  I went to the cinema after work.
2 Why don't we take the bus? **should**
3 I didn't sleep well last night, so I've been tired all day. **because**
4 I think he drives too fast. **shouldn't**
5 He had an accident, but he didn't need to go to the hospital. **after**
6 He's gone to bed because he's not feeling very well. **so**

Exercise 3

Complete the text with one word in each space. Contractions (*shouldn't, doesn't,* etc.) are one word.

Research has shown that if people want to be happier they [1]_____ work so hard and they should spend [2]_____ time with their family and friends. Children shouldn't [3]_____ so much TV, especially if there are a lot of adverts, [4]_____ the adverts make children want things that they can't have. The main thing children need for happiness is love from their parents.

The economist Richard Leyard thinks that the government should do [5]_____ to help. He thinks the government [6]_____ increase taxes [7]_____ people don't work too hard. He also wants provide lessons at school on how to be a good parent, but he [8]_____ think the government should change lots of things because a lot of change makes people unhappy!

13 NATURE

MIGHT AND BE GOING TO

We use *might* + infinitive and *be going to* + infinitive to talk about the future.

We use *be (not) going to* to show certainty – especially about plans we have.

We use *might (not)* to show possibility.

A: *I need to give this book back to Dan.*

B: *I can give it to him, if you like.* **I'm going to see** *him later.*

I **might not go** *to the party. I* **might stay** *at home instead.*

DID YOU KNOW?

We can use *may* instead of *might*.

I **may** *be a bit late. It depends what time my meeting ends.*

We often use these expressions with *might*.

possibly	*I'm not sure*	*I haven't decided*
it depends	*I don't know*	

Exercise 1

Choose the correct option.

1 *We might / We're going to* have a barbecue on Sunday. Would you like to come?
2 *We might / We're going to* be free at the weekend, but I need to speak to my wife first and check.
3 Oh no! It's raining! *We might / We're going to* get really wet!
4 Look at those black clouds up there! *It might / It's going to* rain soon.
5 I might *possibly / definitely* get a new car soon. It depends.
6 *She may / She's going to* come with us. It depends if she can get time off work.

Exercise 2

Match the two parts of the sentences.

1 I might come tomorrow. It depends if
2 I might buy one. It depends how much
3 I might phone you later. It depends what time
4 I might do it this weekend. It depends how
5 I may get the job. It depends how many
6 They may have something you like. It depends what

a I get home.
b busy I am.
c people apply for it, I guess.
d they cost.
e style you want.
f my girlfriend wants to.

PRESENT PERFECT TO SAY HOW LONG

We can use the present perfect to talk about the duration of something (how long) from the past to now. When we say the duration, we sometimes use *for* at the start of the time phrase, but it's also OK not to use it.

A: *How long* **have they been** *there?*

B: *For about six years now.*

A: *How long* **have you had** *him?*

B: *Ten years.*

We've been *here a year now.*

Exercise 1

Correct the mistake in each sentence.

1 How long you been here?
2 How long you have lived here?
3 How long have you did that?
4 She has that dog for five years.
5 I live here for three months now.
6 I don't have had it very long.

Exercise 2

Complete the responses by putting the words in brackets in the correct order.

1 A: How long have you had your cat?
   B: (about / ten / for / years)
2 A: How long have you been together?
   B: (time / now / a / long / quite / – / ten / nine / or / years / maybe)
3 A: How long have you been married?
   B: We met in 2004 – (now / is / twelve / so / it / years).
4 A: How long have they known each other?
   B: (long / not / very / – / a / months / only / few)
5 A: How long has she worked there?
   B: Ages. She started in 1997 – (twenty / now / so / years / is / almost / it).

REVISION

Exercise 1

Rewrite the sentences using *might* to show possibility.

1 They said it's going to rain later.
2 I'm definitely not going to be in the office tomorrow.
3 She's going to call you this afternoon.

Rewrite the sentences using *be going to* to show certainty.

4 It said there might be a storm tonight.
5 We might go to Bulgaria for our holiday this year.
6 My dad might drive us to the station.

Exercise 2

Complete the present perfect sentences using the past participles of these verbs.

be	feel	know	have	live	see	want

1 How long have you two _____ each other?
2 How long has he _____ unemployed?
3 How long have you _____ here in Liverpool?
4 How long have you _____ to be a doctor?
5 I've _____ this cold for two weeks now.
6 That's the best film I've _____ for a long time.
7 I haven't _____ this good for a long time.

Exercise 3

Correct the mistake in each sentence.

1 I don't might see you tomorrow.
2 We is going to finish the work by Tuesday.
3 She is been there for twelve years now.
4 I don't going to do it. I'm too busy.
5 They might probably move to the country next year.
6 How long they are lived there?

14 OPINIONS

WILL / WON'T FOR PREDICTIONS

We can use *will / won't* (= will not) + infinitive to make predictions about the future in the same way as we use *be (not) going to* + infinitive. They both show certainty.

*It***'ll be** *fine.*
It **won't be** *a problem. I'm sure of it.*

think + will

We often use *will* (but not *won't*) with *I think / don't think ...* .
*I think he***'ll ge***t the job.*
*I don't think I***'ll go***. (NOT I think I won't go.)*

We usually ask questions using *do you think + will* + infinitive.
*Do you think you***'ll see** *her tonight?*
Who do you think **will win***?*
*Do you think you***'ll ever** *(= at any time in your life)* **have** *kids?*

will probably

We can add *probably* to show we're not 100% sure. Note the different position with *will / won't*.
*We***'ll probably go** *somewhere in Greece.*
It **probably won't make** *any difference.*

Exercise 1

Choose the correct option.

1 I think *they'll / they'll to* finish it next year.
2 They said *there'll be / there be will* snow tonight.
3 When *will the meeting start / will start the meeting*?
4 She *won't / won't not* be happy about it.
5 I'm sure they *don't will / won't* be late.
6 I don't think *you'll / you won't* pass the exam.
7 I *probably won't / won't probably* see you before then.
8 What *will / will be* your parents do about it?

DID YOU KNOW?

We often use *(don't) expect* and *doubt* with *will*.
Expect means you think something will happen.
Doubt means you think something is unlikely to happen.
I **don't expect** *I'll pass my exam. I haven't done enough work.*
We can complain if you want, but I **doubt it'll** *make any difference. (= I don't think it will)*

Exercise 2

A Put the words in the correct order to make predictions.

1 take / you / a / need / I / expect / will / to / test
2 be / don't / will / necessary / it / expect / I
3 quite / year / I / will / expect / difficult / next / be
4 offer / doubt / will / they / the / me / I / job
5 expensive / it / be / I / will / very / doubt
6 him / can / doubt / but / listen / ask / I / he / I / will

B Rewrite sentences 4–6 above using *think* instead of *doubt*.

ADJECTIVE + *TO* + INFINITIVE

We can describe or give our opinion about an action / situation using the pattern below.

It can be means 'it sometimes is'.

			Adjective	Action / situation
It	is was can be	really very quite	easy difficult dangerous	**to find** work in computing. **to find** the time. **to really know** people. **to walk** at night. **to live** there.

not to do

We sometimes talk about negative situations / actions.
It was difficult **not to tell people***, but I didn't say anything until I knew the baby was OK.*
It was stupid **not to ask for help***.*

Exercise 1

Complete the sentences with the correct verb. Use *to* + infinitive or *not to* + infinitive.

read	park	vote	see
find	walk	offer	worry

1 It was quite difficult _____ somewhere to live.
2 It's perfectly safe _____ round there at night.
3 It's almost impossible _____ the car in town.
4 I think it is very rude _____ a drink to a visitor.
5 I think it can be helpful _____ children's books when you study a new language.
6 It's interesting _____ the differences between the two countries.
7 I think it's important _____ about making mistakes.
8 I think it's stupid _____ in the elections.

More patterns with adjective + *to* + infinitive
Look at these other examples of adjective + *to* + infinitive.
It was **crazy to spend** *so much money on a car.*
It's **too late to phone** *them now.*
It's **too cloudy to go** *to the beach. Let's do something else.*

DID YOU KNOW?

We can show we're talking from personal experience by starting sentences *I find it / I found it* instead of *it is / it was*.
I **find it** *difficult to make friends.*
I **found it** *easy to find work when I lived there.*

Exercise 2

Match the two parts of the sentences. Translate the sentences into your language.

1 It's too far away
2 It was too warm
3 I think it's wrong
4 It's too early
5 It can be fun
6 I found it difficult

a to make friends when I was there.
b to go skiing when we were there.
c to travel there every day.
d to spend the day shopping.
e to ever use violence.
f to know what will happen.

REVISION

Exercise 1
Change the sentences into negatives (–) or questions (?).

1 They'll win. (–)
2 He'll get the job. (?)
3 It was difficult to laugh in that situation. (–)
4 I'll probably see you before Christmas. (–)
5 I think the economy will improve this year. (–)
6 It's easy to find work. (?)

Exercise 2
Complete the sentences with the correct form of the verb in brackets (*to / not to* + infinitive or *will / won't* + infinitive).

1 It's important _____ the contract carefully. (read)
2 Do you think the Social Democrats _____ the election next year? (lose)
3 It can be very expensive _____ here. (eat out)
4 I think it's good _____ and meet new people. (travel)
5 Do you think it's easy _____ abroad? (move)
6 It definitely _____ soon. You'll have to wait. (not happen)
7 It's bad _____ someone when they need it. (help)
8 I don't think it _____ any difference to the result. (make)

Exercise 3
Correct the mistake in each sentence.

1 It was lovely see you again.
2 It don't will cost too much.
3 What you will do with the money you won?
4 Was difficult to learn Russian?
5 It's difficult don't think about it.
6 It's no rude to talk about money in my country.

15 TECHNOLOGY

BE THINKING OF + -ING
We use *be thinking of* + *-ing* to talk about plans we are not 100% sure of, but have already thought about.
I'm thinking of doing a Web design course next year.
We're not thinking of buying a new one yet.
Where are you thinking of going?

Exercise 1
Write full sentences using *be thinking of* and the ideas below.

1 I / think / join a gym.
2 What brand / you / think / buy?
3 They / think / move sometime next year.
4 I hope he / not / think / leave the company.
5 Who / you / think / ask?
6 They said on TV that they / not / think / change the price.
7 Which university she / think / apply to?
8 I / think / try to make my own computer.
9 Why / he / think / retire? He's only 48.
10 Please tell me you / not / think / marry him!

DID YOU KNOW?
When we use *be thinking of* + *-ing*, we often then ask for recommendations.
A: **I'm thinking of** buy**ing** my dad some new clothes, but *I don't know any good shops.* **Can you recommend anywhere**?
B: *Well, there's a good place for older men in the centre of town. It's called Carter's.*

Exercise 2
Match the questions 1–6 with the recommendations a–f.

1 My brother is thinking of doing an English course next year. Can you recommend anywhere?
2 We're thinking of going to the cinema later. Can you recommend anything?
3 I'm thinking of changing the mobile phone company I use. Can you recommend anything?
4 My sister's thinking of buying a new car. Can you recommend anything?
5 We're thinking of going somewhere warm over Christmas. Can you recommend anywhere?
6 I'm thinking of getting a pet for my younger brother. Can you recommend anything?

a Well, you could try Dubai. It's always hot at that time of year – and not too expensive.
b I'm not really sure, to be honest. I haven't seen any films for ages!
c Well, I use Blue and they've always been great – very reliable and good value for money.
d That's a nice idea. Cats are always good – and they need less attention than dogs!
e Well, I spent two years at Cambridge House and really enjoyed it. I had great teachers.
f You're asking the wrong person, I'm afraid. I can't drive, so I don't know much about it.

ADVERBS

-ly
We form descriptive adverbs by adding *-ly* to an adjective.

Adjective	Adverb
a **bad** man	do **badly**
a **quick** run	solve it **quickly**
an **easy** exercise	check it **easily**
a **successful** sportsman	develop it **successfully**
an **efficient** service	work **efficiently**
a **slow** computer	drive **slowly**
a **quiet** room	leave **quietly**
a **happy** child	work **happily**
a **nice** day	play **nicely**
a **safe** place	keep it **safely**

Irregular adverbs
The most common irregular adverb to describe a verb is *well*. A few adverbs have the same form as the adjective, such as *fast* and *long*.

Adjective	Adverb
a **good** time	do it **well**
a **fast** train	change **fast**
a **long** time	not last **long**
a **hard** job	work **hard**
a **late** night	go out **late**
early morning	get up **early**
a **loud** noise	talk **loud** / **loudly**

Modifiers

We can modify descriptive adverbs with *quite*, *very*, *really* and *too*.

*The economy's doing **quite** badly.*
*I had a problem, but the company solved it **very** quickly.*
*Things are changing **really** fast.*

For more information on modifiers, see Unit 6.

Exercise 1

Complete the sentences using adverbs formed from the adjectives in the box.

bad	easy	good	late	nice
early	hard	happy	long	slow

1 A: Can you speak more _____? I can't follow.
   B: Oh yes, sorry. So ... what ... I ... said ... was ...
2 A: The bank has an app I use. It allows you to manage your money really _____,
   B: Yeah – my bank has something similar.
3 A: You look tired.
   B: I am. I went to bed _____ and had to get up _____.
4 A: How did his exam go?
   B: Oh! It went really _____. He's a bit upset about it because he worked quite _____.
   A: What a shame. Still, I'm sure he'll do better next time.
5 A: I don't like their website. The search doesn't work very _____, so it's difficult to find what you want.
   B: Yeah, I know, but the main page is designed _____.
6 A: My son can spend all day quite _____ playing video games.
   B: That's like my son. We sometimes have to give him a time limit so he doesn't play too _____.

Comparatives

We can make comparatives in the same way as with adjectives.

*I'm sure he'll do **better** next time.*
*LED lights last **longer than** other lights.*
*Can you speak **more slowly**? I can't follow.*
*They hope the cells will work **more efficiently** in the future.*

For more information on comparatives, see Unit 6.

Exercise 2

Complete the second sentence in each pair with the correct adverb, so the two sentences have the same meaning. In 6–8 you need a comparative.

1 a It's not a very efficient system.
   b They don't organise things very _____.
2 a I didn't sleep very well.
   b I slept quite _____ last night.
3 a The app is a safe place to keep all your passwords.
   b It allows you to keep all your passwords _____ in one place.
4 a The app provides a quick and easy solution.
   b The app solves the problem _____ and _____.
5 a We didn't leave early enough.
   b We left too _____.
6 a Don't speak so quietly.
   b Can you speak a bit _____?
7 a I'm not improving – I got a better mark in my last test.
   b I think I'm doing _____ than I was before.
8 a I need to do more work for my next test.
   b I need to study _____ for my next test.

REVISION

Exercise 1

Rewrite each sentence as a positive statement (+), a negative statement (–) or a question (?), using the pronoun in brackets.

1 I'm thinking of changing jobs. (? / she)
2 Is he thinking of making his own website? (– / we)
3 They're not thinking of having children yet. (+ / I)
4 Are you thinking of buying a new one? (+ / he)
5 She's thinking of applying for a Master's. (– / I)
6 We're not thinking of selling the company. (? / they)

Exercise 2

Choose the correct option.

1 He's a very *confident / confidently* speaker.
2 It's a really old car. It's really *slow / slowly*.
3 I got home really *late / lately* last night.
4 My gran drives really *slow / slowly*.
5 I'm not very *well / good* at maths.
6 You speak Italian very *good / well*.
7 He's quite *bad / badly* at tennis, but he tries really *hardly / hard*.
8 I understand Chinese quite *good / well*, but my pronunciation is *awful / awfully*.

Exercise 3

Correct the mistake in each sentence.

1 He really quickly speaks!
2 Where you thinking of moving to?
3 I'm thinking to complain to the company about it.
4 You look really nicely in that suit.
5 He's studying hardly for his exams at the moment.
6 The camera works perfect now.
7 We're thinking get married next year.
8 You drive too fastly.

16 LOVE

PAST CONTINUOUS

To make the past continuous, we use *was / were + (not) +* the *-ing* form of the verb.

*I **was working** in a Second Life nightclub when one night I met my future husband.*
*We **were driving** home from another appointment when we suddenly saw it – the house of our dreams!*

We often use the past continuous and the past simple in the same sentence. We use the past continuous to show one action started and was already in progress at the time that a past simple action happened.

*We **were** both **doing** a Spanish course when we **met**.*

To link the two actions together, we often use the word *when*.

*I **was shopping** in town **when** I saw one on sale.*
*We **were** both **working** in the same office **when** we met.*

We can also start with the past simple.

*I **saw** one on sale **when I was shopping** in town.*

DID YOU KNOW?

We often use a negative past continuous clause + a clause with *so* and the past simple.

We **weren't getting on** very well, **so I started** spending a lot of time online.

I **wasn't feeling** very well, **so I just went** home and went to bed.

She **wasn't enjoying** it, **so she decided** to stop and do something else.

Exercise 1

Complete the sentences with the past continuous form of the verbs in brackets.

1 Sorry I didn't answer your call. I _____ (talk) to someone on another line when you called.
2 What _____ (you / do) when you heard the news?
3 It _____ (not / work) very well, so I took it back to the shop.
4 We _____ (have) dinner when my sister suddenly told us she was pregnant!
5 They _____ (not / get on) very well, so they decided to break up.
6 We _____ (sit) in the cinema when he suddenly tried to kiss me. It was horrible!

Exercise 2

Match the two parts of the sentences.

1 We were studying at the same university when
2 I first met him when
3 They were living in Syria when
4 She broke her leg when
5 It was a lovely surprise. They were all waiting for me when
6 Sorry I didn't answer, but you phoned when

a he was working in a café near my office.
b she was skiing in Scotland.
c the war started, so they decided to leave.
d I arrived at the airport.
e I was sleeping.
f we first met.

WILL / WON'T FOR PROMISES

To make promises, we usually use *will / won't*.
We sometimes add *I promise*.

A: *Dad, can we go to the cinema today?*
B: *Sorry, I'm too busy. I'll **take** you next week, I **promise**.*

We can also use *will / won't* in short answers.

A: *You need to be careful.*
B: *I will*.

A: *Don't forget.*
B: *I won't*.

Exercise 1

Choose the correct option.

1 I promise *I'll / I won't* tell anyone.
2 I'll come with you. *You'll / You won't* have to go on your own.
3 Don't worry. *I'll / I won't* be there on time.
4 *I'll / I won't* bring you back a nice present, I promise.
5 A: Have you spoken to the bank yet?
   B: *I'll / I won't* do it as soon as possible.
6 A: I hope you're not going to do that again.
   B: Don't worry. *I will / I won't*.
7 A: Take care.
   B: *I will / I won't*.

Exercise 2

Write a promise to follow each request. Use the words in brackets. The first one is done for you.

1 Can she go on her own? (be careful)
   Can she go on her own? She'll be careful.
2 Could I borrow some money? (pay back)
3 Can I borrow your umbrella? (lose)
4 Is it OK if some friends come over tonight? (make noise)
5 Can I borrow your jacket? (look after)
6 Could we have a break? (be back)
7 Could I stay with you? (stay)

REVISION

Exercise 1

Rewrite the sentences as statements (+), negatives (–) or questions (?), using the pronouns in brackets.

1 I was working yesterday, so I couldn't answer your email. (– / he)
2 I was living there when they met. (? / you)
3 I will tell him. (– / I)
4 I was paying attention during the meeting. (– / they)
5 Will you do it for me? (+ / I)
6 We were cycling when the big storm started. (? / you)
7 She wasn't listening when you made that promise. (+ / we)
8 Was he driving too fast when the accident happened? (+ / I)

Exercise 2

Complete the sentences with the correct form of the verbs. Use the past simple for one verb and the past continuous for the other.

1 I _____ in the park when I _____ my leg. (play, hurt)
2 I _____ 20 euros when I _____ home. (find, walk)
3 We _____ when we _____ for a train. (meet, wait)
4 I _____ to one of her concerts when she _____ in a band. (go, play)
5 We _____ a few times when I _____. (move, grow up)
6 He _____ down a quiet road when a car _____ him and his horse. (ride, hit)
7 She _____ the course, so she _____ to stop. (not / enjoy, decide)
8 They _____ friends in Peru when the earthquake _____. (visit, hit)

Exercise 3

Correct the mistake in each sentence or dialogue.

1 I call you tonight, I promise.
2 What you were doing when this happened?
3 I will always to love you.
4 I was runing down the street when I fell and hurt my arm.
5 The children was all studying quietly when I went into the classroom.
6 Someone was stealing my bike when I was buying some things in the shop.
7 A: Don't be late.
   B: I don't.
8 A: What did he say?
   B: I don't know. I wasn't listen. Sorry.

IRREGULAR VERBS

present	past simple	past participle
be	was/were	been
become	became	become
begin	began	begun
break	broke	broken
bring	brought	brought
build	built	built
burn	burnt / burned	burnt / burned
buy	bought	bought
catch	caught	caught
choose	chose	chosen
come	came	come
cost	cost	cost
cut	cut	cut
do	did	done
draw	drew	drawn
drink	drank	drunk
drive	drove	driven
eat	ate	eaten
fall	fell	fallen
feel	felt	felt
fight	fought	fought
find	found	found
fly	flew	flown
forget	forgot	forgotten
get	got	got
give	gave	given
go	went	gone
have	had	had
hear	heard	heard
hurt	hurt	hurt
keep	kept	kept
know	known	known
learn	learnt	learnt / learned
leave	left	left

present	past simple	past participle
lend	lent	lent
light	lit	lit
lose	lost	lost
make	made	made
mean	meant	meant
pay	paid	paid
put	put	put
read	read	read
ride	rode	ridden
run	ran	run
say	said	said
see	saw	seen
sell	sold	sold
send	sent	sent
sing	sang	sung
sit	sat	sat
sleep	slept	slept
speak	spoke	spoken
spell	spelt	spelt
spend	spent	spent
stand	stood	stood
steal	stole	stolen
stick	stuck	stuck
swim	swam	swum
take	took	taken
teach	taught	taught
tell	told	told
think	thought	thought
throw	threw	thrown
understand	understood	understood
wake	woke	woken
wear	wore	worn
win	won	won
write	wrote	written

INFORMATION FILES

FILE 1

Unit 3 page 27   **CONVERSATION PRACTICE**

Student A

You want to go to a supermarket, a restaurant, a church, a language school and a bookshop.

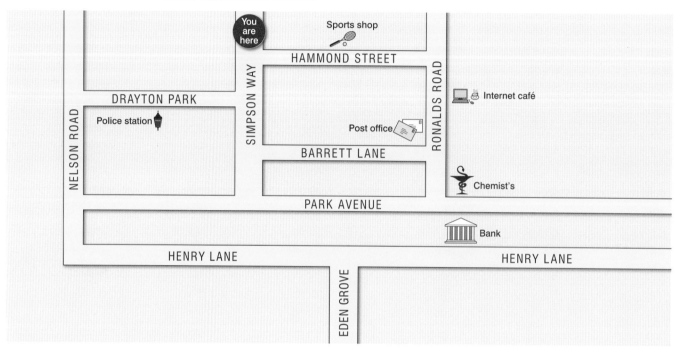

FILE 2

Unit 4 page 36   **VOCABULARY**

Student A

A Ask Student B when these days are. Write the dates.

Immaculate Conception, Italy	_____
Teacher's Day, China	_____
Human Rights Day, South Africa	_____
Independence Day, India	_____
Student B's birthday	_____
The next public holiday	_____

B Complete the dates below. Then answer Student B's questions.

Labour Day, Bolivia	*1st May*
Unity Day, Germany	*3rd October*
Youth Day, Morocco	*12th August*
Father's Day	*The first Sunday in June*
My birthday	_____
The next public holiday	_____

C Check with B that you wrote the correct dates.

Unit 3 page 27   CONVERSATION PRACTICE

Student B

You want to go to a sports shop, a bank, a post office, an internet café and a chemist's.

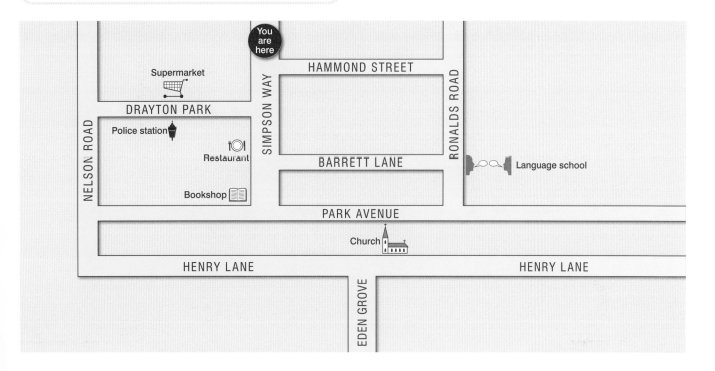

Unit 4 page 36   VOCABULARY

Student B

A   Complete the dates below. Then answer Student A's questions.

Immaculate Conception, Italy	*8th December*
Teacher's Day, China	*10th September*
Human Rights Day, South Africa	*21st March*
Independence Day, India	*15th August*
My birthday	_____
The next public holiday	_____

B   Ask A when these days are. Write the dates.

Labour Day, Bolivia	_____
Unity Day, Germany	_____
Youth Day, Morocco	_____
Father's Day	_____
Student A's birthday	_____
The next public holiday	_____

C   Check with A that you wrote the correct dates.

Student B

Use the table below to help you give information about trains to Hope.

TRAINS TO HOPE	LEAVE	ARRIVE	CHANGES	COST		PLATFORM
slow	4:15	7:28	direct	**Single** 1st: £180 2nd: £135 **Return** 1st: £210 2nd: £165		13
fast	4:45	7:15	direct	**Single** 1st: £288 2nd: £250 **Return** 1st: £314 2nd: £265		9
slow	5:45	8:45	change at Sheffield	**Single** 1st: £35 2nd: £42 **Return** 1st: £35 2nd: £55		11

Student B

Adnan

I came here two years ago because of the war in my country. It was dangerous to live there. Of course, there is crime here – someone stole my bike once – but it's not dangerous.

People here complain about the health service, but for me it has been great. I was injured in the war and when I came here, I had treatment. The doctors were kind and efficient, and it was free. People here are polite, but it's difficult to really know them. In my country, our home was always open. There were always lots of friends and family sharing food, talking, laughing. I really miss that. My friends here are other foreigners. We play football in the park every Sunday.

I've found cleaning and building work here. It's not what I want to do, but wages are OK, so I can support my family. One day, I hope I'll go back home and do a more important job. When I go, I would also like to take the climate with me! I know it rains a lot here, but back home, it's too hot and there's not enough water.

Student A

- Ask your partner what these foods are. Listen to your partner's explanation. Write the word in your own language. Then, look at your partner's photos and check. Did you have the right word?

almonds	coriander	mussels
cabbage	mackerel	strawberry

- Answer your partner's questions. Use the photos to help you explain what the foods are. Use actions or draw if you need to. Don't let your partner see your photos.

B: *What's a carrot?*

A: *It's a vegetable. It's orange and long.*

noodles   chickpeas   plum

prawns   chilli   goat

Unit 10 page 89 **CONVERSATION PRACTICE**

Student A

Use the table below to help you give information about trains to Hull.

TRAINS TO HULL	LEAVE	ARRIVE	CHANGES	COST		PLATFORM
slow	9:15	12:35	change at Leeds	**Single** 1st: £175 2nd: £125 **Return** 1st: £245 2nd: £185		3
slow	9:45	12:45	direct	**Single** 1st: £160 2nd: £110 **Return** 1st: £200 2nd: £150		7
fast	10:05	12:30	direct	**Single** 1st: £325 2nd: £155 **Return** 1st: £380 2nd: £225		7

Unit 11 page 99 **CONVERSATION PRACTICE**

MENU

◎ STARTERS

Soup • Salad

◎ MAIN COURSES

Pizza • Steak • Fish • Chicken

◎ DESSERTS

Ice cream • Chocolate cake • Cheese

◎ DRINKS

Red wine • White wine • Beer

Water • Orange juice

Unit 10 page 90 **READING**

Paragraph 3 is not true.

A photo of the 'Ferrari taxi' was shown on the internet, but the taxi wasn't real. Someone used image-editing software to create the photo and then they invented the story about how much the taxi cost.

FILE 11

Unit 5 page 49 **SPEAKING**

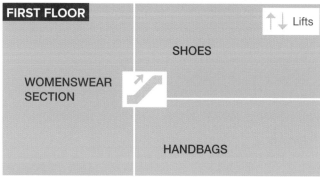

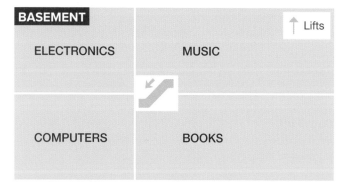

- It's over there.
- It's on the bottom / top shelf / by the till / on this floor / on the fourth floor.
- Try the sports section / the third floor.
- Take the lift / escalator.
- When you come out of the lift, … / When you get off the escalator, …
- … turn right / turn left.
- … it's in front of you / behind you / at the back / in the corner.
- It's next to the jeans / the beauty department.

FILE 12

Unit 11 page 100 **VOCABULARY**

Student B

- Answer your partner's questions. Use the photos to help you explain what the foods are. Use actions or draw if you need to. Don't let your partner see your photos.

  A: *What's a carrot?*

  B: *It's a vegetable. It's orange and long.*

- Ask your partner what these foods are. Listen to your partner's explanation. Write the word in your own language. Then, look at your partner's photos and check. Did you have the right word?

chickpeas	goat	plum
chilli	noodles	prawns

AUDIO SCRIPTS

▶ TRACK 1

1 beach
2 factory
3 river
4 nurse
5 businesswoman
6 church
7 countryside
8 waiter
9 mosque
10 museum
11 office
12 government
13 airport
14 university
15 police officer
16 traffic
17 shop assistant

▶ TRACK 2

I = Ivy; M = Miguel

I: Hi. Come in. Sit down. How are you?
M: Fine.
I: I'm Ivy. I'm a teacher here. What's your name?
M: Miguel.
I: Right. Hi. Nice to meet you. And what's your surname, Miguel?
M: Sorry?
I: Your surname. Your family name.
M: Oh, sorry. Hernandez.
I: OK. Her-nan-dez. Is that right?
M: Yes.
I And where are you from, Miguel? Spain?
M: No, I'm not. I'm from Mexico.
I: Oh, OK. Which part?
M: Chihuahua. It's a city in the north.
I: Is it nice?
M: It's OK. It's a city. Factories. Business. Some things are nice.
I: Is it hot?
M: Now? No, it's not hot now. In June, it's very hot. 30. 35.
I: OK. And what do you do?
M: Again?
I: What do you do? What's your job?
M: Oh, I'm police.
I: Really? You're a police officer?
M: Yes – sorry. I'm a police officer.
I: Interesting. Is it a good job?
M: It's OK. It's a job.

▶ TRACK 3

1 How are you?
2 Where's your granddad from?
3 My parents are from Spain.
4 I'm a receptionist in a hotel.
5 It's not a good job.
6 Tokyo's a very big city.
7 How old is Miguel?
8 Are we late?
9 Are you cold?
10 It's a boring place.

▶ TRACK 4

1
A: Hello.
B: Hi. It's Jan, isn't it?
A: Yes.
B: What do you do, Jan?
A: I'm a doctor.
B: Really? Where do you work?
A: In a hospital in Warsaw.

2
C: So, Lara, what do you do?
D: I'm a teacher.
C: Oh, really? Where do you work?
D: In a secondary school in Bristol.
C: Do you enjoy it?
D: Yes, it's great.
C: What do you teach?
D: French.
C: That's good. Sorry, I don't speak French!

3
E: Where are you from, Marta?
F: Brazil.
E: Oh, OK. Which part?
F: I live in Rio Branco – in the north.
E: I don't know it.
F: Ah. It's a small city.
E: What do you do there?
F: I'm a civil servant.
E: OK. Where do you work?
F: In a local government office.
E: Do you enjoy it?
F: Yes, it's OK.

4
G: What do you do, Filippo?
H: I'm a waiter.
G: Where do you work?
H: In a café in the centre of town – near the cathedral.
G: OK. Do you enjoy it?
H: Not really. I want a different job.
G: Oh? What do you want to do?
H: I don't know – maybe become a police officer.

▶ TRACK 5

/djə/
/də jə/
/dʊː jʊː/
1 Where do you live?
2 Who do you live with?
3 How do you go there?
4 What time do you get up?
5 When do you go to bed?

▶ TRACK 6

1 There are a lot of nice shops near my house.
2 Is there a university in your town?
3 There's a beautiful old mosque in the town centre.
4 There aren't any hospitals in the area.
5 There's an expensive restaurant near here. It's famous!
6 There are some beautiful houses in the old part of the city.
7 There are some nice little places to eat on the beach.
8 There's an airport outside town.
9 Are there any cinemas in your town?
10 There aren't any schools in the village. We go to the next town.

▶ TRACK 7

wɪtʃ, læŋgwɪdʒ, jʊː, laɪk, waɪf, rɪ, tel, weɪ, ləʊkəl, res, wɒnt, west, liːs

▶ TRACK 8

1 Which languages do you speak?
2 I don't like English food.
3 His wife's a receptionist in a hotel.
4 He's a waiter in a local restaurant.
5 Do you want to go swimming in the river?
6 She's at university in west London.
7 He wants to be a police officer.
8 Where does your brother work?

UNIT 2

▶ TRACK 9

1 doing sport
2 dancing
3 singing
4 meeting new people
5 playing computer games
6 walking
7 cooking
8 reading
9 going to a concert
10 watching TV
11 listening to music
12 swimming
13 playing the guitar
14 going out for dinner
15 going to the cinema
16 drawing

▶ TRACK 10

A: Do you like doing sport?
B: No, I'm really bad at it. What about you?
A: Yeah, I think it's great. I love playing tennis and basketball. Do you like walking?
B: No – it's boring. What about you?
A: Yeah, it's OK. I like going to the park. I sometimes walk there.
B: Do you like playing computer games?
A: No, not really. What about you?
B: Oh, I love it. It's really good fun. I play every day – a lot! Do you like going to the cinema?
A: Yes, I do. It's great.
B: I love it too. Do you want to see *Love Train*?
A: No. I don't like love films. I like horror films.
B: Oh.

▶ TRACK 11

1 I need to go.
2 I want to learn to drive.
3 Try to use the words you learn.
4 My daughter wants to get a new phone.
5 I try to study English every day.
6 We need to buy some things later.

▶ TRACK 12

1

A: Do you like watching football?
B: Yeah. It's OK. Why?
A: Well, do you want to watch the match on Saturday?
B: Where?
A: In a café in town. It's on TV.
B: OK. What time does it start?
A: Five.
B: So what time do you want to meet?
A: Is four OK? We want to get a place to sit.
B: OK. Where do you want to meet?
A: Outside Green Street train station?
B: That sounds good. So four o'clock outside Green Street station.
A: Yes. See you there.

2

B: Do you like Italian food?
C: Yeah, I do. I love it.
B: Do you want to meet for lunch on Sunday? There's a really nice Italian restaurant near here.
C: Yeah. That sounds good. What time do you want to meet?
B: Is one OK?
C: Yes, sure. Where?
B: Outside the cathedral?
C: OK. Great.

▶ TRACK 13

M = Matty, S = Simon, C = Camilla

1

M: OK. Let's take a break! There's a café next door if you want a coffee.
S: Eh? What?
C: It's a break. He says there's a café next door.
S: Oh. OK, thanks.
C: Do you want to have a coffee?
S: Oh … yeah, but I don't have any money.
C: That's OK. I have some money.
S: Are you sure?
C: Sure. You buy another day.
S: OK, thanks. How long is the break?
C: Oh, I don't know. Teacher! Teacher!
M: Yes, Camilla.
C: How much time do we have?
M: Twenty minutes.
C: Twenty. OK. Thanks.
M: Oh, and Camilla – call me Matty, not 'teacher'!
C: Oh. OK! Sorry … Matty.

2

C: Er … um teacher, er Matty?
M: Yes. Camilla.
C: Do we have any homework?
M: Oh yes. Everyone! Look on page 157. The Grammar reference. OK? So do Exercise 2 on 'going to' and then in Revision do all three exercises.

S: All?

M: Yeah. And then try to learn some vocabulary from today's class.

S: This is a lot of homework.

M: Do you think so?

C: No, it's not much homework. I think Simon is lazy!

S: Maybe.

M: No, I don't think so! Simon, try to do it. Do some every day – five or ten minutes.

S: OK. Maybe.

A: OK, everyone. Thanks. See you next week.

3

M: OK everyone, nice to see you again. My name's Matty. Before we start, everyone tell each other your names.

M: OK. Stop there! Oh, hello Simon.

S: Hi ... er, sorry, ... I'm late.

M: That's OK. Sit down. There's a place next to Camilla.

S: Er, OK.

M: OK. So everyone. Look at page 57 now. See Exercise 1. What's the answer to number 1? Anyone? Camilla?

C: Close the window.

M: Yes. That's right. OK, everyone – you find the other answers.

S: Teacher! I don't have a pen.

M: Oh, right. Does anyone have a pen? Thanks, Camilla! Oh, and Simon, call me Matty, not 'teacher'.

S: OK. OK. Er.. Teacher – what does 'turn off' mean?

M: Um ... er ... Do you have a dictionary?

S: No. ... Oh, Camilla, thanks. Camilla, do you have any paper?

▶ TRACK 14

/kləʊ/, /kʌ/, /ge/, /gəʊ/, /geɪ/, /eɪk/, /ɜːk/, /æks/, /siː/, /saɪ/, /ɪz/, /eɪz/

▶ TRACK 15

1 Do you want to take a break?

2 That shop never closes.

3 We sometimes go to the countryside.

4 My son plays a lot of computer games.

5 I get home from work at six.

6 We don't get much homework.

7 I want to relax on Saturday.

8 He seems very nice.

▶ TRACK 16

1 Do you have any money?

2 I don't need any help, thanks.

3 What time do you want to meet?

4 There are a lot of places to visit here.

5 I don't need to do much homework tonight.

6 He usually gets up at six and starts work at seven.

UNIT 3

▶ TRACK 17

1 share food

2 wash some clothes

3 a post office

4 put on make-up

5 a supermarket

6 hang up the washing

7 the bathroom

8 set the table

9 sit in the kitchen

10 dry my hair

11 clean the house

12 get dressed

13 a department store

14 go to a chemist

15 the living room

16 a sports centre

▶ TRACK 18

1

A: I need to buy some shoes for my son. Are there any shoe shops near here?

B: How old is he?

A: Six.

B: Try Kid's Stuff – it's a clothes shop for kids. They sell nice shoes.

A: OK. Where's that?

B: It's on New Street. There's a big bookshop on the right, and it's next to that.

A: OK. Thank you.

2

C: Are there any restaurants near here? We want to get something to eat.

D: There aren't really any places in this area. Try the supermarket on Dixon Road. They have sandwiches and salads.

C: Dixon Road?

D: Yeah. Do you know it?

C: Yes, I think so.

D: Well, the supermarket's on the left there – opposite the small park.

C: Great. Thanks for that.

3

E: Is there a bookshop near here? I want to buy a phrasebook.

F: No, sorry. Maybe try Jeffer's. It's a department store on Chester Street. I think they sell books and things for tourists.

E: Sorry. Where?

F: It's on the corner of Chester Street and Hale Road.

E: OK. Sorry. Can you show me on the map?

F: Yes, sure. Look. We're here – on Simpson Lane and there's Hale Road and that's Chester Street there. The department store's on the left – next to a big clothes shop. It's called Jeffer's.

E: OK. Great. Thank you.

▶ TRACK 19

1

A: Simon!

B: What?

A: Look at this room!

B: What?

A: It's a mess!

B: What?

A: I can't walk across it without breaking something!

B: It's not bad.

A: Can you tidy it, please?

B: Later.

A: Now, please!

B: But, mum!

A: Now!

B: OK, OK.

2

C: Wh ... what te ... temperature is the air-conditioning on?

D: 17.

C: Ca ... can you turn it up? I'm co ... cold.

D: It's not cold.

C: P ... please.

D: OK.

C: Thanks.

3

E: What did he say?

F: 'It's not you, it's me.'

E: Oh ... and what was that?

F: 'I don't love you anymore.'

E: OK ... What? Can you turn it up? I can't hear it.

F: It's old age, Dad. Is that OK for you?

E: Yes, thanks.

G: Can you turn the TV down? I need to study and I can't concentrate.

▶ TRACK 20

1 I can't sleep.
2 Can you help me?
3 Can I use your bathroom?
4 Can you turn up the music?
5 I can't find my book.
6 Can I wash some clothes?
7 We can't come next week.
8 He can't drive at the moment.

▶ TRACK 21

/faɪ/, /bæ/, /bɑː/, /pʊ/, /ʌp/, /lʌv/, /lɪv/, /pæl/, /pəʊ/, /pleɪ/, /pliː/, /flæ/, /fɪ/, /fɔː/, /ve/, /frɪ/

▶ TRACK 22

1 I need to find a bank.
2 She's in the bathroom, putting on make-up.
3 They have a lovely living room.
4 I want to send this package to Poland.
5 Put the plates in the sink, please.
6 My flat's on the left – opposite the post office.
7 A friend has four sofas in her flat!
8 There's a plate of vegetables in the fridge.

UNIT 4

▶ TRACK 23

1 enjoy the nightlife
2 watch a football match
3 be annoyed
4 rent a boat
5 get some flowers
6 have a picnic
7 get back home
8 have a cold
9 see a film
10 walk in the mountains
11 do some shopping
12 laugh
13 snow
14 celebrate your birthday
15 stay in a hotel
16 go sightseeing

▶ TRACK 24

1

A: Hi, Helga. How are you?

B: OK, but very tired!

A: Oh. What did you do at the weekend?

B: We went to a rock festival.

A: Yeah?

B: Yeah. It was fantastic.

A: Really? Who did you see?

B: Oh, lots of bands! The Hives, The Strypes. Who else now? Oh, yes. I saw The Loons on Saturday night. They were good.

A: Sounds great.

B: Yeah, it was great, but I didn't sleep much.

2

C: Hello.

D: Hi, how are you? Did you have a nice weekend?

C: Yes, it was OK.

D: What did you do?

C: Nothing much, really. I did some shopping on Saturday morning. I played tennis, watched TV – the usual things.

D: It sounds OK.

C: Yeah, I needed to relax.

3

E: Did you have a good weekend?

F: Not really.

E: Oh! That sounds bad. What did you do?

F: Nothing! I was ill. I had a bad cold. I stayed in bed all weekend.

E: Oh, no! Are you OK now?

F: Yes, but I need to work now!

4

G: Detlev! Hi! How are you?

H: Good.

G: Did you have a nice weekend?

H: Yes, it was great.

G: What did you do?

H: Well, some friends came to visit, so I showed them round the city.

G: That sounds nice. Where did you go?

H: Well, on Saturday, we went to the cathedral and then had a picnic in the park, and in the evening we went into the old town. Then on Sunday, we went to the market in the morning, and then I cooked lunch for everyone.

G: That sounds great.

H: It was. It was lovely.

▶ TRACK 25

1 My friends visit me a lot.
2 We visited the cathedral.
3 I played a game of tennis with a friend.
4 I tried to phone you yesterday to arrange to play tennis.
5 I wanted to go out last night, but it rained.
6 I met a friend and we chatted all night.
7 We often walk together and chat.
8 We walked along the river and had a picnic.

▶ TRACK 26

1 January the first
2 October the nineteenth
3 March the eighth
4 November the second
5 June the twenty-fourth
6 the third Monday in January

▶ TRACK 27

1

The night before the holiday, we made a fire on the beach with some friends. We sat round the fire all night and we drank and ate and sang songs and laughed. We had a great time. Some of my friends swam in the sea, but I didn't. The sea wasn't very warm. It usually isn't in June. Then on the 24th, I slept until four in the afternoon.

2

I wasn't in Russia in March, I was in London for work, so I missed the holiday. They don't have this holiday in the UK. It was sad. On Women's Day, men usually treat us very well. They do nice things and give us presents. But I didn't go out for dinner. I didn't get any flowers. I didn't have anyone to say nice things to me. I just sat in my hotel room and watched TV! It wasn't very nice.

3

For the holiday, we went to Snowshoe Mountain in West Virginia. The snow's good in January. We left on Saturday the 16th at three in the morning and we drove to the mountains. It was good because there weren't many cars on the road. We got there at eight and spent the whole weekend skiing. It was very clear and sunny. There wasn't a cloud in the sky. We had great views. We came home on the afternoon of the holiday Monday, but the traffic was bad. We didn't get back home to Washington until two in the morning.

▶ TRACK 28

/djə/
/dɪ djə/
/dɪd jɔː/

1 Did you go on holiday anywhere?
2 Where did you go?
3 Who did you go with?
4 Did you have a good time?
5 Where did you stay?

▶ TRACK 29

/uːn/, /aʊnd/, /ent/, /mən/, /maʊnt/, /æm/, /deɪ/, /drəʊ/, /tɪd/, /tɪk/, /tɪn/, /təl/, /ɪst/, /aɪt/

▶ TRACK 30

1 We drove round the country.
2 We went to Germany in June.
3 We missed our flight when we came home.
4 We went walking in the mountains.
5 We rented a boat and swam in the river.
6 We spent a day in the capital city.
7 We had a fantastic time.
8 The weather was warm and sunny.

▶ TRACK 31

1 The bank's on this road on the right.
2 I think she lives on her own.
3 Can you turn it up? I can't hear it.
4 How long were you there for?
5 There wasn't anyone I knew there.
6 I'm sorry. I didn't hear what you said.

UNIT 5

▶ TRACK 32

1 a bar on the top floor
2 the menswear department
3 a man with a brown jumper
4 take the lift
5 a young woman with a blue top
6 have a sale
7 work in a bakery
8 go up the escalator
9 choose a cake
10 look round the market
11 fruit and vegetables
12 queue to pay
13 business is growing
14 a woman with a green dress
15 the cheese section
16 steal some jeans
17 a woman with a leather jacket

▶ TRACK 33

1

A: Who's next?
B: Me.
A: What would you like?
B: Can I have some apples?
A: These ones?
B: No, those red ones.
A: How many would you like?
B: Six.
A: OK. Anything else, my love?
B: Yes. Those things there. What do you call them in English?
A: These?
B: Yes.
A: Peaches. Do you want the yellow or the orange ones?
B: Three yellow ones.
A: There you go. That's three pounds ten altogether. Thank you. Next?

2

C: Those look nice.
D: Mmm. That yellow one especially.
C: Hello. Do you speak English?
E: A little.
C: You see the yellow cake? Is it lemon?
E: Yeah.
C: Mmm. Can we have some of that?
E: How much? Like this?
D: A bit more. That's fine.
C: And the brown one above it – with the orange stuff on top? What's that?
E: That's coffee cake with orange.
C: OK. I'll have a piece of that.
E: Like this?
C: That's great.
E: Five euros forty-six.

3

F: English?
G: Yes. How much are those?
F: Depends. seven dollars fifty, ten, fifteen dollars. Which do you like?
G: How much is that red one?
F: This one?

G: No, the other one, there at the top. With 'Egypt' on it.

F: This one?

G: Yes.

F: Fifteen.

G: Really?

F: For you, two for twenty five.

G: You have another one like that?

F: Of course.

G: What size?

F: Any size.

G: OK. What about two for twenty dollars?

F: OK. What size do you want?

G: Can I have one in medium and a small one? Thanks.

F: Here you are.

▶ TRACK 34

thirteen	fourteen	sixteen
thirty	forty	sixty

▶ TRACK 35

1 That's eighteen euros exactly.
2 That's seventy dollars and sixteen cents altogether.
3 Everything is reduced by fifteen percent.
4 Those are thirteen ninety-nine at the moment – reduced from seventeen.
5 It costs fourteen thousand pounds new.
6 Our apartment cost two hundred and forty thousand when we bought it.

▶ TRACK 36

1 The shops in town are having sales at the moment.
2 I'm working very hard at the moment.
3 My mother's not here. She's doing the shopping.
4 The economy's growing fast at the moment.
5 My football team's doing really well now.
6 You're really improving.
7 Some friends are staying with me at the moment.
8 My brother's studying at university.

▶ TRACK 37

1

A: Excuse me. Do you sell batteries?

B: Yes, madam. They're over there, by the till.

A: Really?

B: No? Let's see. Yes, look. They're there. On the bottom shelf.

A: Oh, yes. Thanks. Oh, wait! They don't have this kind. It's for a camera.

B: Oh, right. Try the basement. Take the lift over there and the camera section is in front of you when you get out. Ask an assistant.

A: OK. Thanks.

B: You're welcome.

2

C: Did you see that?

D: What? That woman with the blue coat?

C: Yeah. She put that perfume in her bag!

D: I know. Tell the security guard.

C: No, you tell him.

D: Why me? You saw her first!

C: No – I didn't.

D: Oh, wait! Someone's talking to her.

C: Oh dear ...

3

E: Hi there.

F: Where are you?

E: I'm still on the bus, but we're coming down Oxford Street now.

F: Oh, OK. Well, I'm just queuing to pay for these things.

E: Did you get what you wanted?

F: Yeah, I got a pair of jeans and a really nice skirt and two tops.

E: That sounds a lot!

F: They were all in the sale.

E: Right. Anyway. Where do you want to meet?

F: There's a café on the fourth floor.

E: Is there?

F: Yeah. Go in the main entrance and up the escalator and when you get off on the fourth floor, it's behind you. It's at the back of the store in the left corner.

E: OK – I'm sure I can find it. See you in a moment.

4

G: Excuse me. Are these all the sizes you have?

H: Yes.

G: OK. Can I see if these fit?

H: Of course. The changing rooms are over there in the corner. Next to the jeans.

G: Oh, OK. Thanks. How many items can I take to try on?

H: Six.

G: Great. Thanks.

▶ TRACK 38

/ɪŋ/, /vɪŋ/, /θɪŋ/, /ʃɜː /, /ʃən/, /ɪʃ/, /ɪtʃ/, /ɪdʒ/, /tʃuː/, /tʃiː/, /dʒiː/, /dʒʌ/

▶ TRACK 39

1 Which one is cheaper?
2 Choose what you want.
3 They're selling everything they can.
4 My English is really improving.
5 She's wearing jeans and an orange jumper.
6 Can you manage with all those bags?
7 There's a big fish section in the market.
8 He's just changing his shirt.

UNIT 6

▶ TRACK 40

1 solve the problem
2 a boring class
3 police training
4 cause a problem
5 study Engineering
6 help each other
7 a Law student
8 pass the exam
9 a lazy student
10 learn to ride a bike
11 teach PE
12 an angry boss
13 a creative person
14 a modern university
15 a strange teacher
16 make clothes
17 borrow some money
18 learn Arabic

▶ TRACK 41

1
A: So what do you do, Imke?
B: I'm a student.
A: Oh, OK. What're you studying?
B: I'm doing a degree in Marketing.
A: Right. And what year are you in?
B: My first. I only started this year.
A: How's the course going?
B: Really well. It's great. I'm really enjoying it. It's very interesting and the other students are very nice and friendly too, so that's good.

2
C: So what do you do, Tom? Are you working?
D: No, I'm a student at university.
C: Oh, right. What're you studying?
D: Geography.
C: Really? What year are you in?
D: My second.
C: And how's it going?
D: Not very well, actually. I just find it boring.

3
E: What do you do? Are you working?
F: No, I'm not, actually. I'm at the local technical college.
E: Oh, right. What're you studying?
F: Engineering.
E: Wow! OK. What year are you in?
F: My third. I finish next year.
E: And how's it going?
F: OK, but it's quite difficult. It's a lot of work!
E: I'm sure. Well, good luck with it.

▶ TRACK 42

1 How are you?
2 Where are you from?
3 What are you studying?
4 What year are you in?
5 Are you enjoying it?
6 Are you good at English?
7 Are you doing anything now?
8 Are you hungry?

▶ TRACK 43

1 Astrid
I'm doing a great course at the moment. I'm learning to make clothes. It's every Monday and Wednesday evening from 6.30 to 9 and it lasts for ten weeks. It's quite expensive, but it's really good. The teachers are very helpful and I'm learning a lot. I love seeing what the other students make as well. I want to change my job and work in fashion, so doing this course is a good start.

2 Peter
We had a training session at work last week. It wasn't very long – it only lasted about an hour – but it was awful. My boss told everyone to go, so we didn't have any choice. It was about how to make good decisions. I didn't learn anything new. I was quite angry by the end of it.

3 Kate
I'm learning to ride. I started taking classes about six months ago and I ride once or twice a week. It depends how busy I am. I grew up in the countryside and when I was young I always wanted to ride and have a horse, but my parents didn't have much money so I didn't have the chance. I'm really enjoying the lessons. My teacher is very patient and I'm getting quite good now.

4 Neil
I'm doing an online Creative Writing course at the moment. My wife started it with me, but she stopped. She didn't like it because it's an open course and she said it was strange doing it with thousands of other students. On the course, we watch lots of videos and people comment. Then we do our own writing. I'm trying to write a novel. I'm spending about ten hours a week on it. Another thing I like about the course is there's no exam at the end. I hate taking exams. I always fail.

▶ TRACK 44

/e/, /ə/, /ɜː/, /ɔː/, /lə/, /lɔː/, /lɜː/, /en/, /ɜːn/, /ʃən/, /mənt/, /ɜːs/, /ɔːz/

▶ TRACK 45

1 It causes a lot of problems.
2 The last course was more interesting.
3 The government's made education worse.
4 My classmates are quite friendly.
5 We learned a lot about the law.
6 The sports teacher's very popular.
7 I spent four hours preparing the talk.
8 The training at work was very boring.

▶ TRACK 46

1 My son's studying Law at university.
2 I'm learning to ride a horse at the moment.
3 Excuse me. I'm looking for the changing rooms.
4 Some of my classmates aren't very friendly.
5 Your English is better than mine.
6 It was much warmer last summer.

UNIT 7

▶ TRACK 47

1 dead
2 clever
3 old friends
4 funny
5 look after children
6 repair a car
7 a wedding
8 strict
9 feed the dog
10 do some housework
11 do the washing
12 nursery school
13 very fit
14 husband
15 male and female
16 surprised

▶ TRACK 48

1
A: Do you have any brothers or sisters, Zoe?
B: Yes, I do. I have two brothers.
A: Oh, right. How old are they?
B: Well, I'm the middle child. My older brother's 28 and my younger one is nineteen.
A: What do they do?
B: Neil – my older brother – is a teacher, and my younger brother, Tim, is in his second year at university.
A: Oh, OK. What's he studying?
B: Chemistry.

2

C: Did you go out yesterday?

D: Yeah, I did. I met my cousin and his girlfriend for a drink.

C: Oh, OK. Is he visiting?

D: No, he lives here. He's English.

C: Really?

D: Yes. My uncle Giorgio met my aunt Ruth in London and they stayed in England.

C: So, how old is your cousin?

D: Nineteen. He's a year younger than me.

C: Do you have any other cousins here?

D: No, I don't, but I have twelve back in Italy.

C: Really? How many aunts and uncles do you have?

D: Nine. My dad has eight brothers and sisters!

3

E: So, are you married, Ted?

F: Yes, I am – 30 years next year.

E: Wow! Really?

F: Yep.

E: So, what does your wife do?

F: She's a nurse.

E: And do you have any children?

F: Yeah, just one son – Ted junior. He's finishing college this year.

E: Really? OK. What's he studying?

F: Medicine. He wants to be a doctor.

▶ TRACK 49

Really? Really? Really?

▶ TRACK 50

1 My dad has ten brothers and sisters.
2 My brother's fifteen years older than me.
3 My wife is a nurse.
4 It's my birthday today.
5 My grandma's 98.
6 My sister's in her last year at school.

▶ TRACK 51

1 Johan and I grew up together. We first met at school and later we shared a house together in Malmö. He's very creative. He's a photographer and he lives in New York now, but we're still very close. We talk all the time. We're friends for life, I'm sure.

2 I only know Miguel because my husband works with him. I don't really get on with him very well, but what can I do? They were already friends when we met and I respect that. He likes going out a lot. He goes to parties all night. I think he's a bit stupid. He's 38, but he thinks he's still 21! He also sometimes says stupid things about women.

3 In some ways, Claire and I don't know each other at all. She lives in Wisconsin and I live in Leeds. We never meet face-to-face. We only meet in chat rooms and we talk through Messenger. She's very sensitive and she really understands me. My friends think I'm crazy, but when I leave college, I want to go to the US and meet her in person!

4 Liu Bing – or Auntie Liu as I call her – isn't really my aunt. She's an old friend of my mum's. They went to school together and she came to our house a lot when I was a kid. She's a strong and confident woman, and she made me feel good about myself. When I moved to Shanghai, she helped me find a place to live and a job, so now she's not only my mother's friend, she's mine as well!

▶ TRACK 52

/griː/, /glɪ/, /miː/, /kɪ/, /fɪ/, /fiː/, /ʃiː/, /swɪ/, /sɪ/, /strɪ/

▶ TRACK 53

1 We agreed to meet tonight.
2 I'm not very confident about my English.
3 I need to feed my kids.
4 She's my best female friend.
5 She swims a lot, so she's very fit.
6 I need to leave at six.
7 We're sisters, but we're not very similar.
8 Why is your dad so strict with your sister?

UNIT 8

▶ TRACK 54

1   the main square
2   grow fruit
3   move house
4   destroy a building
5   win the lottery
6   provide help
7   go fishing
8   have a check-up
9   go to the library
10 a romantic dinner
11 a big clock
12 do some exercise
13 build a house
14 save money
15 get a taxi
16 get married

▶ TRACK 55

1

A: Hey ... um ... Katie ... listen, do you want ... um ... do you have time for a coffee?

B: No, sorry, I don't. I'm going to study in the library and do some reading for my Literature course.

A: Oh, OK. Well, maybe later?

B: I can't really. I'm not going to have time. I'm just going to go home because I really need to study. I have my exams next week, you know, so ...

A: Oh, right. Well, good luck with them. What about after your exams? Do you want to go out somewhere then? Maybe dinner one night?

B: I'm really sorry, but I can't. I ... I have to work that night. Bye.

A: But I didn't say which night!

2

C: So what're your plans for today?

D: Oh, I need to write a few emails, so I'm going to find a café with Wi-Fi and do that – and I have to check the details of my flight for next week as well, so, you know. What about you? What're your plans?

C: I'm going to go running by the river later. I need to do some exercise!

D: Good idea! What about tonight? Are you going to be busy then?

C: No. Why? Do you want to meet somewhere?

D: Yes, OK. Where?

C: How about in the main square at eight?

D: OK. Great.

C: Then I can show you some nice places where there aren't too many tourists.

3

E: Are you going to go to the meeting?

F: No, I'm not. I'm going to meet some clients and have lunch with them.

E: Oh, right. Where are you going to eat?

F: A new French place in Harajuku.

E: Oh, that sounds good.

F: Yeah. What about you? What're your plans?

E: I have to give a presentation at the meeting, but after that I'm going to go out somewhere. Do you want to come?

F: Maybe, yeah. Call me later, OK?

E: OK.

F: Great. See you.

▶ TRACK 56

going to

1 Where are you going to go?
2 I'm going to leave tomorrow.
3 What time are you going to get up?
4 Some friends are going to visit.
5 How long are they going to stay?
6 He's not going to come.

▶ TRACK 57

A: What're your plans for later?

B: I don't have any. Why? Do you want to meet somewhere?

A: Yes. Great. Where?

B: How about in the main square, under the big clock?

A: Yes, fine. What time?

B: Is six OK?

A: It's quite early.

B: Oh, sorry. Well, how about seven thirty?

A: Perfect! See you later. Bye.

▶ TRACK 58

1

I'm from the Czech Republic, but at the moment, I'm living in Manchester. I'm doing a degree here. I also work part-time and I'm saving money because, after university, I'd really like to go to China to study kung fu. I practise three times a week here, and I'd like to take it to the next level.

2

I work for a big design company in São Paulo, but I'd like to leave and start my own business sometime in the next two or three years. I don't like having a boss. I'd like to work for myself. I'd also like to start a family, have children, but maybe that has to wait!

3

I'm going to retire next year, after working for 38 years. It's going to be strange, but I'm looking forward to it. I'd like to spend more time gardening. I have a small piece of land and I'd like to grow my own fruit and vegetables. I'd also like to spend more time with my wife and children.

4

I'd like to be really famous. I'd like to have my own TV show and I'd like to have lots and lots of money. I'd like someone to drive me round in a big car and I'd like to eat in expensive restaurants – and I'd like everyone in the world to know my name!

▶ TRACK 59

1 I'd really like to spend a year in South America.
2 I'd really like to meet him sometime. I love his music!
3 My brother would like to learn how to cook.

4 She'd like to change jobs sometime soon.
5 I wouldn't like to be famous!
6 It's a nice apartment, but I wouldn't like to live in that area.
7 Would you like to get something to eat after class?
8 Would you like to come shopping with me tomorrow?

▶ TRACK 60

/eɪ/, /aɪ/, /uː/, /eɪv/, /aɪv/, /uːv/, /eɪt/, /feɪ /, /deɪ/, /baɪ/, /laɪ/, /duː/, /juː/

▶ TRACK 61

1 They're going to create 800 new jobs.
2 I'm going to drive there, so I can take you.
3 I do exercise every day to keep fit.
4 The university has a famous library.
5 I'd like to move to a nicer place.
6 The school provides all the books.
7 I'm saving money to buy a motorbike.
8 It's going to improve the situation.

▶ TRACK 62

1 She's not going to like the idea.
2 I don't have to work tomorrow, but my wife does.
3 What time are you going to arrive tomorrow?
4 I'd really like to stop working and travel more.
5 Would you like something to eat?
6 My daughter still lives at home, but my sons don't.

UNIT 9

▶ TRACK 63

1 get a great view
2 go up a tower
3 visit a palace
4 make a mess
5 call an ambulance
6 hurt myself
7 break a glass
8 fall down
9 win the match
10 an exciting ride
11 forget to bring
12 lie on the beach
13 start crying
14 buy fresh fish
15 lose the game

▶ TRACK 64

A: Have you been to Istanbul before?

B: Well, it's my first time, but Harry's been here before.

C: Yeah, once – but it was for work. I didn't see much then.

A: When did you arrive?

B: Friday. We're really enjoying it.

A: So where have you been?

B: Well, this morning we went round the Bazaar. That was great. Then we went over to Galata and walked round there.

A: Did you go up the Galata Tower?

C: No. There was a long queue and we didn't want to wait.

A: Really? You get a great view from the top.

C: Yeah, I heard. Another time, maybe.

A: Have you been to Topkapi Palace?

B: Yes, we went there at the weekend. It's amazing, and it's so big!

A: I know. How long did you spend there?

B: All day! We were tired at the end.

C: Yeah, really tired!

A: I'm sure.

B: We also went to the Hagia Sophia.

A: Did you? I've never been in there.

B: But you live here!

A: I know, but sometimes you don't think about visiting places when they're near.

B: That's true. We live in London and I've never been to Buckingham Palace.

A: So, what are your plans for this evening?

C: We'd like to go out for dinner somewhere, but we're not sure where.

A: Well, have you tried the fish here?

B: No, we haven't.

A: Oh, you should! It's very good – very fresh. There's a great place quite near here. I can take you there, if you want.

C: Oh, that sounds great. Thank you.

▶ TRACK 65

1

A: Have you seen my glasses?

B: No. Have you checked in your jacket pocket?

A: Yeah. They're not there. They *were* on the table before.

B: Maybe they've fallen on the floor.

A: I can't see them. Can you?

B: No. You went to the toilet. Did you look there?

A: No. ... I've found them!! They were by the sink!

2

D: Sammy! No!

C: Can I help?

D: Yes, sorry. My son's thrown the plate on the floor.

C: Don't worry. These things happen. Let me clean everything.

D: Do you have a cloth or some tissues? There's sauce on my trousers.

C: Oh, yes, of course. And do you want more spaghetti for your son?

D: Er ... no, that's OK.

3

E: Do you have any water?

F: Yeah – there's some in the bag.

E: I can't see any.

F: Really? I filled a bottle this morning.

E: No. There's no bottle.

F: It's not in the pocket?

E: No.

F: I guess I left it at home, then.

E: Don't worry. I can buy some.

4

G: Ow!

H: What have you done?

G: I've cut my hand.

H: Fffff.

G: Do you have a plaster or something?

H: Yeah, but go to the sink and wash it under the cold water first.

5

I: I think we've come the wrong way

J: It's just two or three more streets.

I: Please. Can we ask someone?

J: Oh ... OK. Excuse me. Do you speak English?

K: Sure.

I: We're looking for Stockmann's.

K: Oh! You've come the wrong way. Do you have a map?

J: Yes, but it's not very good.

K: Let me look. OK. You're here ... and Stockman's is here. So you need to go back and then turn right here.

J: OK. Thanks.

I: I told you it was that way.

▶ TRACKS 66 & 67

1 Have you seen my keys?

2 I've forgotten your name.

3 Someone's taken my bag.

4 What have you done?

5 I've broken a glass.

6 Our bags haven't arrived.

7 We've missed our flight.

8 Where's Martin gone?

9 Has anyone called the police?

▶ TRACK 68

/æ/, /ɒ/, /aʊ/, /əʊ/, /æn/, /aʊn/, /raʊ/, /rəʊ/, /læ/, /lɒ/, /əʊl/, /gɒ/, /əʊk/

▶ TRACK 69

1 Sorry. I've broken your window.

2 I forgot to tell you.

3 I found it on the floor.

4 We lost the match.

5 Have you planned your holiday?

6 I can show you round the town.

7 He sounded sad when we spoke.

8 He stopped me and stole my phone.

UNIT 10

▶ TRACK 70

1 a lovely pool

2 a lot of crime

3 get off the train

4 go to the gym

5 get in the car

6 an animal on the line

7 vote for it

8 charge for the motorway

9 wait on the platform

10 pay in cash

11 get a haircut

12 cycle in a bike lane

13 watch a live band

14 travel first class

15 taste delicious

16 park the car

17 change money

▶ TRACK 71

A Hello. I'm sorry. Do you speak English?

B: Of course. How can I help?

A: Hi. We'd like two tickets to Groningen, please.

B: Groningen. Certainly. Travelling today?

A: If possible, please, yes.

B: No problem. The next train is at 12.25, so you have lots of time.

A: Good.

B: A single or return?

A: Return, I think, but we're not sure when we're going to come back.

B: Ah, so it's probably best to buy two singles. Return tickets only last one day.

A: Oh, OK. How much are the single tickets?

B: First class is fifty-two euros fifty and second class is twenty-seven euros ten.

A: Two second class is fine, thank you.

B: That's fifty-four euros and twenty cents, please. How would you like to pay?

A: Is Visa OK?

B: Yes, of course. Please enter your PIN. Great. Thank you.

A: Thank you. What platform does the train leave from?

B: You need platform six, and you have to change at Hilversum.

A: Oh, really? It's not direct?

B: No, there are no direct trains to Groningen from here.

A: I see. How long does the journey take?

B: It's about two and a half hours in total. You have to wait thirty minutes in Hilversum. You arrive around three o'clock.

A: OK. And it's platform six, yes?

B: Yes, platform six at 12.25.

A: OK. Thanks for your help.

C: Did you get the tickets OK?

A: Yes, it's at twenty-five past twelve. What time is it now? Do we have time for a coffee?

C: Yeah – plenty of time. It's quarter to twelve.

▶ TRACK 72

1 Quarter to seven.
2 Five to twelve.
3 Twenty-five to three.
4 Ten to ten.
5 Talk to me.
6 I'd love to go to Thailand.
7 We have to change here.
8 I don't have to go to work today.

▶ TRACK 73

A: Good evening, sir, madam. How can I help you?

B: Hi. We'd like to go out for dinner. Where's the best place to eat?

A: Try Captain Nemo's. It's a lovely little restaurant by the sea. It's not the cheapest place in town, but the fish there is really excellent.

C: Oh, that sounds great. Do we need to book?

A: I can do that for you, if you like. What time would you like your table?

B: About half past eight?

C: Yes, that sounds fine. What's the easiest way to get there? Can we walk?

A: Not really. It takes about half an hour to walk there. It's probably best to take a taxi. Would you like me to book one for you?

C: Yes, please. That's great.

B: Oh, there's one other thing, before I forget. We'd like to buy some presents. Where's the best place to go shopping?

A: There's a nice market in the main square tomorrow. They have some nice things. Try there. It starts at around eight and goes on until about two.

B: It sounds perfect. Thanks for your help.

A: No problem. It's my pleasure.

▶ TRACK 74

/wʊ/, /wɜː/, /haː/, /ʊk/, /aːk/, /gʊ/, /dʒɜː/, /fɜː/, /duː/, /paː/, /ruː/

▶ TRACK 75

1 I booked a return ticket.
2 You can't park the car near here.
3 Their flight's at half past two.
4 The train journey took too long.
5 Which route do you prefer?
6 First-class seats aren't good value.
7 It's the worst place in the world.
8 Would you like me to ask?

▶ TRACK 76

1 She's one of the funniest people I know.
2 I've never been there, but I'd love to go.
3 There's too much pollution and there are too many cars on the road.
4 I visited them in Madrid a few weeks ago.
5 There aren't enough chairs here for everyone.
6 I need your help. Something terrible has happened.

UNIT 11

▶ TRACK 77

1 a lot of spices
2 order food online
3 a cookery book
4 ask for the bill
5 fried chicken
6 buy some sweets
7 steak and chips
8 look at the menu
9 a lot of garlic
10 want to lose weight
11 a pregnant mum
12 cut some onion
13 tomato soup
14 sell soft drinks
15 a vegetable dish
16 a fruit dessert

▶ TRACK 78

A: Hello. I'm sorry. Do you speak English?

B: A little, yes.

A: Great. Can we have a table for two, please?

B: Have you booked?

A: No, I'm afraid we haven't.

B: Ah. We are very busy tonight. Can you wait ten minutes?

A: Yes.

C: Can we see the menu, please?

B: Of course.

C: Ah. You don't have English menus?

B: We don't. I'm sorry, but I can help you. This is chicken, this is fish – but I don't know the name of the fish in English – this is steak, this is soup and this is a bird – I don't know the name – it's similar to a chicken, but smaller. It's very, very good. I recommend this.

C: Oh. I'd like to try that, please.

B: Certainly, madam. And for you, sir?

A: The fish, please.

B: I'm sorry, sir, but the fish is finished. We don't have any more.

A: Oh, right. Well, can I get a steak, please? Well-cooked. No blood.

B: As you prefer.

B: Can I take your plates?

C: Thank you. That was delicious.

B: Would you like any dessert?

A: No, I'm fine. I'm really full. Can we have the bill, please?

B: Of course. One moment.

B: Here you are.

A: Thanks. Does this include service?

B: Yes, we add 15 per cent.

C: OK. Thank you.

▶ TRACK 79

1 For starters, I'll have the soup, please.
2 I'd like the chicken, please.
3 Can I get a steak, please?
4 Can I have the ice cream?

▶ TRACK 80

1

A: Are you ready to order?

B: Yes. Thanks. I'll have the salad for starters, please.

A: Certainly. And for your main course?

B: Can I get the chicken, please?

A: I'm afraid the chicken's finished.

B: Really? Oh. OK. Well, can I have the fish then, please?

2

C: Would you like any dessert?

D: Yes, please. Can I get the ice cream?

C: Of course. And for you, madam?

E: I'm really full. I'll just have a coffee, please.

C: With milk – or without?

E: Without, please, so just black.

▶ TRACK 81

1

A: So where do you want to eat?

B: I don't mind. I eat anything.

A: Yes, me too.

C: Actually. I don't eat meat.

A: Oh, really?

C: Yeah, but if the restaurant has some fish or vegetable dishes, that's OK.

A: Have you been to the place on the corner?

C: No.

B: Me neither. What's it like?

A: It's nice. It's Italian – more or less.

B: OK. That's fine with me.

C: Me too.

2

A: Did you go away anywhere in the summer?

B: Yeah, we went to Australia.

A: Really? I'd really like to go there.

C: Oh, I wouldn't.

A: No? Why not?

C: It's too far and I don't like planes.

B: It IS a long way, but it's amazing. You should go.

C: Hmm. I'm not sure. What's the food like? Is it all meat and barbecues?

B: No, not at all! There's lots of great Asian food and all kinds of different things.

A: Yeah. I saw a programme about it on TV.

C: Really?

B: Yeah. In fact, I had some of the best food I've ever had there.

A: It sounds great. I'd LOVE to go there. When I have more money – or time.

3

A: What are you going to have?

B: I can't decide.

A: Me neither.

C: Hmm. it all looks delicious. What about the mussels?

A: Oh, I don't like seafood.

C: Really? I do! I love it.

B: Me too. Don't you like *any* seafood?

A: Not really. I've eaten prawns before, but I prefer meat.

B: OK.

C: OK. I've decided. Talking of prawns, I'm going to have the prawn curry.

B: Hmm. Good choice. I saw Jamie Oliver on TV last night and he made a prawn curry.

C: Oh yeah. I saw that too. Maybe that's why I thought of it!

B: Yeah.

A: OK, I think I'll have the steak.

B: Oh, right – decisions, decisions. OK. I'm going to have the lamb.

▶ TRACK 82

/weə/, /ɪə/, /nɪə/, /hɪə/, /bɪə/, /blʌ/, /eəri/, /nʌts/, /ʌn/

▶ TRACK 83

1 Do you know anywhere good to eat near here?
2 I hate the taste of beer.
3 I'd like my steak well-cooked – no blood.
4 She can't eat any dairy products.
5 Here are your drinks.
6 I can't eat nuts because they make me ill.
7 It has a very unusual taste.
8 There's a great vegetarian restaurant near here.

UNIT 12

▶ TRACK 84

1 it's badly damaged
2 she's a bit upset
3 I burnt my hand
4 she's fallen asleep
5 my stomach hurts
6 protest against it
7 have a big smile
8 complain to the staff
9 put on sun cream
10 read the news
11 fans celebrating
12 get some fresh air
13 stop infection
14 a big storm
15 put ice on it
16 stop shouting!

▶ TRACK 85

1

A: Are you OK?

B: Yeah, I'm OK. My stomach hurts a bit.

A: Maybe you should lie down.

B: No, it's OK. I think I'm just hungry.

A: Are you sure?

B: Honestly, I'll be fine after I have something to eat.

2

C: Hi, it's Johnny.

D: Johnny! How are you?

C: Basically, I'm OK, but I fell off my bike and I've broken my arm!

D: Oh dear. Maybe we should cancel the meeting for tomorrow.

C: No, it's OK. It's my left arm, so I can write.

D: Are you sure?

C: Yeah, honestly, it's fine. It doesn't really hurt.

3

E: Are you OK?

F: No, I feel a bit sick.

E: Maybe you should go out and get some fresh air.

F: Yes, I think I will. I'll be back in a moment.

E: OK. Take your time. There's no rush.

4

G: Are you OK?

H: Yeah, yeah.

G: Have you been to the doctor?

H: No. It's just a cold.

G: Are you sure? You have a very bad cough. I really think you should see someone. Maybe it's an infection.

H: Honestly, it'll be fine in a couple of days.

5

I: Are you OK?

J: Yeah, I'm fine. My back hurts a bit, that's all.

I: Maybe you shouldn't play tennis, then.

J: It's OK. I told Kevin I'm going to.

I: Yeah, but are you sure you can play?

J: Yeah, I'll be fine after I warm up.

▶ TRACK 86

1 You should try it.
2 We should go.
3 I should stop.
4 You should call him.
5 They shouldn't be here.
6 He shouldn't do that.

▶ TRACK 87

1 I got the bus to work. I was lucky because there was a seat. I sat and read my book. It was quite a nice journey.

2 When I got to work, we had a meeting. The boss was quite angry. He shouted a bit and told us we need to work harder. It was really horrible, but I tried not to cry.

3 After the meeting finished, I sat and thought about everything I had to do. I got a headache. I sent a few emails and tried to concentrate.

4 I had lunch with my aunt. She lives near work. She always makes me smile. I felt better after seeing her.

5 In the afternoon, I went to see some clients. It was a successful afternoon. I sold a few things, and it's always nice meeting people.

6 Back in the office, I had to answer about 30 emails. It was slow and not very interesting.

7 After work, I had to wait for the bus for half an hour and then it was full, so I couldn't sit and read.

8 When I got home, I went for a run with my friend, Viv. We're going to go on holiday together, so we talked about that. It was a lovely warm evening.

9 After dinner, I watched the news on TV. I wanted to watch a film as well, but I fell asleep on the sofa.

▶ TRACK 88

/haʊ/, /ɜːθ/, /hɜːr/, /hæ/, /hed/, /həʊ/, /helθ/, /hæf/, /hɒs/, /hʌŋ/, /ðə/, /weðər/, /wɪð/, /wɪðaʊt/

▶ TRACK 89

1 How are you going to celebrate your birthday?
2 How did you hurt your hand?
3 I had a headache, so I stayed at home.
4 It's really bad for your health.
5 I have to go to hospital.
6 I'm really hungry because I haven't eaten all day.
7 I'm happy the weather is warm.
8 Do you want your coffee with milk – or without?

▶ TRACK 90

1 We eat quite a lot of rice and fish.
2 I was sick after I ate some seafood.
3 There aren't many places to eat near here.
4 Maybe you should tell him you're feeling stressed.
5 They didn't have any tables, so we didn't eat there.
6 I don't think we should pay more than thirty pounds for it.

UNIT 13

▶ TRACK 91

1 an icy road
2 a bit windy
3 a cloudy day
4 a farmer using chemicals
5 an empty road
6 climb a hill
7 pick up rubbish
8 the top of a wall
9 scared of spiders
10 check the forecast
11 a warm summer's day
12 a crowded street
13 surrounded by fields
14 chase each other
15 want attention
16 jump off a mountain
17 don't let it bite
18 it smells bad

▶ TRACK 92

1

A: What do you want to do tomorrow?

B: I don't know. What's the forecast?

A: It's going to be quite hot. They said it might reach 35 degrees.

B: Really? Why don't we go to the swimming pool?

A: Oh, we could do. Which one?

B: The open-air one – and we can have lunch at the café.

A: OK. Let's do that.

2

C: What do you want to do today?

D: I don't know. What's the forecast? It looks a bit cloudy.

C: It said it might rain this morning, but it's going to be dry this afternoon.

D: OK. Well, why don't we relax this morning and then go for a walk this afternoon?

C: Could do. Where?

D: How about taking the car and going to the hills?

C: OK. Let's do that. We haven't been to the hills recently.

3

E: Do you want to go away at the weekend?

F: I'm not sure. What's the forecast?

E: I think it's going to be cold. They said it might snow.

F: Really? Why don't we just stay here? I don't want to drive if there's snow or ice on the roads.

E: That's true. Maybe we should do some shopping for Christmas.

F: We could do. When exactly?

E: Early on Saturday morning. We can take the train.

F: Can we be back before the football starts?

E: Maybe. What time?

F: It starts at three.

E: I guess – if we go early.

F: OK. Let's do that. We have to do it sometime.

▶ TRACK 93

1 There might be a storm later.

2 They said it might snow tonight.

3 I might go for a run after class.

4 We might go to Spain in the summer.

5 I might not come to class tomorrow.

6 I might have to work this weekend.

▶ TRACK 94

1

A: Hey, did I tell you? I have foxes in my garden.

B: Really? Living there?

A: I think so, yes. I see them quite a lot, anyway.

B: Wow! So how long have they been there?

A: For a few months, I guess.

B: And are they OK? I mean, do they cause problems?

A: Not really, no. Well, sometimes they use the garden as a toilet ... but I love having them there and watching them play.

B: Have they ever tried to come inside?

A: Once, yes. They stole one of my shoes, actually! I found it outside the next day – half-eaten.

B: Oh!

A: I haven't had any problems recently, though, because I have a cat now and I think they're a bit scared of her!

2

C: Look. This one's a picture of my dog. Here.

D: He's huge!

C: I know. He weighs fifty-one kilos.

D: Really? That's amazing. What's his name?

C: He's called Sheriff.

D: And how long have you had him?

C: Five years. I got him when we moved out of the city. We have more space now, so ...

D: Mmm.

C: He's very friendly. He always jumps on you when you come home.

D: Woah! Scary!

C: No, it's fine. And he's very funny too. I mean, he plays very well with our cat, Kira. He chases her around – and they've never had any fights or anything.

3

E: What's that noise?

F: That? Oh, we have rats in the house. Didn't I tell you?

E: No. How annoying! How long have you had them?

F: Well, we've been here a year now and they've been here the whole time.

E: Ugh!

F: I know. They eat our food and I worry they'll bite the kids one day.

E: So what're you going to do?

F: Well, we've tried all kinds of things already, but nothing has worked, so I think we need to pay someone to come in and kill them.

▶ TRACK 95

1 A: How long have you had your cat?
   B: Two years.

2 A: How long have you been together?
   B: A few months now.

3 A: How long have you been married?
   B: For 15 years now.

4 A: How long have they known each other?
   B: Not very long.

5 A: How long have you lived in this house?
   B: All my life!

6 A: How long has she worked there?
   B: Ages.

▶ TRACK 96

/kr/, /kraɪ/, /kraʊ/, /dr/, /draɪ/, /tr/, /tri/, /træn/, /str/, /striː/, /streɪ/

▶ TRACK 97

1 I love living in the countryside.

2 I don't take public transport because of the crime.

3 The streets in the centre are always crowded.

4 I need to drive a friend to the station.

5 It's always dry in April.

6 I agree it was a very strange article.

7 He lives three streets from me.

8 There are lots of problems with transport.

UNIT 14

▶ TRACK 98

1 a strong economy

2 extra wages

3 arrive at the border

4 there's been a murder

5 get treatment

6 use violence

7 don't get on well

8 leader of a team

9 advert for a musical

10 injure herself

11 lost the election

12 start peace talks

13 more efficient

14 a scary film

15 have insurance

16 support each other

17 go and see a play

▶ TRACK 99

1

A: Have you ever seen a film called *28 Days Later*?

B: No, I haven't. I've heard of it, but I've never seen it. What's it like?

A: It's brilliant. It's really, really scary. It's about a terrible disease that makes people hungry for blood, and they want to kill.

B: Really? It sounds very violent!

A: Yeah, it is, but it's great! It's a very clever film. It's not a normal horror movie. It's also about the environment and politics and everything.

B: It sounds terrible – definitely not my kind of film!

A: No, it's great! Honestly!

2

C: Have you seen that new musical *Dogs* yet?

D: Yes, I have. I saw it last week, actually.

C: Oh really? We went to see it last night. What did you think of it?

D: It was OK. Nothing special. It was quite entertaining in places, I suppose, but the story was stupid.

C: Really? Do you think so? I thought it was brilliant – one of the best things I've seen in a long time.

D: Yeah? OK.

C: The dancing and the music were great and it was very funny. I couldn't stop laughing!

D: But what about the ending? It was so predictable!

C: Not for me! I found it really sad. I started crying!

D: Really? Oh well. I suppose we just don't share the same tastes.

▶ TRACK 100

1 Tomorrow's general election will probably be the closest in many years. Both the People's Party and the Popular Front say they expect to win, but most people think that they will probably have to share power. Voting starts at seven in the morning and closes at ten, and they're expecting the final result early on Monday morning.

2 The country's largest chemical company, NBE, has said that it is going to cut five thousand jobs. The company lost 385 million dollars last year and now plans to close its two biggest factories in the north of the country.

3 Abroad, peace talks between Adjikistan and Kamistan have failed and there are worries that war will now follow. The two countries disagree about where the border between them should be.

4 Next, pop music. Last year's TV Idol winner, Shaneez, has got engaged. The singer is planning to marry her boyfriend of two months, actor and model Kevin Smith.

5 And finally, France go into their important World Cup match against Brazil tonight without their captain and star player, Florian Mendy. Mendy injured himself in training yesterday and there's now a chance he won't play in the rest of the competition.

▶ TRACK 101

1 It'll be fine.
2 I probably won't vote this year.
3 It won't be easy.
4 It won't cost much.
5 I think he'll have a few problems.
6 We'll probably be a bit late.
7 We won't win.
8 It won't kill you. You'll live.

▶ TRACK 102

əns: violence, difference, insurance

mənt: treatment, environment, government

ʃən: election, situation, solution

▶ TRACK 103

1 I've noticed a few differences.
2 There were celebrations when she won the election.
3 The government should do more for the environment.
4 They stole my phone, but I had insurance.
5 The president didn't comment on the situation.
6 There's no easy solution to unemployment.
7 My insurance paid for my treatment.
8 I really hate all violence.

▶ TRACK 104

1 She's lived there all her life.
2 How long have you known about this?
3 It's difficult not to worry about what will happen.
4 You can try, but I don't expect it'll change things.
5 I doubt the economy will be stronger next year.
6 They said it's going to be hot and there might be a storm.

UNIT 15

▶ TRACK 105

1 produce electricity
2 very heavy
3 plug it in
4 shelves of food
5 various apps
6 read the instructions
7 do a search
8 install solar power
9 save energy
10 press the button
11 I dropped it
12 design a website
13 try to repair it
14 keep files
15 change the battery

▶ TRACK 106

1

A: Do you know much about computers?

B: A bit. Why?

A: I'm thinking of buying a laptop. Can you recommend anything?

B: Well, it depends. How much do you want to spend?

A: I'm not sure – about five or six hundred pounds.

B: OK. Well, for that price, try a Bell. They have quite a lot of memory, they're not too heavy and the battery lasts quite a long time.

A: That sounds perfect. Thanks.

2

C: What happened to your phone?

D: Oh, I dropped it last night and broke the screen.

C: Oh, how annoying!

D: I know. I'll need to replace it, but I'm actually thinking of getting one of those new model 8s everyone's talking about.

C: The Kotika ones?

D: Yeah.

C: Ooh! I see. Someone's feeling rich, then!

D: Why? What? Are they really expensive?

C: Well, they're not cheap ... but they are amazing phones. I mean, they look great, they're nice and light and they've got a huge screen, so they're great for playing games and watching videos on.

D: Wow. OK. Well, I guess I should have a look at one this weekend, then.

3

E: Hi. How're you?

F: Oh hi. What're you doing here?

E: I'm trying to find a birthday present for my brother. It's taking me ages.

F: What kind of thing are you looking for?

E: Well, I'm thinking of buying him a digital camera, but I don't know much about them!

F: Well, Bonny does a really good one. It's quite strong, so it won't break if you drop it ... , it takes really good pictures – even in the dark – and it's not very expensive either.

E: OK. Well, that sounds good.

▶ TRACK 107

1 b c d e g p t v
2 f l m n s x z
3 a h j k
4 q u w
5 i y
6 o
7 r

▶ TRACK 108

1 A: www.peiterzx.co.gu. That's p–e–i–t–e–r–z–x dot co dot g–u.

   B: OK, p–e–i–t–e–r–z–x dot co dot g–u.

   A: Yes.

2 A: My email's nomashy@jmal.com. That's n–o–m–a–s–h–y at j–m–a–l dot com.

   B: OK, n–o–m–a–s–h–y, that's all one word, right?

   A: Yes. At jmal dot com.

3 A: Flat four, 65 Farquhar Drive. That's f–a–r–q–u–h–a–r and d–r–i–v–e.

   B: OK. Flat four, 65 Farquhar Drive – f–a–r–q–u–h–a–r.

   A: That's right.

▶ TRACK 109

1 How many computers do you have in your home?
2 How long is your computer on every day?
3 How often do you check your email?
4 How many emails do you get every day?
5 What kind of mobile phone do you have?
6 What do you use your phone for?
7 Have you ever done anything stupid on your computer?
8 If you buy a piece of technology, how do you learn to use it?
9 What do you do if you have a problem with a piece of technology?
10 How often do you buy a new piece of technology?

▶ TRACK 110

1 How many computers do you have in your home?
   a None.
   b One.
   c Two or more.
2 How long is your computer on every day?
   a Maybe an hour or two – if I turn it on.
   b Four or five hours. Most of the evening.
   c I never turn it off.

3 How often do you check your email?
   a Maybe once a day, maybe less.
   b Two or three times a day.
   c I check it all the time on my phone.
4 How many emails do you get every day?
   a Nought to ten.
   b Ten to thirty.
   c Thirty to a hundred.
5 What kind of mobile phone do you have?
   a The most basic pay-as-you-go phone.
   b An OK phone with quite a good camera. It does everything I need it to do.
   c The very best, latest model.
6 What do you use your phone for?
   a What do you mean? Phoning people, of course!
   b I use the camera, I listen to music, and I sometimes play games.
   c Apart from the camera, I use the diary, Facebook, maps – all kinds of things. I can't list them all.
7 Have you ever done anything stupid on your computer?
   a Yes. I've deleted files on my computer by accident.
   b Yes. I sent an email to the wrong person once.
   c No, of course not.
8 If you buy a piece of technology, how do you learn to use it?
   a I ask someone to show me the very basic things.
   b I read the instructions and learn to do a few things. I'm not interested in the complicated things.
   c I just start playing about with it and teach myself. To find out more detailed things, I watch videos or look at the instructions or the website.
9 What do you do if you have a problem with a piece of technology?
   a Get angry, shout and jump up and down – until someone tells me I need to plug it in.
   b Check it's plugged in and, if it is, call someone to repair it.
   c Check everything is plugged in. Turn it off and on again – and if it still doesn't work, I repair it myself.
10 How often do you buy a new piece of technology?
   a Hardly ever. Why do I need it when my old things work?
   b Sometimes. Some new things are better, and I change them when my old things break.
   c All the time. I like to have all the latest things.

▶ TRACK 111

/ɑ:/, /æ/, /ɪ/, /eɪ/, /eə/, /ɒ/, /ə/, /ɔ:/

▶ TRACK 112

1 The software allows you to manage your money.
2 It's a really amazing app.
3 I need to change the battery on my camera.
4 It's not hard to create a nice website.
5 They damaged the wall when they installed the machine.
6 It allows you to translate any language.
7 I save all my files in various places.
8 I have to repair my washing machine.

UNIT 16

▶ TRACK 113

1 hold the baby
2 Don't slip!
3 make an appointment
4 I'm jealous!
5 protect your head
6 knock at the door
7 encourage each other
8 celebrate their anniversary
9 musical instruments
10 negotiate the price
11 be in love
12 go to a nightclub
13 remove the paint
14 plant some flowers

▶ TRACK 114

1
A: Did I tell you Owen's going to move in with his girlfriend?
B: I didn't know he had a girlfriend! How long have they been together?
A: Two or three months, I think.
B: That's not long! What's she like?
A: She's nice, and she's very good-looking!
B: That's great. I'm pleased for him. So, where are they going to live?
A: Pickwick somewhere.

2
C: Did I tell you my brother Gerrard is going to get married?
D: No. When's the wedding?
C: Next May sometime.
D: That'll be nice. So what's his partner like?
C: She's quite annoying, actually. We don't really get on.
D: Oh dear.

3
E: Did I tell you Fiona and Kieran are going to get divorced?
F: No! Why's that?
E: I think she wanted kids, but he didn't.
F: Oh, that's sad! How long have they been married?
E: Not very long. Four years, I think.
F: What a shame. They're both such nice people.
E: I know. I hope we can stay friends with both of them.

4
G: Did I tell you I have a date on Friday?
H: No. Who with?
G: A guy in my French class.
H: So what's he like?
G: He seems very nice. He's quite quiet, but he's funny.
H: Is he good-looking?
G: Yeah, not bad. He's quite tall and he has lovely eyes.
H: OK. So what are you going to do?
G: We're going to have a drink together and then we're going to meet some of his friends for karaoke.

▶ TRACK 115

1 My husband and I spent two years looking for the right place to live. We didn't look seriously to begin with, but then I got pregnant and we had to find somewhere fast. We saw five houses every weekend for four months, but didn't like any of them. One day, we were driving home from another appointment when we suddenly saw it – the house of our dreams! And, incredibly, it was for sale. We knocked at the door and offered the price they were asking for it immediately.

2 When I was a kid, I always loved music and musical instruments. For my twelfth birthday, my uncle gave me a guitar – and it was love at first sight. My uncle was a really important person for me at that time. He was playing in a band at the time, and I went to see them one night. That had a big influence on me. After that, the guitar became the centre of my world. I played it 24 hours a day, seven days a week. Later, I studied music at university and now I make guitars for a living. All because of that special day!

3 I love Second Life, an online world where you create virtual characters – you design them, choose their names and then create lives for them. Last year, I was in a relationship, but we weren't getting on very well, so I started spending a lot of time online. I was working in a Second Life nightclub when one night I met my future husband. He came in and it was love at first sight. His 'character' soon asked my 'character' to marry him and I said yes. We were married online in July. He then asked me in the real world and I accepted. We haven't actually met yet, but he's the one for me.

▶ TRACK 116

1 I was **do**ing some **shop**ping when I **met** an **old friend**.
2 She was **ru**nning for the **bus** when she **fell**.
3 They were **wor**king in **Greece** when it **ha**ppened.
4 I **was**n't en**joy**ing it, so I **left**.
5 She **was**n't **fee**ling **very well**, so she **went home**.
6 We **were**n't **get**ting **on**, so we **bro**ke up.

▶ TRACK 117

/aʊ/, /ʌ/, /ɔː/, /ɒ/, /ʊ/, /uː/, /əʊ/, /ə/

▶ TRACK 118

1 Her baby was born on Monday.
2 I control how long my son spends on the computer.
3 Those flowers look lovely.
4 It's polite to hold the door open for people.
5 Knock on the door before you go in.
6 Her boyfriend's not very good-looking.
7 I'd love a house of my own.
8 You don't have to remove your shoes.

▶ TRACK 119

1 We met when we were both studying in Germany.
2 I'm thinking of asking her to marry me.
3 I won't do anything without talking to you first.
4 I saw it when I was staying in New York.
5 He crashed because he was driving too fast.
6 I'll tell you when I hear more news.

Outcomes Elementary
Student's Book

Hugh Dellar and Andrew Walkley

Publisher: Gavin McLean

Publishing Consultant: Karen Spiller

Development Editor: Clare Shaw

Editorial Manager: Scott Newport

Head of Strategic Marketing ELT: Charlotte Ellis

Senior Content Project Manager: Nick Ventullo

Manufacturing Manager: Eyvett Davis

Cover design: emc design

Text design: Alex Dull

Compositor: emc design

National Geographic Liaison: Leila Hishmeh

Audio: Tom Dick & Debbie Productions Ltd

DVD: Tom Dick & Debbie Productions Ltd

Student Book ISBN: 978-1-305-09346-1
Student Book w/o Access Code ISBN: 978-1-305-65191-3

National Geographic Learning
Cheriton House
North Way
Andover
UK
SP10 5BE

Cengage Learning is a leading provider of customized learning solutions with employees residing in nearly 40 different countries and sales in more than 125 countries around the world. Find your local representative at **www.cengage.com**.

Cengage Learning products are represented in Canada by Nelson Education Ltd.

Visit National Geographic Learning online at **ngl.cengage.com**
Visit our corporate website at **www.cengage.com**

CREDITS
Although every effort has been made to contact copyright holders before publication, this has not always been possible. If contacted, the publisher will undertake to rectify any errors or omissions at the earliest opportunity.
Photos
6 (tl) © Jim Jurica/iStockphoto; 6 (tr) © Digital Vision/Getty Images; 6 (ml) © Golden Pixels LLC/Shutterstock.com; 6 (mmt) © Creatas/Jupiterimages; 6 (mmb) © BGSmith/Shutterstock.com; 6 (mr) © g-stockstudio/Shutterstock.com; 6 (blt) © PhotoDisc/Getty Images; 6 (blb) © Devy Masselink/Shutterstock.com; 6 (br) © Joe Gough/Shutterstock.com; 7 (t) © Janne Hämäläinen/Shutterstock.com; 7 (mt) © RubberBall Selects/Alamy Stock Photo; 7 (mbl) © macbrianmun/Shutterstock.com; 7 (mbm) © Kheng Guan Toh/Shutterstock.com; 7 (mbr) © Monkey Business Images/Shutterstock.com; 7 (bl) © Howard Sayer/Shutterstock.com; 7 (bm) © Digital Vision/Getty Images; 7 (br) © Kzenon/Shutterstock.com; 8 © Frontpage/Shutterstock.com; 10 © Graham Prentice/Alamy Stock Photo; 11 © Agencja Fotograficzna Caro/Alamy Stock Photo; 12 (t) © ziggy_mars/Shutterstock.com; 12 (m) © Tom Hanslien Photography/Alamy Stock Photo; 12 (bl) © trekandshoot/Shutterstock.com; 12 (br) © Marques/Shutterstock.com; 14 (tl, mmt, blt, br) © PhotoDisc/Getty Images; 14 (tr) © Glow Images/Getty Images; 14 (ml) © AVAVA/Shutterstock.com; 14 (mmb) © Diego Cervo/Shutterstock.com; 14 (mr) © Thinkstock Images/Jupiterimages; 14 (blb) © Somos Images/Corbis; 15 (t) © criben/Shutterstock.com; 15 (mt) © Digital Vision/Getty Images; 15 (mbl) © PhotoSmart/Shutterstock.com; 15 (mbm) © lukaszfus/Shutterstock.com; 15 (mbr) © Creatas Images/Jupiterimages; 15 (bl) © Monkey Business Images/Shutterstock.com; 15 (br) © Yang Liu/Corbis; 17 © Nick David/Getty Images; 18 © Hybrid Images/Getty Images; 19 (t) © Caiaimage/Tom Merton/Getty Images; 19 (bl) © Vladimir Godnik/Getty Images; 19 (br) © Helder Almeida/Shutterstock.com; 20 © Cultura RM/Alamy Stock Photo; 21 (tl) © SuperStock; 21 (tr) © urfin/Shutterstock.com; 21 (mr) © Cengage Learning; 21 (bl) © PhotoDisc/Getty Images; 21 (br) © Image Source/SuperStock; 22 (tl) © DigitalStock/Corbis; 22 (tr, bl) © John Foxx Images/Imagestate; 22 (br) © Zoran Karapancev/Shutterstock.com; 24 (tl) © BananaStock/Jupiterimages; 24 (tr) © Rob Byron/Shutterstock.com; 24 (ml) © Patrick Strattner/Getty Images; 24 (mmt) © Ford Photography/Shutterstock.com; 24 (mmb) © Iriana Shiyan/Shutterstock.com; 24 (mr) © PhotoDisc/Getty Images; 24 (bl) © Kalle Singer/bilderlounge/Jupiterimages; 24 (bm) © Lana Smirnova/Shutterstock.com; 24 (br) © Don Hammond/Design Pics/Corbis; 25 (t) © Everett Collection/Shutterstock.com; 25 (mt) © DigitalStock/Corbis; 25 (mbl) © Digital

Printed in Greece by Bakis SA
Print Number: 01   Print Year: 2016

Cover

Illustrations

Text
The publisher would like to thank Sustainable Development Solutions Network (SDSN) for the world happiness data.

Acknowledgements
The publishers and authors would like to thank the following teachers who provided the feedback and user insights on the first edition of *Outcomes* that have helped us develop this new edition: Rosetta d'Agostino, New English Teaching, Milan, Italy; Victor Manuel Alarcón, EOI Badalona, Badalona, Spain; Isidro Almendarez, Universidad Complutense, Madrid, Spain; Ana Bueno Amaro, EOI Roquetas de Mar, Almería, Spain; Isabel Andrés, EOI Valdemoro, Madrid, Spain; Brian Brennan, International House Company Training, Barcelona, Spain; Nara Carlini, Università Cattolica, Milan, Italy; Karen Corne, UK; Jordi Dalmau, EOI Reus, Reus, Spain; Matthew Ellman, British Council, Malaysia; Clara Espelt, EOI Maresme, Barcelona, Spain; Abigail Fulbrook, Chiba, Japan; Dylan Gates, Granada, Spain; Blanca Gozalo, EOI Fuenlabrada, Madrid, Spain; James Grant, Japan; Joanna Faith Habershon, St Giles Schools of Languages London Central, UK; Jeanine Hack; English Language Coach.com, London, UK; Claire Hart, Germany; David Hicks, Languages4Life, Barcelona, Spain; Hilary Irving, Central School of English, London, UK; Jessica Jacobs, Università Commerciale Luigi Bocconi, Milan, Italy; Lucia Luciani, Centro di Formaziones Casati, Milan, Italy; Izabela Michalak, ELC, Łódź, Poland; Josep Millanes Moya, FIAC Escola d'Idiomes, Terrassa, Catalonia; Rodrigo Alonso Páramo, EOI Viladecans, Barcelona, Spain; Jonathan Parish, Uxbridge College, London, UK; Mercè Falcó Pegueroles, EOI Tortosa, Tortosa, Spain; Hugh Podmore, St Giles Schools of Languages London Central, UK; James Rock, Università Cattolica, Milan, Italy; Virginia Ron, EOI Rivas, Madrid, Spain; Coletto Russo, British Institutes, Milan, Italy; Ana Salvador, EOI Fuenlabrada, Madrid, Spain; Adam Scott, St Giles College, Brighton, UK; Olga Smolenskaya, Russia; Carla Stroulger, American Language Academy, Madrid, Spain; Simon Thomas, St Giles, UK; Simon Thorley, British Council, Madrid, Spain; Helen Tooke, Università Commerciale Luigi Bocconi, Milan, Italy; Chloe Turner, St Giles Schools of Languages London Central, UK; Sheila Vine, University of Paderborn, Germany; Richard Willmsen, British Study Centres, London, UK; Various teachers at English Studio Academic management, UK.

Authors' acknowledgements
Thanks to Karen Spiller and Clare Shaw, and to Dennis Hogan, John McHugh and Gavin McLean for their continued support and enthusiasm.
Thanks also to all the students we've taught over the years for providing more inspiration and insight than they ever realised.
And to the colleagues we've taught alongside for their friendship, thoughts and assistance.